Ann Snyder

The civil war from a southern standpoint

Ann Snyder

The civil war from a southern standpoint

ISBN/EAN: 9783337224585

Printed in Europe, USA, Canada, Australia, Japan

Cover: Foto ©ninafisch / pixelio.de

More available books at **www.hansebooks.com**

Confederate Memorial, Nashville, Tenn.

THE CIVIL WAR

FROM A SOUTHERN STAND-POINT.

BY MRS. ANN E. SNYDER,
NASHVILLE, TENN.

"We wore ourselves out whipping the enemy."—*General Cobb.*

PRINTED FOR THE AUTHOR.
PUBLISHING HOUSE OF THE M. E. CHURCH, SOUTH.
J. D. BARBEE, AGENT, NASHVILLE, TENN.
1890.

DEDICATION.

THE AUTHOR OF THIS BOOK DEDICATES IT

To Mrs. Harriet Maxwell Overton,

AS A SMALL TESTIMONIAL TO HER DEVOTION TO THE CONFEDERATE CAUSE, BOTH IN THE STORMY TIMES OF WAR AND IN THE QUIETER TIMES OF PEACE—

A DEVOTION THAT FOUND A PRACTICAL EXPRESSION

IN THE AMELIORATION OF THE SOLDIERS' LIFE, AND IN ASSISTING THEM TO MEND THEIR BROKEN FORTUNES AFTER HAVING DONE THEIR DUTY TO THEIR COUNTRY.

PREFACE.

There have been quite a number of histories of the late war between the States, both from a Northern and from a Southern stand-point. The former have been so partisan as to force one to believe that the South has hardly been fairly represented; for the manner in which the Confederate side of the great struggle is discussed in the common school hastories eminating from Northern sources, and which, from a lack of something better, are necessarily used in our schools, would make one entirely dissatisfied with the actions of the Southern people, from the very beginning of the war to its end. But, fortunately, there is another side to the question, and one, too, which approaches nearer to the truth, and it is this side which the author of this little book has endeavored to give; and in doing this she has used freely whatever available sources were at hand, condensing the materials as much as possible, so as to bring them into the compass of the present small volume.

The objection to the histories that have been written from a Southern stand-point is that they are usually of too large and bulky a character for the general reader, and as a result one is often astonished to find how very much the mass of our people are wanting in a knowledge of the glorious contest which they made. Moreover, the histories just referred to are rather personal in character, in that they are attempts to explain why this or that battle was lost or won, thus introducing much recrimination and a large amount of useless discussion. In the present work every thing of this nature is so far avoided that it is rather the record of how the *private* soldier fought, written in a plain, unvarnished style. Therefore, with the earnest hope that the book may prove an aid in recalling to the minds of our people how grandly and nobly those brave hearts that wore the gray struggled through four long years for their cause, in behalf of which so many gave their lives, the author sends it forth into the hands of the public.

INTRODUCTION.

It seems proper to say that I am writing this introduction on short notice. The work was assigned to one far more capable and widely known than myself, who lately felt compelled to decline the service. It was then pressed upon me by the author and others with a kindness and generosity which obliged me, though not well prepared, to accept, and to discharge the duty thus imposed as best I could. I have seen it stated that in judging of a book Goethe was accustomed to ask three questions: "What does the author propose to do? Is what he proposes worth doing? How has he done it?" Let us try to keep these criteria in mind. As the effect of the perusal of a book and the estimate which the reader puts upon it depend so much upon his getting and taking with him a right view of the design of the author, I call special attention thereto. That design, as set forth by the writer of this volume in her preface, is definite and restricted. It is an effort to correct, as far as possible, any false statements which have come from Northern partisan writers placing the South under severe and unjust condemnation; and believing that the masses are largely ignorant in regard to the war, she aims also to furnish a book better suited to the general reader, and especially the young, than any now before the public, giving much prominence to the service of the private soldier, who deserves more praise than is usually given him, "as houses, cities, States, and institutions of all kinds among men have always owed very much more to men whose names have been lost than to those whose names have been preserved." There is no purpose to displace other larger and more exhaustive works which treat at great length and with ability of the many complex military, civil, and social problems growing out of the war; but it is a simple, direct, well-connected, fair, and modest statement of the Southern side of the conflict by an earnest Southern woman, an enthusiastic lover of the Confederate cause, who relies upon truth as its defense.

That what she proposes is worth doing will, I think, be admitted without question. It is said that "history is philosophy teaching by example," and its chief value is truth, and the greatness and value of truth is its helpfulness. "It is our duty not to ridicule the affairs of men, nor deplore, but simply to understand them." These weighty words justify every effort to obtain correct history. We are safe in saying that "ignorance allows even great souls—souls grown too great for personal selfishness—to find relief in what they believe unselfishness even in national and ecclesiactical selfishness." Could we learn and rightly use the lessons of history, we would not allow the vast energies of our being to be expended along narrow lines and in small fields.

To aid in carrying out her purposes and give additional interest to the volume, the author has secured a valuable appendix, which treats of the following subjects: "The South Justified," "Religion in the Southern Army," and "The Institution of Domestic Slavery in the Southern States." These are carefully prepared, and the last two are full of interest and valuable contributions to history, while the first treats of what is, to some extent, a living issue, for although the war has shown secession to be impracticable, a number of able and conservative statesmen and jurists deny that this proves it to be wrong, and who, while they have no wish to incite to its exercise, still claim that it is justifiable as a Constitutional right. From the very origin of American history it has been predicted that there would be a union of self-governing States covering the continent. Even with a homogeneous population in the beginning, on account of our various climatic and other influences, the problem is a difficult one—namely, the formation of a Government "elastic enough to suit all sections and strong enough to hold all together for the needed co-operation and progress." Any calm and wise student of our history must see, it seems to me, " that not an empire, not an autocracy, not a limited monarchy, would realize this great ideal, but States united, not welded but fluent, each as perfectly free to discharge the functions of statedom by securing the liberties and promoting the progress of its people as if it were the only State on the globe," yet bound to all the other States, the prosperity of the whole being the prosperity of each—States worthy of union worthily united. In perfecting such an august consummation, which plainly must be the work of years, it is quite easy to perceive, to borrow a beautiful figure, " how there might be many who could see more clearly the value of the Union than that of constitutional liberty, and how there might be others in whose eyes the union of States would be to the liberty of States as the casket is to the crowned jewel it contains, or the human body to its spiritual inhabitant."

As to how well the author has succeeded in her effort the reader must decide, and to do so fairly he should keep in mind the design of the work and think calmly of the great struggle and what may be the final outcome. In my judgment, all who thus act must go beyond the pinched patriotism of sectional animosities, and while deeply deploring the war with its sad physical and sadder moral effects, honor the heroic effort of the South. Although the work is intensely Southern, its spirit is excellent, all severity being carefully avoided by the author. I bespeak for it a cordial welcome at the hands of a generous public. R. Lin. Cave.

Nashville, Tenn., March 26, 1890.

CONTENTS.

CHAPTER I.
	PAGE
THE CAUSES	15
The Slavery Question	17
States' Rights and Centralization	23

CHAPTER II.
THE SECESSION OF THE STATES	27
The Confederacy Established	29
The First Gun	31
The Emancipation Proclamation	33
Battle of Bethel	36
The Confederates Win at Manassas	40

CHAPTER III.
AFFAIRS IN MISSOURI	47

CHAPTER IV.
BATTLE OF CHEAT MOUNTAIN	51
Cumberland Gap	54

CHAPTER V.
AFFAIRS IN KENTUCKY	57
General Polk Attacked by the Federals	58
Death of General Zollicoffer	61

CHAPTER VI.
FORT DONELSON—PERMANENT ORGANIZATION	64
The Battle of Fort Donelson	64
The Confederates Evacuate Nashville	67
A Permanent Organization	68

CHAPTER VII.
AFFAIRS ON THE WATER	69
A Confederate Naval Victory at Hampton Roads	69

CHAPTER VIII.

	PAGE
GENERALS VAN DORN AND SIBLEY IN THE WEST	73
Battle of Elk Horn	74
In the Far West	75

CHAPTER IX.

ISLAND NO. TEN—SHILOH—NEW ORLEANS	77
The Great Battle of Shiloh	78
Fall of New Orleans	82

CHAPTER X.

GALLANT DEFENSE OF RICHMOND	84
Kernstown—Jackson Repulsed	85
Jackson's Successes in the Valley	85
Jackson Defeats the Federals at Port Republic	87
Activities on the Chickahominy	89
Mechanicsville—Malvern Hill	90

CHAPTER XI.

A SERIES OF IMPORTANT EVENTS	94
The Battle of Boonsboro	103
Surrender of Harper's Ferry	104
Battle of Sharpsburg	105

CHAPTER XII.

MOVEMENTS IN THE WEST AGAIN	109
Battle of Perryville, October 8	113
In the South-west	115
Battle of Corinth	117
Guerrilla Warfare in Missouri	119

CHAPTER XIII.

CAMPAIGN IN NORTHERN VIRGINIA	121
General Hindman's Success in Arkansas	125
Cavalry Exploits	126

CHAPTER XIV.

MURFREESBORO—GALVESTON—ARKANSAS	128
Capture of Galveston	133
Surrender of Arkansas Post	134
Confederate Rams Attack the Federals in Charleston Harbor	135

CHAPTER XV.

	PAGE
IMPRESSMENT—BATTERIES AND GUN-BOATS	137
Federals Attack Fort McAllister	138
The Federals in Front of Vicksburg	138
The Federals Repulsed from Charleston	141

CHAPTER XVI.

CHANCELLORSVILLE—VICKSBURG—GETTYSBURG	143
Death of General Jackson	147
Loss of Vicksburg	148
Invasion of Pennsylvania	149
Battle of Gettysburg	150

CHAPTER XVII.

SIEGE OF CHARLESTON—MORGAN'S RAID	154
General Morgan's Raid	158

CHAPTER XVIII.

CHICKAMAUGA—MARTIAL LAW IN KENTUCKY	162
Battle of Chickamauga	163
Martial Law in Kentucky	167

CHAPTER XIX.

RAPPAHANNOCK—MISSIONARY RIDGE	170
Skirmishes on the Rappahannock	170
Missionary Ridge	174

CHAPTER XX.

MINOR OPERATIONS IN THE WEST	180
Virginia and Tennessee Border	181
Lincoln's "Peace Proclamation"	183
Attack upon New Berne, N. C.	186
Battle of Ocean Pond	187

CHAPTER XXI.

INVASION OF MISSISSIPPI AND ALABAMA	189
Legal Enactments	191
Federal Cavalry Raids	192
Federal Expeditions from New Orleans and Vicksburg	193
General Forrest in Kentucky	195
Confederates Retake Plymouth, N. C.	196

CHAPTER XXII.

	PAGE
In Virginia Again	198
Cold Harbor	203
The Western Part of Virginia	204
Attack upon Petersburg	205
Other Reverses of the Enemy	206
The Loss of the "Alabama"	207

CHAPTER XXIII.

General Sherman in the South	209
General Forrest at Guntown	213
General Early's Raid	213
General John Morgan Invades Kentucky	215
General Price in Missouri	215
The "Peace" Question	216

CHAPTER XXIV.

Naval Operations—General Grant in Virginia	220
Destruction of the "Florida" and "Albemarle"	221
The Attempts upon Richmond	221
Sheridan's Raid in the Valley	224
Battle of Cedar Creek	225
General Breckinridge in East Tennessee	227

CHAPTER XXV.

Operations of Generals Sherman and Hood	228
Battle of Nashville	230
General Sherman's March	231
Attempts upon Wilmington	232
Fall of Charleston and Columbia	234

CHAPTER XXVI.

The End	237
Peace Conference	238
Closing Conflicts	239
The Surrender	241
General Order No. 9	243

APPENDIX.

	PAGE
THE SOUTH JUSTIFIED	245
RELIGION IN THE SOUTHERN ARMY	271
Prison Service	295
THE INSTITUTION OF DOMESTIC SLAVERY IN THE SOUTHERN STATES	304

ILLUSTRATIONS.

CONFEDERATE MEMORIAL, NASHVILLE, TENN	Frontispiece.
FORT SUMTER IN 1861	30
BATTLE BETWEEN THE "MONITOR" AND THE "MERRIMAC"	72
DESTRUCTION OF COTTON AT THE TAKING OF NEW ORLEANS	83
HARPER'S FERRY	104
DESTRUCTION OF THE "HATTERAS" BY THE CONFEDERATE STEAMER, "ALABAMA," ADMIRAL SEMMES COMMANDING	136
GENERAL LEE BEFORE THE "BATTLE OF THE WILDERNESS"	200
THE "SUMTER" RUNNING THE BLOCKADE, AND CHASED BY THE FEDERAL SHIP, "IROQUOIS"	220
COLONEL JOHN OVERTON'S RESIDENCE, GENERAL HOOD'S HEADQUARTERS AT THE BATTLE OF NASHVILLE	230
MR. WILMER MCLEAN'S RESIDENCE, WHERE GENERAL LEE SURRENDERED	242

THE CIVIL WAR

FROM A SOUTHERN STAND-POINT.

CHAPTER I.

The Causes.

FROM the very character of the people that settled what is known as the Northern or, more strictly, the New England States, and those that settled in the Southern section of the country, one can easily see that in the course of the peculiar development of each natural and distinct lines of difference will be the result. Consequently, in the narration of the momentous struggle of the eventful years from 1860 to 1865, it is eminently proper to briefly outline the causes that led up to it, going back to colonial days, to explain the heated antagonism that fell like the burst of a storm-cloud upon the country.

The emigrants that settled the New England States were, for the most part, religious malcontents. The memory of Marston Moor and Cromwell was still fresh, and the royal head of Charles rolling from the block was not the act of a distant past, but was close enough in time to be a reality. The restoration came, and with it the Puritan thought he saw all the results of his hard-fought victories swept away. Next to that personal devil which ever accompanied and contested with him in every good resolution, this Puritan hated the house of Stuart and all the nobles that took their stand by its fortunes. Consequently, after having emigrated from the mother country, these feelings became more intense in character. In their new home, the foundations of which were laid from the persecutions which produced the civil war in England, they began to construct a civilization peculiarly their own—a civilization which was a strange compound of persecution and bigotry. The exiles that had been made homeless by persecution and intolerance in turn sent to the mercies of the pitiless savage whoever might differ with them in religion or opinion. Forgetful of their own unhappy past, they became the very incarnation of those very qualities which had made England to them an unkind step-mother. The district that they had settled in was barren and rocky. Much labor and care were necessary to get from the apparently unwilling soil its products and fruits. Consequently agriculture was followed only as a matter of necessity. This encouraged the growth of cities and city life, which thrived marvelously as time passed on.

Turning now to those colonies of the South, history shows a civilization founded and developed purely imitative in character, differing in every essential feature from that developed at the North. These emigrants were neither political nor religious refugees, but they were rather acting under the impulse of a venturesome age that made them leave their island home and seek the El Dorado of the new world. Nor were they all English. The Huguenots came over. Those who had followed the white plume of good Henry of Navarre united their race and lineage with the descendants of the victors of Cressy and Poitiers. Here was a commingling of royal blood. The soil of this new country was fair and fertile beyond compare. Consequently the greatest inducements were held out to the agriculturist, and, as a natural result, city life was discouraged and the growth of large plantations inevitable.

The Slavery Question.

Into both sections—thus begun, indeed, under the same circumstances, but differing widely both as to the character of the people who settled them and the nature of the civilizations that must necessarily follow—negro slavery was introduced, that system which was one day to kindle a fire which would light the world with its awful glare.

The slave is never a profit to his owner save in agricultural pursuits. Therefore in the New England States he was very soon found to be out of place and a loss to his owner, while at the South he became a very necessary and essential feature of the farm and the plantation. Being in demand, the people of the New England States found no difficulty in disposing of the slaves in their possession at a fair price to the large plantation-owners at the South. But so soon as they were rid of this apparently useless feature of their civilization it was discovered that slavery is a curse and slave-holding a crime, and therefore the logical conclusion to one admitting the major premise was that all Southern people were criminals in the sight of Heaven.

From the nature of the two sections, as already outlined, one can see that a cause, however slight, may beget an antagonism which will grow in intensity as the years go by, until, finally, to natural divisions and distinctions artificial ones will be added. Among the latter differences the question of slavery became the all-important one; and one, too, that at a very early date in the history of the country created more bitter and more intense opposition than one would expect from the nature of the question alone.

That the people of the North should so soon become horrified at an institution which they themselves once countenanced, and should allow their opposition to it to assume the character of a fanatical hatred, would indeed be a very problematical question of itself alone; but when one remembers the innate intolerance of the people—narrow and lacking in breadth of judgment and liberality of opinion, together with that old nature nurtured in the mother country and transplanted to American soil, and which did not change nor alter itself with its changed surroundings and conditions—then the question is no longer a problem. One almost feels that the battle of the Cavalier and the Roundhead is to be fought over again. This American Puritan could not appreciate that broad, liberal, free civilization that was developing at the South; for it seemed to be rich where his was poor. Its prosperity was a marvel and a wonder to him; the very gladness of its life contrasted sharply with his own, which a narrow creed had settled into such hard places.

Moreover, the natural and necessary product of a noble civilization is a noble and a princely manhood. Consequently the slave-holding States, by sheer force of a superior intellectuality, dominated the National Government and affected the character of all legislation by the impress of their masterly minds. The inevitable effect of this upon the North was to create and to foster that feeling of jealousy that naturally existed, to add fuel to the fires of slavery agitation, and to widen sectional lines.

As far back as 1787 controversies arose in regard to the slavery question, and the convention of delegates from the New England States which met at

Hartford, Conn., in 1814, though ostensibly called for other purposes, really owed its conception to a jealousy of the political power of the slave-holding States. Besides, even as early as this time, there was such a strong under-current of hostility at the North that it showed itself in an effort to prevent representation in Congress from the South; and threats of secession, which was afterward thought so criminal and illegal on the part of the South, were heard from that section which had for its war-cry the upholding of the Constitution and the preservation of the Federal Union.

In 1820 the admission of the State of Missouri furnished a cause for battle between the discordant elements. The result of this legislation was the so-called Mason and Dixon's line, which, while it produced a temporary peace, gave sectional divisions and feelings a distinctness and definiteness that they had never had before; for, with something like prophetic vision, the aged Thomas Jefferson wrote to a friend in regard to the measure: "It [the question of slavery] sleeps, but is not dead. A geographical line coinciding with a marked principle, moral and political, once conceived of men, will not be obliterated; every new irritation makes it deeper."

With this new dividing line making matters concrete, so to speak, where, before, they were abstract, the agitation of the slavery question was intensified into a kind of religious fanaticism which made a war on the South necessary, almost, to the salvation of one's soul. This spirit is illustrated in the remarks of Dr. Tyng, a prominent minister of New York City, and one, too, of more than local celebrity, in presenting Bibles to certain notorious roughs of that city, known as "Billy Wilson's men." Though commending to them the Book of peace, he declared that in carrying the horrors of a bitter and relentless war into the Southern States they were propitiating the favors of Heaven, and it would count much in the final salvation of their souls. That this question became a species of religious fanaticism is shown in the spirit of the ministers of the Northern Methodist Church, which finally became so bitter as to produce a permanent separation into two distinct bodies; and in the character of that famous novel by Mrs. Harriet Beecher Stowe, "Uncle Tom's Cabin," which, from its pathetic coloring, and coming just at a time when the popular mind of the North was ready to receive any thing which might represent the Southern people as criminals and barbarians, exercised a tremendous influence. And this same influence has not lost its power even at the present day; for the leopard cannot change its spots, and some sections of the North are ever ready to believe that old, false tale of horrors in regard to the South.

Discussions, resolutions, debates, and abuse took a

practical shape when that incarnation of rank fanaticism, John Brown, with his deluded followers, invaded the soil of Virginia with the purpose of inciting servile insurrection among the happy and contented slaves of that old Commonwealth. This demonstration of Brown was no spasmodic, abnormal outbreak, but rather the natural outcome of that spirit at the North which at once was more than ready to sympathize with his movement, and to declare his example worthy of emulation, and not only one of the chiefest of the earthly virtues, but also a service to God.

The certain tendency of Northern opinion is again shown in the nomination by the Republican party for Speaker of the House of Hon. John Sherman, who publicly recommended a book known as the "Helper Book," which advocated a murderous uprising of the slaves at the South. One short quotation will be sufficient to suggest the line of procedure to which this leading representative of the Republican party had committed himself: "Frown, sir; fret, foam, prepare your weapons, threaten, strike, shoot, stab, bring on civil war, dissolve the Union; nay, annihilate the solar system, do what you will, you can neither foil nor intimidate us; our purpose is fixed as the pillars of the eternal heavens. We have determined to abolish slavery, and so help us God we will!" These utterances in the calmness of the present seem rather like the rabid vaporings of insanity than the expressions of reason, yet the book is clearly characteristic of that frenzy into which the North had worked itself.

STATES' RIGHTS AND CENTRALIZATION.

When in any community or associations of men there develop certain principles and opinions that grow and increase in force and intensity to such an extent as to call into existence two distinct divisions completely discordant and out of harmony with each other, so that the peace and welfare of either the one or the other is threatened, then naturally a question of permanent separation arises. With this question there also arises another hardly secondary in importance—viz., as to the character of the original contract into which they entered, its terms and its obligations; whether union was voluntary or otherwise, and what were the causes that led to it.

The causes that have been before enumerated produced just such a state of circumstances in the United States. Consequently there arose two very widely divergent interpretations of the Federal Constitution, its powers and its limitations, technically called "States' rights" and "centralization." The former opinion was held to by the Southern States, and meant that each individual State had certain rights and privileges which were not surrendered when it went into a *voluntary* federation or league with the other States. On the other hand, the opposition, taking as their motto that celebrated saying of Andrew Jackson, "The Federal Union must and shall be preserved," denied to the individual States any rights or liberties that a majority might not take from them at any time they might see fit, and that a strong, centralized government might inflict any laws or prohibitions in regard to local government, however odious or oppressive to the people.

The sentiment of the North crystallized about this latter opinion, the purpose of which looked clearly toward the abolishment of the system of slavery at the South. This system had become so thoroughly inwrought into the very fiber of Southern life that the abolishment of it was like literally tearing a member from the body. It also constituted a principal portion of their wealth and was absolutely necessary to the character of the industry carried on at the South. Therefore, with the certain and sure sweeping away of the vast wealth involved in the slave staring them in the face, together with a sacred principle at stake as old as the first dream of human liberty—that man must be left to the free and unobstructed enjoyment of his property and the pursuit of happiness—the Southern statesmen, as representatives of the people, began to see that they must have recourse to the last means open to the oppressed— revolution. In this case revolution meant secession on the part of the South—a peaceful withdrawal from the compact into which they had gone voluntarily, and from which they might separate whenever from reasonable causes the bond became irksome or oppressive.

In the beginning the original colonies formed a defensive and offensive alliance in the war against Great Britain. At the successful termination of this war this league was formally ratified into the United States of America, with the individual liberties of each State guaranteed. Therefore from the very principle of both the original and the subsequent union, while time may smooth away the differences and divergencies between the various members of this Union, and thus bring the States closer together and render them more compact, it cannot develop a right in any one particular section to interfere with practices and systems in any other, recognized as legal and legitimate at the time of the original Union; for power of this kind belongs to conquest and oppression. It is that which Rome exercised over her provinces gained by the might of the sword, which Bonaparte exhibited after victories in Germany and Italy, and which England showed in her dealings with the American colonies—the natural result of which was to bring on the war of the revolution that made possible the existence of the United States. Therefore, with this view of the character and nature of the Federal Union, it is entirely a misnomer to say that the Southern people were "traitors" in any sense of the word; for to be a traitor one must commit traitorous deeds. Will future history, or rather does the whole past history of the human race define treason as a defense of individual rights, resistance to oppression, or devotion to a principle as deeply rooted as the pillars of heaven and as essential to human happiness as the air is essential to life? Consequently the Southern people would have indeed been traitors to all history had they done otherwise under the circumstances.

CHAPTER II.
The Secession of the States.

WITH such feelings as these prevailing at the South, the election of Abraham Lincoln seemed to bring matters to a focus. The South had hoped that the so-called conservative element at the North would put a check upon the wild rush of that frantic crusade that was being made against her. But Mr. Lincoln being the representative of the most violent and hostile class, the South began to prepare to separate herself from that Union which had ceased to do its duty toward her, which had ceased to guarantee her rights or to even give security to home and fireside, and which had become the oppressor instead of the protector.

Actual withdrawal from the Union was begun December 20, 1860, by the Legislature of South Carolina unanimously passing the ordinance of secession. Six days later Major Anderson, with the United States troops, evacuated Fort Moultrie, in Charleston harbor. In January, 1861, Florida seceded; followed by Mississippi on the 9th of the same month, Alabama on the 11th, Georgia on the 20th, Louisiana on the 26th, and Texas on February 1. Thus, in less than three months after the election of Mr. Lincoln, all the so-called cotton States had left the Union by a unanimous vote of the people, and had secured every Federal fortification except the ones in Charleston harbor. Just one month from the secession of South Carolina, January 21, 1861, Jefferson Davis, of Mississipi, Messrs. Kilpatrick and C. C. Clay, of Alabama, and Yulee and Mallory, of Florida, resigned their positions in the National Houses of Congress. Though in extreme bad health at the time, Mr. Davis made a forcible yet temperate speech that made a solemn and lasting impression upon his hearers. Mr. Clay's speech of resignation was more violent and aggressive in character, for he made a vigorous attack upon the Republican party as the cause of the division that must necessarily separate the two sections.

The State of Virginia was not quite ready to push matters to the extreme of secession. Accordingly, February 4, 1861, the Legislature met and passed resolutions whose purpose was a peaceful and honorable settlement of the difficulties, to be effected by a conference to be held in Washington. At first this line of procedure seemed to meet with a favorable response, so that the convention met at Richmond and held a session of several days' duration, but adjourned without agreeing upon any definite plan of adjustment. Shortly afterward the Legislature was again called together, and an election was held, showing that a majority were opposed to an unconditional secession of the State. Subsequently Tennessee and North Carolina decided to call a convention with a somewhat similar purpose. This apparent reluctance of these States to rush at once into secession encouraged the enemies of the South into thinking that some at least of the slave-holding States would remain in the Union, and tamely submit to the deprivation of their property and rights.

The Confederacy Established.

Meanwhile the six seceded States began to take steps toward establishing a provisional government by a convention of delegates from each assembled at Montgomery, Ala., February 4, 1861. After deliberating four days, this body adopted a Constitution for the Confederate States of America, which differed very little from the Constitution of the United States. In the election of President and Vice-president on the 9th the choice fell unanimously upon Jeff Davis, of Mississippi, and Alexander Stephens, of Georgia. The newly organized government now began active preparations to make good its claim to be numbered among the nations of earth, and took the initiative by taking possession of the different United States forts and arsenals. Fort Moultrie and Castle Pinckney, at Charleston, were captured by the State troops; Fort Pulaski, at Savannah; Mount Vernon, Ala., was taken, with twenty thousand stands of arms; Fort Morgan, in Mobile Bay; Forts Jackson, St. Philip, and Pike, near New Orleans, together with the custom-house and mint; Pensacola Navy Yard; Forts Baraccas, McCrae, and Pickens; the arsenals at both Baton Rouge, La., and Little Rock, Ark.

Martin Crawford and John Forsyth, both of Georgia, were sent as commissioners to Mr. Seward, the Secretary of State at Washington, in regard to Fort Sumter. They were given the verbal assurance that the United States was disposed to acquiesce in their demands to remove the troops from Fort Sumter. But in this the commissioners were deceived, for the United States Government was at this same time making active preparations for a siege and sending re-enforcements, while, with their fleet, which appeared off the harbor April 12, 1861, they were threatening the city of Charleston. These matters were promptly telegraphed to the Confederate Secretary of War, Mr. Walker, who at once ordered General Beauregard to demand the immediate surrender of the fort, and if this demand was refused to proceed to reduce it by force of arms. In reply to General Beauregard's demand to surrender, Major Anderson, the Union commander, wrote as follows: "I have the honor to acknowledge the receipt of your communication demanding the evacuation of Fort Sumter, and to say in reply thereto that it is a demand with which

Fort Sumter in 1861.

I regret my sense of honor and my obligation to my Government prevent my compliance." General Beauregard had now no other course save to accept the gauntlet of war thus thrown down to him. So a little after three o'clock on the morning of April 12 he sent word by his aids to Major Anderson that he would open fire with his batteries just one hour from that time.

The First Gun.

The signal shell that opened in real earnest the awful four years' struggle went from Fort Johnson with its red glare across the gray sky of that momentous dawn, April 12. This was followed by the fire from Fort Moultrie, Cumming's Point, and the floating battery. The Federals endured in silence this cannonading until seven o'clock, when they opened fire with their guns. Toward evening the terrific bombardment by the Confederates began to tell upon the fort. The garrison was driven from the barbette guns, and the parapet walls began to crumble away. The Federal fleet off the harbor remained a passive and inactive witness of the certain destruction of the fort. Why they took no part in the fight is explained by Captain Cox: "As we neared the land, heavy guns were heard, and the smoke and shells from the batteries that had just opened fire on Fort Sumter were distinctly visible. Immediately I stood out to inform Captain Rowan, of the 'Pawnee,' but met him coming in. He hailed me and asked for a pilot, declaring his intention of standing into the harbor and sharing the fate of his brethren in the army. I went on board and informed him I would answer for it that the Government did not expect any such gallant sacrifice, having settled upon the policy indicated in the instructions to myself and Captain Mercer."

Meanwhile on the shore the Confederate troops were in raptures over the prospect of victory, and on the following morning early (April 13) every Confederate battery opened fire upon Sumter, which was replied to vigorously for a time. At eight o'clock smoke was seen issuing from the fort, and its firing was only at long intervals. At half-past one o'clock in the afternoon a shot from Fort Moultrie tore the flag-staff from the walls of Sumter. Seeing the desperate condition of the garrison, and the flames being on the increase, General Beauregard sent three of his aids with a message to Major Anderson, to the effect that, as his flag was no longer flying and his quarters in flames, and, supposing him to be in distress, he desired to offer him any assistance he might need. However, before the aids reached the fort the flag was again flung to the breeze, but only for a short time, for soon the white flag of truce was substituted for it, which meant that after two days of heavy bombardment Sumter had surrendered. It was a joyous occasion in the city of Charleston. The ringing of bells, the pealing of cannon accompanied the shouts of the happy and elated citizens. But in the midst of their rejoicing they did not forget that magnanimity due from the victor to the conquered. As a testimonial to the gallantry of Major Anderson, General Beauregard not only agreed that the garrison might take passage for New York at their own convenience, but also allowed them, on evacuating the fort, to salute their flag with fifty guns.

Proclamation of War.

The fall of Sumter did not disturb Mr. Lincoln. He had calculated the result and the effect upon the country. April 14, 1861, the great proclamation, calling for troops to subjugate in sixty days the grandest people in the world, was sent forth as follows: "Having thought fit to call forth, and do hereby call forth, the militia of the several States of the Union to the aggregate number of 75,000, in order to suppress said combinations, and to cause the laws to be duly executed. The details for this object will be immediately communicated to the State authorities through the War Department at Washington City."

The effect of this proclamation was to make the Northern States a unit against the South. Democrats who had once been friends to her now turned against her, and joined themselves, with the zeal of new converts, to the bitter abolition party; and those who were before mild and conservative now became the fiercest advocates of the war. John Cockraine, a leading member of the Northern wing of the Democratic party, advised the masses to crush out the rebellion and, if need be, drown the South in one indiscriminate sea of blood.

As antagonism begets an antagonism of like proportion and equal degree, so the Southern States, one after another, refused to furnish to the United States Government troops with which to subjugate their sister States. Governor McGoffin, of Kentucky, declared that his State would furnish no troops, but would remain strictly neutral; while Governor Ellis, of North Carolina, replied to the call that he could take no part in violating the laws of the land.

On April 17 the glorious news flashed over the South that proud old Virginia, at last true to her sister States, had adopted the ordinance of secession, with the following patriotic resolutions, that sounded the key-note of Southern thought and opinion: "The people of Virginia recognize the true American principle that the Government is founded on the consent of the governed and the right of the several States of this Union for just cause to withdraw from their association under the Federal Government with the people of the other States, and to erect new Governments for their better security; and that they never will consent that the Federal power, which is in part their power, shall be exerted for the purpose of subjugating such States to the Federal authority."

Virginia was followed by Arkansas May 4; North Carolina, May 20; and Tennessee, June 8.

The light of April 19, 1861, saw the spilling of the first drop of fratricidal blood. The United States troops, in passing through the streets of Baltimore, were attacked by the brave and spirited citizens of that noble city, and for two weeks (full of excitement and terribly suggestive of the tenacity and bitterness of the four years that were to follow) the route was closed to the soldiers. A regiment of Massachusetts volunteers was compelled to move its quarters. Meanwhile the citizens flung to the breeze a Southern banner and were fired into by the troops, whom they in turn attacked with stones and sticks, or whatever weapons might come to hand. Afterward a mass-meeting was held by the thoroughly indignant populace, and addresses were made by the most prominent and leading citizens of Baltimore advocating secession as the only palliation for their wounded honor.

On the same day (April 19) Mr. Lincoln issued his proclamation declaring all the ports of the South in state of blockade, and threatening that any interferance with the vessels of the United States upon the high seas would be considered as nothing less than piracy. Letters of marque had already been issued by the Confederate Government. Just at this time Robert E. Lee resigned his position in the regular army of the United States, to answer the call that his native State had made for his sword and his marvelous military genius. He was at once placed in command in Virginia. On the same day with the issuing of Lincoln's blockade proclamation and the attack upon the Massachusetts troops in Baltimore the Federals evacuated Harper's Ferry.

On the 20th of the following month (May) the seat of the Confederate Government was moved from Montgomery, Ala., to Richmond, Va., where President Davis, as the representative head of the yet untried republic, was accorded a warm and demonstrative welcome.

The first invasion of Virginia was begun by the Federal troops occupying Alexandria (May 4), and the State troops falling back and taking a position at Manassas Junction, under the command of General Bohan, of South Carolina.

Battle of Bethel.

Matters remained in about this situation until the 10th of the following month, when Colonel J. Bankhead Magruder, who was intrenched at Great Bethel Church, nine miles south of Hampton, was attacked by a Federal force under General Pierce four thousand strong. A battery of Richmond howitzers was the first to receive the charge. They retreated from their guns, and Captain Bridges, of the First North Carolina, was ordered to retake them. With a coolness and a deliberation rather characteristic of trained veterans than raw troops, they advanced to the charge in the midst of a terrible artillery fire, and when within sixty yards of the Federals they dashed forward at a splendid double-quick and drove the Federals back in confusion to a position obscured by the dense growth of the timber. After a considerable amount of skirmishing and artillery-firing, the Federals were re-enforced by a column under the command of Major Winthrop. The first lines of his troops wore white bands around their caps, in order, if possible, to deceive the Confederates and take them unawares, for this band was a badge of their own uniform. Besides, they cried out repeatedly: "Don't fire! don't fire!" They crossed the small creek between our line and theirs with exultant cheers, evidently supposing that our work was open at that point, and that by a sudden rush they could make a breach. But this proved a costly delusion when the steady and effective fire of the North Carolina Infantry was turned upon the Federals, who were forced to fall back almost in a rout and with the loss of their commander, Major Winthrop, who had excited the admiration of the Confederates by his conspicuous gallantry. Though this battle was not quite decisive enough to be called a complete victory, yet it was a timely check upon the advance of the Federals.

The partial victory of the Confederates at Bethel was followed by a partial disaster at Rich Mountain, in Randolph County, Va. The main body of Federals, under General MacClellan, twenty thousand strong, were advancing toward Beverly, with the object of getting in the rear of General Garnett, who had been put in command in North-west Virginia. General Garnett had taken a strong position at Rich Mountain, having his forces arranged as follows: Colonel Pegram occupied the mountain with one thousand six hundred men and several pieces of artillery; while General Garnett, with three thousand infantry, six pieces of artillery, and three companies of cavalry, had intrenched himself on the slopes of Laurel Hill. On the 5th of July the Federals took their position at Bealington, directly in front of Laurel Hill; and two days afterward a large force held a similar position opposite Rich Mountain. With the two forces situated thus with respect to each other, General Garnett was informed by Colonel Pegram that he had learned that there were seven thousand men in front of Rich Mountain, with General MacClellan present and in command, and that orders had already been given for an attack in front, while

General Rosecrans had started around by a convenient route with three thousand troops to strike him in the rear; that to guard against that movement against his rear he had placed a piece of artillery with three hundred men at the point where Rosecrans was expected. On the receipt of this note General Garnett at once instructed Colonel Pegram to defend his position at all hazards, which order he gallantly obeyed when the Federals moved in the midst of a pouring rain, through the tangled and pathless woods, to attack them. The Federals were at first disappointed that their attempt to surprise the little band upon the mountain had failed, but they continued to advance under a terrific artillery fire that seemed to tear the forest asunder. Assaulted by more than thrice their number, in both front and rear, the condition of the little band was hopeless from the beginning; yet for more than two hours they maintained the struggle against such odds, until Colonel Pegram saw that their only chance was to try to escape. Colonel Tyler, with the troops under him, succeeded in doing so; but Colonel Pegram, receiving the news that General Garnett had evacuated Laurel Hill, was compelled to surrender the remaining five hundred.

General Garnett conducted his retreat in remarkably good order, considering the difficulties encountered. His course lay through the mountains, over a road hardly wide enough for one wagon to pass. When the tired, weary little band reached the branch of the Cheat River the pursuing Federals fell upon their rear and cut off four companies of Georgians. At Carrack's Ford a brave resistance was made by the Twenty-third Virginia, under Colonel Taliaferro, who occupied the high banks upon the right of the ford. With vigorous cheers for Jeff Davis, they opened an effective fire upon the Federals as they advanced, and their fire was replied to quite warmly; but having exhausted nearly every cartridge, General Garnett ordered them to retire and continue to retreat. At the next ford General Garnett himself fell while trying to form his command to defend the crossing. The brave little remnant, that had literally contested every inch of ground, finally managed to reach Monterey and form a junction with General Jackson.

The Confederate Government now found it necessary to borrow money for the maintenance of its armies; so it made what was known as the "produce loan," having for its basis the great staple, cotton, which was pledged for the redemption of its debts.

The Confederates Win at Manassas.

Up to this time the battles had been comparatively skirmishes. The first real contest was soon to begin. The two armies of Virginia had maneuvered and watched each other warily, like two huge monsters preparing for mortal combat. The Federals were bouyed up by the boasted cry of " On to Richmond!" while the Confederates felt that they were to put to the arbitration of the sword a sacred principle, and that the battle was to take place at the very threshold of home and fireside.

The Federals were under a commander of reputation, and one, too, in whom they had all confidence—General McDowell. The Congress of the United States had given a recess, that all its members might be present at the anticipated victory; politicians forgot for the time their state-craft, merchants withdrew themselves from barter and trade, and mechanics laid aside their tools, that they might see with their own eyes that first of a series of grand victories which were to open the gates of Richmond. The fashionable ladies of Washington forgot even their tenderness in their desire to see their favorites of last night's ball crush the so-called "rebels" and "slave-beaters," and were present in the full regalia of a gala occasion.

The divisions of Generals Longstreet and Bonham confronted the Federals and consumed the 17th, 18th, and 19th of July in preliminary skirmishes, often severe, along the Bull Run and near the north-west junction of Manassas Gap.

General Johnston was ordered at once to form a junction with General Beauregard. He succeeded in reaching Manassas on the 20th, and united the Seventh and Eighth Georgia Regiments and the Fourth Alabama, under General Bee, to Jackson's Brigade, and he then assumed entire command of the forces concentrated here, which now numbered something less than thirty thousand, divided into eight brigades. The Confederates determined to act on the defensive. Soon after sunrise the Federals opened with a heavy cannonading in front of Colonel Evans, and at the Stone Bridge the divisions opposed to each other skirmished for over an hour, during which time the main body of Federals were attempting to cross the Bull Run; which movement was checked, making the formation of a new line of battle necessary. Afterward, Colonel Evans, finding that they had succeeded in making a crossing, moved his left and was attacked by a column sixteen thousand strong, much in excess of his own numbers; while General Burnside appeared from the woods in front, near Wheat's Louisiana Battery. The Federals were further re-enforced by the Second Rhode Island and a mounted battery, while Sloan's South Carolina Regiment came to the assistance of the Confederates. The determined and never-faltering valor of Wheat's Battery soon repulsed the enemy, though their glorious commander fell desperately wounded while leading in a gallant charge. To relieve this point against the overwhelming numbers that were being massed against it, General Bee came with the Seventh and Eighth Georgia, Colonel Bartow with the Fourth Alabama, Second Mississippi, and two companies of the Eleventh Mississippi, together with Imboden's Battery. Thus reenforced, General Evans moved across the plain and took up an advanced position which he must hold against fifteen thousand Federals. A dreadful conflict of an hour's duration now ensued, which showed what mettle the Southern soldiers were made of, and that if the Federals reached Richmond their course would be more than a holiday episode. In their efforts to drive our men from their advanced position the enemy's line was constantly broken and shattered. In the meanwhile General Sherman had crossed the Bull Run, and was threatening our right. Victory seemed almost inclined to the Federals; at any rate "a glorious victory, with the conquest of Richmond," was telegraphed to Washington. The Confederates began to waver somewhat, but were checked for the time by the heroic Bee, and he too, having suffered terribly, was just on the point of being overwhelmed by the mere mass and dead weight of the vastly superior numbers of the enemy, when General Jackson arrived. With the inexpressible grief of his heroic heart depicted on his countenance, he approached Jackson, and said: "General, they are beating us back.". "Sir," said Jackson, "give them the bayonet." With renewed zeal and energy, Bee immediately rallied his men, with the inspiring words: "There's Jackson, standing like a stone wall; let us determine to die here, and we will conquer."

Now was the crisis of the battle. Orders had almost fatally miscarried, so that General Beauregard had to change his plan, which required the greatest amount of manœuvering to retrieve the almost lost field.

By noon it seemed as if all the pomp and glory of war, together with all its horrors and terrors, had been turned loose in this valley filled with smoke, and reverberating and re-echoing with the awful roar of the artillery, above which could be heard the old Southern yell, which had sounded its glad note of victory before, in the wars with the savage, at New Orleans with Jackson, and on the plains of Mexico with Taylor and Scott.

On the side of the Confederates matters were becoming desperate now. Something must be done. Their left seemed to be overpowered. Holmes's, Lindsay's, and Walker's Batteries; Bonham's, Kempker's, Ewell's, and Longstreet's Brigades came up just in time. General Beauregard charged to the front with the Fourth Alabama. At 2 o'clock he issued orders for his entire line to recover the positions they had lost, which was done with a determination that meant victory. Generals Beauregard and Johnston now led a general attack, every regiment being in action. The brave Bee fell mortally wounded at the head of his regiment; a few yards from him a shot pierced the heart of Colonel Bartow, while he was grasping the flag of his command; as he fell, Colonel Fisher was also killed. It now became the enemy's turn to retreat, and after a terrific resistance they were driven across the turnpike.

General Kirby Smith, with Elzey's Brigade of the Army of the Shenandoah and Beckham's Battery, had reached Manassas about noon. The flying Federals had rallied and turned once more against our left. General Johnston ordered General Beauregard to seize the opportunity and throw forward his whole line. The Federals were again driven back to the fields, which were filled with masses of infantry. Thence they scattered in every direction toward the Bull Run. Early's and Cocke's Brigades and Beckham's Battery, with Stuart's Cavalry, continued to play upon the wagon-trains, and so complete was the rout and so thorough was the demoralization that many even begged clothes from the negroes in which to make their escape. The fields seemed covered with the flying blue masses, and the victorious Confederates continued to pursue the panic-stricken Federals. The retreat became simply a wild stampede, with no restraint whatever. The wounded were left uncared for, the dead unburied, and the wagon-trains with their immense stores of ammunition and provisions forgotten, nor did the rout and confusion slacken until Centerville was reached. The grand army that in the morning had turned its face so hopefully and so confidently boastful toward Richmond saw its bright prospects darkened with the going down of the sun, and had turned its back in a disgraceful panic, with a loss in killed and wounded which must have been considerable, though no accurate estimate can be given. As the price of their glorious victory the Confederates laid down 369 noble lives, with 1483 wounded.

CHAPTER III.

Affairs in Missouri.

ABOUT this time interesting events were taking place in the West. The Confederate troops encamped on the outskirts of the city of St. Louis, Mo., had been forced to surrender, and a reign of terror was established by the Dutch Federal soldiers murdering private citizens and seizing ammunition, supplies, and every thing else which they could lay hands upon. To check their ravages and to defend the soil of his State, General Jackson issued a call for fifty thousand troops and appointed General Price major-general, who in turn created eight brigadiers—Parsons, Hindman, M. L. Clark, Harris, Stine, Rains, McBride, and Jeff Thompson. These troops were quartered at Booneville. On the 20th of June the Federals under General Lyons took up their march in that direction.

The barefooted soldiers under General Marmaduke resisted with such signal courage as to surprise the Federals. Colonel Cooke, a brother to that notorious B. F. Cooke who was executed at Charlestown, W. Va., as an accomplice of John Brown, was one of the Federal home guards. These so-called home guards were all asleep in two large barns, which Colonel O'Kane attacked, and routed the inmates, killing 206 and taking 100 prisoners.

This was followed by the severe battle of Oak Hill, which lasted six hours. The Federals had in the field ten thousand men, of whom they lost in killed, wounded, and prisoners two thousand; the Confederates also captured six pieces of artillery and seven hundred stands of arms. General Lyons was present in person to command the Federal troops, while the Missourians were under Generals Slack, McBride, Parsons, and Rains on the left, with Herbert's regiment of Louisiana volunteers and General Price in the center. The Missourians opened an effective fire with their batteries, and then charged the Union forces. Though undrilled, undisciplined, and untrained, they bore themselves with conspicuous gallantry, routing the Federals and putting in full retreat Sigel's boasted "grand army" of Germans.

After the battle the Confederate forces returned to the frontiers of Arkansas, to get themselves ready for their second victory, at Carthage, Mo. Here they were commanded by Generals Parsons, J. B. Clark, and Slack. The character of their equipment and the nature of their discipline were in painful contrast to the perfect preparation and gay trappings of the Federals, whose equipment was complete in every particular. With old, rude field-pieces, charged with pieces of iron, trace-chains, and stones, they replied to the splendid batteries of the enemy. Their coolness and the desperation with which they fought, together with the character of the implements which they used, produced such fear in the lines of the Federals as to force General Sigel to retreat July 4, and their valor called from him the following merited tribute: "Was the like ever seen? raw recruits standing like veterans, bidding defiance to every discharge of our batteries! Such material would make the best troops in the world." This tactician and military scientist looked only to the outward and artificial side of the soldier; he forgot that at the heart, with the purposes that stir it to action, is to be found the material for the real soldier. These brave Missourians were defending home and native land and outraged law, and, consequently, to them the drilling and the execution of the mechanical part of a soldier's art were matters of secondary importance.

The Federal general, Lyons, was left by his own men dead upon this field of carnage, but his body was tenderly cared for by the magnanimous victors, and shipped to friends.

Missouri now wheeled herself into line with the other Southern States, by the Legislature in session at Neosho passing the ordinance of secession.

The battle of Lexington, Mo., added another star to the Confederate crown of victory in the West.

Here were captured three thousand prisoners, among whom were Colonels Mulligan, Peabody, White, Grover, and Van Horn, with eighteen commissioned officers, besides guns and ammunition. There were also taken seven hundred and fifty horses and a hundred and fifty thousand dollars' worth of commissary stores—just what the Confederates were in great need of. Commenting upon this victory, General Price adds another laurel to the soldiers of Missouri: "This battle demonstrated clearly the fitness of citizen soldiery for the tedious operations of a siege."

September 1, at a place called Blue Hills, which gave the name to the battle, General D. R. Atchison and Colonel Sanders attacked the Federals with reckless valor and daring, and drove them ten miles. The Confederates took a number of tents and many camp supplies that the Federals had left in their flight. The Federals received such heavy re-enforcements under General Fremont that General Price thought it best to fall back. The retreat was accomplished successfully, especially through the consummate skill of General Jeff Thompson with his "swamp" brigade.

CHAPTER IV.

Battle of Cheat Mountain.

RETURNING now to the East, we find matters still very active in the neighborhood of Cheat Mountain. At Scay Creek, in the Kanawha Valley, General Wise had repulsed three regiments of Federals, and was sanguine of doing a great work in the valley, when the disaster at Rich Mountain exposed his little army to such peril that he was forced to fall back to Lewisburg, destroying all bridges behind him.

General Floyd surprised the Federals at breakfast at White Sulphur Springs, and attacked them, causing them to stampede in all directions. He then strengthened his position on the Gauley.

General Lee now repaired with re-enforcements to the scene of action, and early in August he arrived in the vicinity of Cheat Mountain and at once made his plans for battle; but on account of some misunderstanding a retreat was caused without the firing of a single gun. Thus having failed to dislodge the Federals, he went to the valley to the relief of Generals Floyd and Wise. At first taking up his head-quarters with General Floyd for the purpose of examining his position, he proceeded thence to Sewell, where he found General Wise with the Federals in front twenty thousand strong, in which position they remained for fifteen days, until General Rosecrans disappeared one night, much to the surprise of General Lee.

General Lee now withdrew from Cheat Mountain to Gauley, leaving General T. J. Jackson behind with twenty-five hundred men completely at his disposal, with whom to do as he pleased. General Jackson was then attacked by the Federals, but gallantly repulsed them, his pickets holding the entire column in check for over an hour, so that they were misled into believing that there was a considerable army in the rear. With this idea they made an almost precipitate retreat.

The severity of the weather now put an end to the campaign in Western Virginia, for awhile at least.

General Floyd, at his own request, was sent to Cotton Mills, where he was attacked by General Rosecrans. He retreated, but managed not to leave his wounded in possession of the Federals. He was then transferred to Tennessee and Kentucky.

The Federal General Stone, being persuaded that no important force of Confederates remained in the Upper Potomac region, began to cross that river Sunday, October 20, at Harrison's Landing. Five companies of Massachusetts troops under Colonel Devins succeeded in making a crossing. A few hours later Colonel Baker took command of these, with orders from General Stone to drive the Confederates from Leesburg, whose force consisted of the brigade of General Evans (one of the conspicuous and heroic actors on the bloody field of Manassas). This brigade was made up of four regiments—the Eighteenth Virginia, Thirteenth, Seventeenth, and Eighteenth Mississippi. Taking up their position on Goose Creek, they bravely awaited the overwhelming number of the Federals. Lieutenant-colonel Jenifer, with four Mississippi companies, held the approaches toward Leesburg; while Colonel Hunter, with the Virginians, became hotly engaged with the enemy in the woods. About two o'clock, seeing that the Federals were being re-enforced, Colonel Burt, with the Eighteenth Mississippi, attacked them on the left flank, and Colonels Hunter and Jenifer moved against their front. Colonel Burt was received with such a heavy fire from the Federals concealed in the woods that he was compelled even to divide his forces in order to avoid a flank movement; but he was soon supported by the Seventeenth Mississippi, under Colonel Featherston, who came into action at a gallant double-quick. The battle now became general along the whole Confederate line, with the exception of the Thirteenth Mississippi, with six pieces of artillery, which was held in reserve. For two hours the Confederates fought with their characteristic methods— a desperation and a valor that were satisfied with nothing short of victory. Against this the Federals could not sustain themselves. They were driven back to the river, with the loss of their commander, Colonel Baker. When Colonel Evans saw them on the retreat he ordered his boys to charge. Naturally the retreat became a rout and a race for life on the part of the panic-stricken Federals in their efforts to reach the other bank of the river. The spectacle of a whole army completely beside themselves with fear, rolling and tumbling, pushing and scrambling down the steep bluffs and banks of the river, in the worst possible confusion, with the shrieks of the drowning added to the other horrors of the battle-field, was simply appalling.

This defeat was named in the Federal Congress "a national calamity," and it was said that "another laurel was added to the chaplet of the rebellion." And rightly too was it a serious cause for alarm at the North, for the superior fighting qualities of the Southern soldier were being demonstrated on every field where he had any thing like equal terms.

CUMBERLAND GAP.

To protect the mountain passes in East Tennessee and Kentucky, that were like open gate-ways, threatening not only those two States, but also the whole South, General Zollicoffer was sent, September 14, with seven thousand troops to Cumberland Gap.

To show that he respected the assumed neutrality of the State of Kentucky more than did the Federals, he sent the following telegram to Governor McGoffin: "The safety of Tennessee required the Confederate authorities to occupy these mountain passes. I postponed this movement until the despotic Government at Washington refused to recognize the neutrality of Kentucky. We have ever felt toward Kentucky as a twin sister; we are as one people in valor, kindred, sympathy, and patriotism." With this he also issued an order that he had come to defend the soil of a sister State, and that no citizen of Kentucky was to be molested in property or liberty. He then continued to advance toward Somerset, driving the Federals before him. He was opposed by a German general, Schoepff, with troops of like nationality, who was deluded into the belief that General Hardee was on his left flank; consequently he performed that famous "wild-cat stampede," fleeing for two whole days, scattering along his course guns, knapsacks, and every thing that would impede men when stripping to run a race. This retreat was continued, and was a case of "the wicked flee when no man pursueth."

In occupying these passes it was the purpose of the Federals to have means open of invading South-west Virginia, getting possession of the salt-works of Western Virginia, and of cutting off communications with Richmond and Memphis. To oppose this design, a small force of a thousand men was raised at Prestonburg by Colonel Williams, but he was forced to retreat before the vastly superior numbers of General Nelson, who boastfully had this insignificant skirmish heralded throughout the North as a great and decisive victory.

CHAPTER V.

Affairs in Kentucky.

AFTER the election of Mr. Lincoln, a Union party was formed in Kentucky, with the purpose of preventing the secession of their State. Resisting all pressure from this quarter, Governor McGoffin refused to respond to Mr. Lincoln's call to furnish troops for the subjugation of the Southern States, which step seemed to meet with the approval of the majority of conservative citizens. In a short time, however, relations between the two extremes of opinion became very much strained. Every "States' rights" paper was suspended; General Buckner united his fortunes with the Confederacy; in complete defiance of law, Ex-governor Morehead, on account of his Southern principles, was arrested in the presence of his family and sent as a prisoner to Louisville. To avoid the same treatment, the following prominent and leading citizens were forced to flee from their homes: Hon. John C. Breckinridge, Ex-vice-president; Colonel G. W. Johnson; T. B. Moore, Secretary of State; William Preston Johnson, former Minister to Spain; Colonel Humphrey Marshall, Ex-member of Congress; and Captain John H. Morgan, afterward so widely celebrated on account of his daring cavalry exploits.

In the meantime the authorities of the State continued to demand that the neutrality of Kentucky be respected; and the Legislature passed special resolutions asking General Polk—who, in the early part of September, had occupied Columbus—to withdraw from their borders. General Polk issued a proclamation declaring that he would act in accordance with their wish if they would force the Federals to do likewise. This proposition was rejected by the adherents of the Federal Government, though they had been the first to violate the neutrality of Kentucky.

To anticipate somewhat, it may be properly stated here that the sympathizers of the South, not being any longer able to endure the treatment which they were suffering at the hands of their opponents, met at Russellville November 18, and on the 20th unanimously adopted resolutions of secession, choosing George W. Johnson Governor and sending commissioners to Richmond asking for admission into the Confederacy. Their prayer was granted, and by the middle of December Kentucky was joined hand and heart with her sister States.

General Polk Attacked by the Federals.

While engaged in finishing his fortifications at Columbus, General Polk was attacked, on the morning of November 7, by a strong force from Cairo. Hearing that General Grant was on the river with gunboats and transports, and trying to land on the Missouri shore, six miles above Belmont, he ordered General Pillow to cross the river at once with four regiments and go to the relief of Colonel Tappan at Belmont. Before they were able to get well settled in their position the skirmishers were driven in, and it was evident that they were engaged with an enemy numerous enough to surround them with a line three deep. The Federals made several vain attempts at a flank movement, both against the left and the right. On the right they were repulsed by the determined resistance of Colonel Tappan's forces, together with the Thirteenth Arkansas and the Ninth Tennessee, commanded by Colonel Russell; while on the left their defeat was due to the deadly fire of Beltzhoover's Battery. Colonel Beltzhoover's ammunition became exhausted, as did also Colonels Bell's and Wright's. In reply to reports to this effect General Pillow gave the order to charge bayonets, which was executed so gallantly and effectively by the whole line that the enemy were driven to the shelter of the woods. Here, however, supported by a large reserve, they forced the Confederates back to their former position, who repeated their bayonet charge again and again, driving the Federals back each time upon their reserves. Soon perceiving the utter uselessness of maintaining such an unequal contest, General Pillow ordered the whole line to fall back to the river-bank. It seemed now that the Confederates must yield the palm of victory to the enemy, when, just at the proper time, Colonel Walker, with the Second Tennessee, crossed the river and came to General Pillow's support. Thus re-enforced, he hastened with all speed up the river, turning the enemy's position and getting in their rear. At this point he was further re-enforced by fresh troops, whom, with the Eleventh Louisiana, he placed under command of Colonel Marks. These proceeded at once, with the support of Colonel Russell, to charge the enemy in the rear, while General Cheatham took a position in sight of the shore to assist Colonel Marks, if necessary. The enemy now turned their attention to the boats, which were used in transporting our troops across the river, and opened a heavy fire upon them. To oppose this movement, Captain Smith's Battery was located on the opposite bank of the river. The Federals now found that they were in a dilemma from which it seemed difficult to extricate themselves; General Cheatham was pressing them on their flank, Colonels Marks and Russell were making matters extremely unpleasant in the rear, while Smith's Artillery was thundering in front of them. Consequently, after but a feeble resistance, they broke and ran in utter confusion. General Polk had, in the meantime, crossed the river, and, with the united commands, he vigorously pressed the pursuit until they reached the surgical head-quarters of the enemy, where they captured much-needed supplies of every character—blankets, clothes, provisions, wagons, horses, etc. To complete the confusion and dismay of the enemy, even after they had reached their boats they were subjected to a destructive fire from our troops, who lined the banks of the river.

In his official report General Pillow said that no further evidence was needed to assure the fact that this small Spartan army, which withstood the constant fire of three times their number for nearly four hours (a large portion being out of ammunition), had acted with extraordinary gallantry, and that complete results had crowned the day.

The Confederates lost, in killed and wounded and missing, 632, while the Federals sustained a loss of fully three times that number. Thus, all things considered, the victory at Belmont was one of the most brilliant of the war.

DEATH OF GENERAL ZOLLICOFFER.

Resuming the narration of the exploits of General Zollicoffer in Eastern Kentucky, we find that he had moved his forces to Mill Springs, on Fishing Creek, January 1, 1862. Here General Crittenden assumed command. The army was in great distress on account of want of provisions for both man and beast, for only one boat-load of supplies had come up from Nashville. The severity of bitter midwinter weather made their situation all the more wretched. However, with such a force, hardly prepared to cope with the enemy even on equal terms, General Crittenden began at midnight to charge General Thomas, with ten thousand men intrenched at Beech Grove. The battle began in real earnest on the morning of January 19, General Zollicoffer leading the front. The charge was gallantly made in the face of a galling fire from the enemy, who were being gradually driven back; when General Zollicoffer, just as he had mounted the crest of the hill around which the battle raged fiercest, was shot by the Federal Colonel Fry, and fell back dead in the midst of his friends, Colonel Battle's noble regiment of Tennesseeans. This unfortunate affair put a new phase upon the battle, by producing a depressing effect upon the soldiers, especially the Tennessee troops, by whom General Zollicoffer was greatly beloved. In spite of his most persistent efforts, General Crittenden was forced to retreat to Monticello, in order to open communication with Nashville.

In the meantime General Albert Sidney Johnston had been placed in command of the Western Army, and his line embraced a position sixty miles below Louisville, on the railroad. The Federals had advanced to Munfordville, and had succeeded in getting a portion of their forces across Green River to Woodsonville, where they were attacked and defeated, December 17, 1861, by General Hindman, with a loss of fifty killed.

General Johnston was forced to abandon his position at Bowling Green, on account of the immense numbers that were threatening him under General Buell, for it is estimated that the Federal force in Kentucky at this time consisted of over a hundred thousand, made up principally of Western men.

CHAPTER VI.

Fort Donelson—Permanent Organization.

THE Confederate Congress, recognizing the importance of the Cumberland and Tennessee Rivers as the key to Nashville and other strong strategic points, made large appropriations for the construction of floating batteries and other defenses.

The enemy, under General Grant, moved up the Cumberland River, and, after a gallant resistance, forced the brave defenders of Fort Henry to surrender. He then proceeded against Fort Donelson. Here General Johnston had sent the best divisions of his troops, as both he and General Beauregard, after a consultation, had concluded that this was the most important point at which they could make their defense.

THE BATTLE OF FORT DONELSON.

Early on the morning of February 13 General Floyd, who had been stationed at Russellville, Ky., reached the scene of action. With the rising of the sun the booming of the guns from one of the boats announced the beginning of the battle, which was continued all day, with heavy cannonading and attacks on several points of our lines, which were completely repulsed, the enemy being forced back to their original position. Thus the strength of our line was well tested.

On the following day no preparation seemed to be made on the part of the enemy for a renewal of their attack; but the activity in the neighborhood of the gun-boats showed that great re-enforcements were coming to a force already thirty thousand strong.

At three o'clock in the afternoon, however, having formed in the shape of a crescent, the fleet of the enemy opened fire, which was replied to so vigorously that the effect of our shot upon the iron-clads could be clearly seen.

New troops by the thousands seemed to be joining the ranks of the enemy. Nor did their fire cease after dark, which kept the Confederates from a much-needed rest. Thus they were forced to watch the whole of that bitter night through, with the mercury ten degrees below zero, and exposed to sleet and snow.

At a consultation held by General Floyd it was seen that their cause was hopeless under the existing circumstances, and the only course left open to them was to attempt to cut their way through the opposing lines of the enemy. Accordingly General Pillow, assisted by Colonel Bushrod Johnson, Colonel Baldwin commanding the Mississippi and Tennessee troops and Colonels Wharton and McCausland commanding the Virginians, moved from his position early in the morning. He found the Federals ready to receive him in front of their camps. A stubborn conflict ensued, desperately fought, with every inch of ground contested. Finally the enemy, fighting bravely, fell back to the Winn's Ferry Road, where General Buckner was defending the Confederate right. They attacked him, and after two hours of hard fighting gained possession of the most advantageous part of his intrenchments. Thus, after a nine hours' struggle, marked on both sides by a desperate courage that showed itself in the number of the dead scattered over the field, the Federals were virtually in possession of all points of advantage and importance. With only thirteen thousand men, weakened by exposure in the trenches, and worn out by the hard fighting, it seemed utterly hopeless for the Confederates to renew the conflict. Therefore surrender was agreed upon; but Generals Floyd and Pillow both refused to surrender either their own persons or their commands, so the unpleasant duty devolved upon General Buckner, who was offered terms by General Grant, in reply to which he wrote: "The distribution of the forces under my command compel me, notwithstanding the brilliant success of yesterday, to accept the ungenerous and unchivalrous terms you propose." The loss on the side of the enemy was conjectured to be about five thousand, and the Confederate loss about one-third of that number.

The Confederates Evacuate Nashville.

Immediately on receiving news of the fall of Donelson General Johnston saw that Nashville could not be defended without the destruction of the city. When his purpose became known a wild panic ensued on the part of the citizens to get out of reach of the advancing enemy. The State Legislature, with Governor Harris in possession of the documents and valuables of the State, fled to Memphis. A great quantity of stores and provisions were lost, though Generals Floyd and Forrest remained and endeavored to ship away as much as possible, that it might not fall into the hands of the enemy. Even large numbers of the wounded had to be left in the hospital, but these were tenderly cared for by the loyal and devoted women of Nashville and the patriotic men. Thus, with the enemy present at their doors, devotion to the principles of secession and love for the South were intensified, and any lukewarmness vanished and gave place to an earnest enthusiasm for their cause. With a noble generosity, and though they knew not how they themselves were to fare in future, they entertained the soldiers of the Confederacy, filling their haversacks and bidding them godspeed in their battle for right.

General Johnston meanwhile had reached Murfreesboro, and was resting the main body of his army there.

A Permanent Organization

was effected by the Confederate Government on the 22d of February, 1862, when affairs did not look so bright for the young Government as in the beginning. It seemed almost impossible, as President Davis himself declared, to furnish adequate protection at all points, both on land and sea; but the best possible measures under the circumstances were being taken. But the financial aspect of the war was at least encouraging, for there was no floating debt, the credit of the Government was unimpaired with the people, and the total expenditure for the year—one hundred and seventy million dollars—was one-third less than that expended by the Federal Congress. Moreover, the recent reverses had a tendency to quicken the energies of the authorities so as to produce vigorous and active measures, among which was the "Conscript Bill." The farmers of the country were also urged to decrease their plant of cotton and put into the soil other things more necessary to the sustenance of man and beast.

The confiscation of property by the Federal authorities, their imprisonment and bad treatment of citizens—all had a tendency, while it exasperated the people, to intensify their devotion to the Confederacy and to strengthen the energy of their resistance to the Federal power.

CHAPTER VII.

Affairs on the Water.

AFTER the abandonment of Columbus by the Confederates, the defense of Island Number Ten—situated in a bend of the Mississippi, thirty miles in length, near the towns of New Madrid and Point Pleasant, Mo.—was intrusted to General Beauregard. This island was looked upon as the chief barrier against the Federals entering the Southern Mississippi. It was considered thoroughly impregnable, having an immense swamp on the Missouri side and on the other side a lake several miles wide.

On the 12th of October the submerged ram, the "Manassas," made an attack upon the Federal squadron near the mouth of the Mississippi River, and succeeded in sinking the "Preble" and driving the others out of the river into the gulf.

A Confederate Naval Victory at Hampton Roads.

The Confederate squadron in the James River was commanded by Franklin Buchanan. The fleet consisted of the "Virginia," which was the remodeled "Merimac" that had been partially destroyed; the steamer "Patrick Henry," twelve guns; the steamer

"Jamestown," two guns; and the gun-boats "Teazer," "Beaufort," and "Raleigh." With these he moved out to Newport News to offer battle to the enemy. Before going into the engagement Captain Buchanan addressed his men as follows: "My men, you are about to face the enemy. You shall have no reason to complain of fighting at close quarters. Remember that you fight for your homes and your country. You see those ships; you must sink them; I need not ask you to do it; I know you will do it."

The Federal ship "Congress" occupied a position below the batteries, at Newport News, while the "Cumberland" was just opposite them. With a determination to sink the "Cumberland" with the "Virginia," Captain Buchanan steamed straight toward her, complimenting the "Congress" with a broadside as he passed, which was returned, but without producing any damage. The shore batteries, together with both ships, now concentrated their fire upon the "Virginia," which kept straight on, raking the "Cumberland" fore and aft with the discharge of her guns, and striking her bow below the waterline with such terrible effect that in fifteen minutes the waters of the ocean rolled over the flag of the "Cumberland," that had been kept floating to the last. The "Virginia" did not rest with this success, but went to serve the "Congress" similarly. On account of the shallowness of the water, she could make but slow progress, her keel being in the mud. However, she managed to get in position above the James River Batteries, though she had to endure a second time the fire of the enemy. In making this movement the Federals were considerably elated, in that they thought the Confederate "terror" had sustained such injuries as to force her to withdraw from the contest. But when she turned a terrible broadside upon the "Congress," producing death and destruction, dismay and confusion was the result. A flag of truce was immediately run up at the masthead, and the commander of the "Beaufort" was ordered by Captain Buchanan to go and take possession of her, with the officers as prisoners, but to allow the crew to land. He also ordered the ship burned.

The prisoners on board the "Beaufort" requested that they be allowed to transfer their wounded from the "Congress," which request was granted; but, violating their plighted honor, they never returned. An attempt was now made to burn the "Congress," which was prevented by the fire from the batteries on the shore. At this failure Captain Buchanan opened upon her with hot shot, and about midnight the citizens of Norfolk were awakened by the explosion of her magazine, and all that was left of the "Congress" were the scattered fragments floating upon the sea.

Captain Buchanan having been severely wounded, Lieutenant Catesby Jones assumed command, and at eight o'clock the next morning the "Virginia" sailed out to engage the new Federal iron-clad, the "Monitor." The latter had the advantage in smallness of size, and consequently of lighter draft and rapidity of movement. For two hours these two vessels poured a terrible fire into each other. Once the "Virginia" ran aground, and, being under the double fire of both the "Monitor" and the "Minnesota," seemed to be in desperate straits; but the crew managed to extricate her, and again turned her batteries upon the enemy. After having disabled the "Minnesota," and twice silenced the fire of the "Monitor," she put back to Norfolk.

These exploits of the "Virginia" created great excitement, both at the North and in Europe, and the immediate effect was that within five days after their defeat at Hampton Roads the Federal Government had appropriated fifteen million dollars for the building of iron-clads.

Battle between the "Monitor" and the "Merrimac."

(72)

CHAPTER VIII.

Generals Van Dorn and Sibley in the West.

AT the close of the year 1861 General Price had occupied Springfield with the purpose of being within reach of supplies and of protecting that part of the State. In the latter part of January, 1862, the Federals were massing large numbers—first at Rolla and afterward at Lebanon. Perceiving that their purpose was to move against him with largely superior forces, he requested aid from the divisions in Arkansas. According to expectation, on the 12th of February the Federals attacked him, forcing a retreat from Springfield. The enemy followed in close pursuit, so that the retreat to Cross Hollows, Ark., was virtually a running fight of five days, for the Confederates had to make their way through by repulsing the attacks of the enemy at every point.

General Van Dorn was appointed by President Davis to take command of the forces in the West. Consequently, hearing of General Price's retreat from Springfield, he moved from his own position at Pocahontas, Ark., and on the 3d of March took charge of the united forces of Generals Price and McCullough.

Battle of Elk Horn.

The Federals, twenty thousand strong, under Generals Sigel and Curtis, were resting at Sugar Creek, waiting for further re-enforcements. Having been joined by General Pike with his command of Indian troops, on the 4th of March General Van Dorn, with a force sixteen thousand strong, took up his march in the direction of Sugar Creek for the purpose of attacking the Federals.

On the morning of the 7th the battle began, and by eleven o'clock it was being fought in real earnest, and by two o'clock in the afternoon the Confederates were on the point of a complete and decisive victory, when both Generals McIntosh and McCullough were killed. Notwithstanding this irreparable loss and the confusion necessarily resulting to the soldiers from the death of their commanders, General Van Dorn continued to press the enemy, so that when darkness put an end to the battle he had gained possession of their intrenchments, together with a large amount of commissary stores. Having recuperated themselves during the night, the enemy renewed the contest on the morning of the 8th. General Van Dorn continued the fight until after nine o'clock, when he began to withdraw his forces in the direction of his supplies. The enemy attempting to follow were checked at once, and the retreat was conducted with the greatest success, and besides the Confederates carried away with them 300 prisoners, four cannons, and three baggage-wagons. They lost about 600 in killed and wounded, while the Federal loss is conjectured to have been fully double that number, though it is not officially known. When the character of the equipment and training of the two armies is relatively considered, the success of the Confederates was all the more a matter of congratulation, for they were poorly armed with old shotguns and rifles, and completely without military drill, while the Federals were well disciplined and furnished with the latest improved weapons.

In the Far West.

After a long march of nearly two hundred miles from Arizona, General Sibley, with two thousand three hundred troops, found himself in the neighborhood of Fort Craig, in which were Union troops to the number of six thousand—one thousand five hundred American soldiers and about five thousand Mexicans. Having crossed the Rio Grande River three miles above the fort, that portion of his troops—about two hundred and fifty in number—under Colonel Pryor first came in contact with the enemy. This division alone for over an hour sustained their incessant fire until the rest of the troops came up. The enemy then moved their whole line forward, but were driven back. With a second attack, however, they forced the Confederates to retreat and take up a new position. Thinking that they had won the day, the enemy moved their battery across the river, which was no sooner done than the Confederates charged them, and with the assistance of Teel's Battery drove them in great confusion from their guns, forcing them to cross the river. In this battle of Valverde (March 21) our forces lost 38 killed and 120 wounded, while the enemy gave their loss as 300 killed, 400 wounded, and 2,000 missing. The Confederates continued their victorious march, forcing the Federals to evacuate both Albuquerque and Santa Fe, and to retreat to Fort Union, a strong fortification sixty miles northeast of Santa Fe.

CHAPTER IX.
Island No. Ten—Shiloh—New Orleans.

ON the 15th of March the Federal fleet of gun-boats, under the command of Flag-officer Foote, began the bombardment of Island No. Ten, which had been fortified with great skill by General Beauregard. An incessant and ceaseless cannonading was kept up between the gun-boats and the batteries until April 8 without giving any convincing sign of victory to either side; but the people of the South were strengthened by daily reports from the scene of action that it was absolutely impossible for the Federal forces to take the fort. Under these circumstances, on the 5th General Beauregard left to take charge of operations on the Tennessee River, and the command of the island devolved upon General MaCall, who allowed the enemy to construct a canal twelve miles long across the peninsula at New Madrid. This canal gave them possession of the river below the island. Then, in order to avoid surrender, with the infantry and Stewart's Battery, General MaCall, on the night of April 6, managed to reach the Tennessee shore, leaving in the hands of the enemy seventy cannons, large quantities of ammunition, the floating batteries, and four steamers.

The Great Battle of Shiloh.

In massing all of his forces at Corinth General Beauregard's purpose was to cut off the enemy's communication between the South and East. Here he assembled a magnificent army—the very flower and chivalry of the South. General Johnston moved from Murfreesboro and joined him here; also two divisions of General Polk's forces at Columbus, together with several regiments of troops from Louisiana and a force from Mobile; consequently few battle-fields of the South witnessed such a gathering of men, both as to their number, the quality of the troops, and the character of their discipline.

General Grant occupied a position at Pittsburg Landing, awaiting the arrival of General Buell, who was rapidly hastening from Nashville to join him. To strike the enemy at once, and thereby prevent the effectiveness of this junction by a victory before it could be accomplished, was the purpose of General Beauregard. In keeping with his plan, he began the disposition of his troops on Thursday, the 3d of April, expecting to make the attack on Saturday, but the condition of the roads was such as to make progress so slow that one day was lost in the preparation, and a fatal day it was! After skirmishing somewhat late Saturday evening, the great battle was opened early Sunday morning, April 6, by General Hardee advancing against the camp of the enemy and taking them by surprise, finding them undressed and in the preparation of breakfast. However, they quickly formed to meet our forces, which were advancing in three lines, with General Hardee commanding the front, General Bragg the center, and General Polk the rear. With the driving in of the pickets, a sublime artillery duel began the work of death, and the coolness and splendid composure of the raw recruits of the Confederates under this test gave a prophecy of the magnificent courage which they displayed on that memorable day. Rising from the ground upon which they were lying that the discharges of the artillery might pass over, they rushed forward, crushing every thing before them with the force of a hurricane. Broken in ranks, the enemy rallied behind trees and in the underbrush, only to be again repulsed and driven back. The scenery is described as follows: "Far up in the air shells burst into flames like shattered stars, and passed away in little clouds of white vapor; while others filled the air with a shrill scream, and burst far in the rear. All along the line the faint smoke of the musketry rose lightly, while from the mouth of the cannon sudden gusts of intense white smoke burst up all around."

The attack of the Confederates was compared by General Beauregard, in his official report of the battle, to an "Alpine avalanche." Inspiring examples of personal valor displayed by general and field officers made the Confederate soldiers invincible. At half-past two General Johnston, commander-in-chief of the Confederate forces, fell mortally wounded. Riding up to him, Governor Harris, who was a volunteer aid, asked if he was badly hurt, to which the dying hero replied: "Yes; and I fear mortally." He fell from his horse, and soon expired. This sad affair was prudently kept from the army. The Confederates still continued to push the enemy to the Tennessee River, and at six o'clock in the evening the last position was carried. The fruits of this victory were great. The Confederates were in possession of all the encampments of the enemy between Owl and Lick Rivers. On Sunday General Beauregard established his head-quarters at the little church at Shiloh. The soldiers slept on their arms. The situation of both armies was critical, but General Grant was relieved by the glistening bayonets of Buell across the river. On seeing them he was heard to remark to one of his officers: "To-morrow they will be exhausted, and then we'll give it to them with fresh troops." General Buell advanced, and was hailed to the field of slaughter with cheers. The battle again began to rage with fury; hour by hour the terrible struggle continued. With fresh troops they constantly thinned the ranks of our worn-out soldiers. To avert further sacrifice of human life General Beauregard determined to withdraw, since it was impossible to contend against such heavy reenforcements—all fresh troops. Approaching General Breckinridge, he said: "General Breckinridge, it may be you will have to sacrifice your life; this retreat must not be a rout: you must hold the enemy if it takes your last man." "Your orders shall be executed," said the chivalrous Breckinridge. "Our poor boys are weary and hungry, yet we can trust them." They stood guard, and closely watched the enemy, who decided not to try the contest again for awhile, so badly had they been whipped; for they had lost nearly all of their artillery, over three thousand prisoners, including a division commander (General Prentiss), several brigade commanders, an immense supply of subsistence and ammunition, and a large amount of means of transportation. Against the Confederates were engaged the commands of Generals Prentiss, Sherman, Hurlburt, Smith, and McClernand—all told, forty-five thousand finely equipped men. The Confederate forces consisted of thirty-eight thousand. From their almost reckless daring, the Confederates suffered much in the loss of officers. General Gladden, of South Carolina, fell mortally wounded; also Governor George W. Johnson, of Kentucky, while engaged in the thickest of the battle; General Bray had two horses shot from under him; General Breckinridge was twice struck; Major-general Hardee had his coat torn by minie-balls; General Cheatham received one in the shoulder; General Bushrod Johnson was wounded in the side; Colonel Adams, of Louisiana, Colkit Williams, of Memphis, and General William B. Bate, of Tennessee, received severe injuries; and Colonel Blythe, of Mississippi, was among the killed. Our loss in this terrible slaughter was 10,699, while the Federal loss was 15,000. General Beauregard retired to Corinth as a strategic point, where Generals Van Dorn and Price united their forces with his.

Fall of New Orleans.

New Orleans was considered impregnable. The forts of Jackson and St. Philips were only looked upon as outer lines of defense. The city was occupied by a large force under General Lovell, and in its harbor was a fleet consisting of twelve gun-boats, one iron-clad steamer, and the famous ram "Manassas." The enemy's fleet engaged was forty-six sail, carrying two hundred and eighty-six guns and twenty-one mortars, the whole under the command of Admiral Farragut. On the 24th of April the Federal fleet opened fire on the boats, which was vigorously returned. In one hour several of their boats succeeded in passing the forts, the first one having our "night signal" flying, which allowed her to pass the Confederate batteries unmolested. On receiving the news the whole city was thrown into intense excite-

Destruction of Cotton at the Taking of New Orleans.

ment. The conflict between the two fleets was of a dreadful character. The Confederates fought with desperation against the overwhelming numbers until their vessels were driven on shore and burned by their commanders. The "Manassas" was sunk, and the great iron-clad, "Louisiana," was not in good working order. General Lovell withdrew his army to save the city from destruction. The evacuation was begun April 24. As soon as the Federal fleet came in sight of the city the work of destruction began. For five miles along the river on the levee the cotton was piled and burned. Great ships and steamers wrapped in fire floated down the river. Fifteen thousand bales of cotton were consumed. The city was left under charge of Mayor Monroe. The people were heart-broken when General Butler took possession May 1.

CHAPTER X.
Gallant Defense of Richmond.

TURNING now for a brief glance at civil affairs, the Government at Washington—exasperated by the prolongation of a war which they thought they would be able to end in a few weeks, astonished at the success of Confederate arms, and alarmed at MacClellan's failure to take Richmond; yielding to the popular clamor—determined upon extreme measures. Consequently the Secretary of War issued instructions to the commanding generals to seize upon any and all private property, and to make complete use of it, without any compensation whatever.

At the South the Government began to despair of foreign recognition. In fact, the disaster at New Orleans put an end to all their hopes in this respect. The rapidly increasing numbers of the enemy, drawn from every State in Europe, made necessary a change in the manner of recruiting troops. Therefore, in May, 1862, the conscript law was passed; which—while it created a considerable amount of opposition among the people, inasmuch as they considered it a reflection upon themselves—reorganized the army and furnished a regular, systematic method of filling the depleted ranks.

Kernstown—Jackson Repulsed.

On the 23d of March we find the ever active Jackson attacking the Federals at Kernstown, a place near Winchester, Va., with about six thousand troops, among which was Captain McLaughlin's Battery, with Colonel Ashby's Cavalry. The battle continued from four o'clock in the afternoon until darkness set in, when General Jackson fell back to Cedar Creek, having sustained a loss of one hundred in killed and wounded. Of this retreat the Federal General Shields said: "Such was the gallantry of the Confederates and their high state of discipline that at no time during the retreat did they give way to panic."

With the Federal forces enveloping Richmond, both from the land and from the river, vigorous and active operations on the part of the Confederates now became necessary. But their anxiety from the direction of the water was relieved somewhat by the brilliant repulse of the enemy's gun-boats, in their attack upon the batteries at Drewry's Bluff, which were under the command of Captain Farrand. Here, May 15, they were driven back with great loss of life.

Jackson's Successes in the Valley.

To draw off, if possible, the overwhelming concentration of forces which was taking place immediately around the city General Jackson was sent into the Valley of Virginia, with a small division, and he immediately began that series of wonderful military exploits that have placed him in the front rank of earth's great captains. Consequently, on May 8, he proceeded to attack General Milroy, with twelve thousand troops, at McDowell. Late in the afternoon Jackson—outnumbered thrice by the enemy—began the contest, which was decisively ended by the irresistible charge of Johnson's Brigade (Virginia Volunteers and the Twelfth Georgia Regiment), and just at the going down of the sun the Federals fled in complete confusion from the field. This was a costly victory to Jackson, in that he lost fully three hundred and fifty, killed and wounded. The enemy are conjectured to have lost something in the neighborhood of seven hundred.

With characteristic energy, he did not wait for the Federals to move against himself, but with rapid marches he astounded the Federal General Banks by falling upon that portion of his forces stationed at Front Royal, and taking a quantity of artillery and fourteen hundred prisoners, May 23. General Banks, thoroughly alarmed, fled toward Winchester, and was further frightened by Jackson striking his retreating column in the rear, May 24. However, the Federal forces managed to reach Winchester, only to be again struck, on the 25th, by their terrible enemy. So completely were they demoralized that they hardly made any resistance, and only succeeded in escaping by a superior running ability, which the Federal commander virtually admits in his report, when he says: "Pursuit by the enemy was prompt and vigorous; but *our movements were rapid.*" These victories were very profitable to the Confederates, in that they only lost a few men and captured four thousand prisoners and a vast quantity of supplies.

JACKSON DEFEATS THE FEDERALS AT PORT REPUBLIC.

Retaining possession of his booty, General Jackson fell back from Winchester between the two forces of Fremont and Shields—the former numbering twenty thousand and the latter ten thousand. He thence directed his march toward Port Republic, and on reaching this place he was attacked by Fremont on the morning of Sunday, the 8th of June, while Shields's Division was coming upon the other bank (east) of the Shenandoah River. Thus, so to speak, between two fires, he left that portion of his troops under General Ewell to engage Fremont, while, with the remainder, he kept Shields on the other side of the river.

Holding a superior position, and displaying a remarkably good judgment in the management of the fight, when night came it was found that General Ewell had driven the Federals back, with a loss of two thousand in killed and wounded, while his own loss was less than two hundred.

Under cover of darkness Jackson moved his forces across North River, leaving only a few behind to prevent Fremont from following him immediately. Therefore, early Monday morning he began his attack on the enemy, who were waiting to receive him on the east bank of the Shenandoah. At first General Jackson could only engage the Federals with a portion of his forces, as the rest had not arrived from Port Republic. So well directed was the fire of the enemy that for a time it seemed that our men could not stand its volleys of death, which were then fast thinning their ranks; but fresh troops from Port Republic were rapidly coming to their assistance. Moreover, General Taylor, with the Louisiana Brigade, surprised the enemy by coming out from the woods upon them, and charging right upon the mouths of their cannon. The whole line of the enemy now gave way and broke and fled in disorder, while the Confederates pursued for twelve miles, taking five hundred prisoners. Our loss was considerable, and among the dead was the brave and chivalrous Ashby, who, after his second horse was killed under him, was leading his devoted Virginians on foot, when he was shot, with these words of command on his lips: "Men, cease firing; charge, for God's sake charge!"

Thus, having swept the enemy completely from the valley, Jackson retired to Brown's Gap to rest his victorious but tired legions for a few days.

Activities on the Chickahominy.

The north was now straining every energy for the capture of Richmond, and had put under the command of General MacClellan a magnificently equipped army, which was trying to encircle the city with its lines. By the 30th of May General Johnston found the enemy in front of him, on the Chickahominy River, so he determined to attack them the next day at dawn. But for some reason General Huger, who had been ordered to support Generals Longstreet and Hill, failed to appear; which delay kept the two latter waiting until two o'clock in the afternoon, when they opened the battle without his expected assistance. D. H. Hill's brave troops charged nobly forward, penetrating the enemy's camp and driving them from each new line of intrenchments, behind which they would make repeated stands when re-enforced by fresh troops. When night put an end to the contest, while the victory was thoroughly complete in this quarter, the enemy having been driven for two miles, yet it was found that they had managed to hold their position on the right; but there was every indication that darkness only saved them from the same defeat which their line suffered at other points.

In this battle our loss was a little over four thousand. To compensate for this, the enemy lost eight thousand men, ten pieces of artillery, and six thousand muskets.

General Johnston having been wounded, the command of the Confederate forces for the defense of Richmond devolved upon General Lee.

On the morning of June 1 the enemy made an attack upon our lines, but after some hard fighting were repulsed with considerable loss.

Mechanicsville—Malvern Hill.

The enemy had so posted and arranged their forces along the course of the Chickahominy that their line extended fully twenty miles on both sides of this stream, with the purpose of threatening Richmond with a siege.

That series of splendid battles along this now celebrated little stream was begun by General Jackson, Thursday, June 26, driving a portion of the enemy from the north bank, near the Brooke Turnpike.

General A. P. Hill had crossed the river at Meadow Bridge; and at Mechanicsville, without waiting for General Branch, who was trying to join him, he hurled his column of fourteen thousand men against the enemy, who resisted stubbornly until night put an end to the conflict, when they retreated down the stream to Powhite Swamp.

On Friday, with General A. P. Hill in the center, and Generals Longstreet and D. H. Hill coming down the Chickahominy, and General Jackson toward the left at some distance, an advance movement was made against the enemy. The Confederates rushed furiously to the attack, and by eight o'clock in the evening they had succeeded in pushing the shattered forces of the enemy from the north to the south side of the Chickahominy.

A feature of this day's fight worthy of relating in detail was the brilliant assault of General A. P. Hill upon that portion of the Federals stationed at Gaines's Mills. The fortifications at this point were strong and well constructed, so that the enemy were able to resist his repeated attacks until he was supported by General Pickett's Brigade, from General Longstreet's Division. Even with these, matters were in doubt until Whiting's Division made a masterly "double-quick" charge, and, by superior valor, drove the enemy from defenses which they ought to have been able to maintain against almost any force.

Thus, having been defeated at almost all their strongholds on the north bank, with communications with Washington cut off, the Chickahominy barring their way in front, Generals Longstreet, Magruder, and Huger pressing close upon their rear, it seemed that escape for the enemy was hopeless. However, on Sunday morning it was discovered that they had deserted their fortifications in confusion, and had massed their forces five miles north-east of Darbytown, at a place known as Frazier's Farm. Finding them in this position, on Monday the forces of Generals Longstreet and Hill moved forward unsupported by a single battery of artillery, while the enemy received them with a terrible fire from both infantry and artillery. With as brilliant a courage as had ever illustrated the annals of any war, the Confederates continued their advance in the midst of a perfect storm of shot and shell, gradually driving the Federals back, until by half-past eight in the evening they were in possession of their guns and fortifications. Darkness did not check the victorious advance of the Confederates, for they still continued to press the enemy until the latter were heavily re-enforced. From their hard struggle of the day the Confederates were already tired and worn out. Consequently they slowly retreated before these fresh troops. With cheers the now exultant enemy followed them; but once more, with knightly courage, the Confederates gathered together their flagging energies, and beat the overconfident Federals back. At eleven o'clock General Magruder's Division arrived, and occupied the battle-field, giving General Hill's exhausted heroes an opportunity for a much-needed rest.

On Tuesday the Federals again took up their retreat, and were followed by General Magruder, who came up with them strongly intrenched on Carter's Farm. Just one hour later he attacked them; but after repeated charges in the very face of death itself, both from the guns of the enemy in front and from the huge shells that were sent from their gunboats in the river, two miles distant, he was forced to fall back in the darkness, giving the Federals a chance to continue their retreat through the swamps.

In this battle, known as Malvern Hill, the Confederates added another page to their glorious record for courage and endurance by a frightful loss of life.

CHAPTER XI.

A Series of Important Events.

JUST when the two great armies in Northern Virginia were marshaling their forces for the great conflicts on the Chickahominy, further South an inspiring victory was gained by the Confederates. At Secessionville, on James Island, near Charleston, S. C., a large force of the enemy made an attack on the intrenchments of Colonel J. G. Lamar. Three times they charged the works, beginning at four o'clock on the morning of June 16, but each time they were driven back with great loss, and by ten o'clock they retired in great confusion, leaving behind them four hundred killed and wounded and prisoners.

After Shiloh, General Beauregard, with forty-seven thousand troops, had intrenched himself at Corinth, Miss., where he tried in vain to get the ninety thousand of the enemy to attack him. Failing in this, on the morning of the 30th of May he evacuated Corinth, and successfully retreated to Baldwin; thence on the 7th of June he moved his forces to Tupelo, a more advantageous position.

The enemy continued their successes on the Mississipppi River by taking Memphis, Tenn., June 6.

Then they turned their attention to Vicksburg, Miss., but here their navy, hitherto invincible, met an unexpected repulse. After a siege of six weeks, during which time they threw twenty-five thousand shells into the city, they abandoned their fruitless efforts against it.

Between the 4th and 28th of July General John Morgan effected that famous raid of his which reflected so much credit upon the prowess of Southern cavalry. Setting out from Knoxville, Tenn., with rangers from Georgia, Texas, and Tennessee, he pushed his forces right into the midst of a country infested on all sides by the enemy, creating the greatest consternation and fear, taking from them seventeen of the Kentucky towns that had fallen into their possession, capturing a large number of prisoners with three thousand stands of arms at Lebanon, Ky., and then returning to his original starting-place with a loss of less than one hundred men.

With this brief summary of military operations in the West, attention is again turned to those ever interesting scenes in Virginia which have made every foot of this historic old Commonwealth a battle-ground and a Confederate victory, through which the military student of all after times may find illustrated the highest ideals of his art and the loftiest examples of soldierly courage and endurance. On the 23d of July General Pope signalized his transfer from the

West to the Army of Northern Virginia by issuing an order to the effect that all citizens within his lines who would not take the oath to the Federal Government should be considered spies, and as such should be subjected to the extremest penalties of military laws; and that any one who had violated this oath should be shot and his property confiscated. A further order, equally cruel in its provisions, was issued. The purpose of this law was to hold certain prominent citizens as hostages, to be shot in case any Federal soldier should be killed by the so-called "bushwhackers." In other words, should any Southern citizen, in exercising the sacred prerogatives of his manhood, attempt to defend the threshold of his home against the robber or the assassin, and in this attempt should slay the violator of his household gods, then his friend and neighbor, in the hands of the enemy, would pay the penalty with his life.

Pope now took up his line of march toward the interior of Virginia, and succeeded in penetrating to a point as far as ten miles east of Port Republic. Against this movement General Jackson was sent. On hearing that the latter had crossed the Rapidan, Pope sent General Banks to put a check upon him. On the morning of August 12 General Ewell's Division moved forward and took a position at Culpepper Court-house, and at twelve o'clock they opened upon the enemy with their artillery. At four o'clock in the afternoon the battle was begun in real earnest by the attack of General Early's Brigade upon the right flank of the enemy. The brave General Winder perished as he was leading Jackson's Division into action. The enemy now took the aggressive by charging through an open corn-field with their cavalry, which produced a temporary confusion; but the Confederates soon recovered themselves, and turned such an effective fire upon them that many a horse went back riderless to the Federal lines, followed by the remainder of the cavalry in the greatest confusion. For two hours the battle raged, victory inclining first to one side, then to the other, until the darkness of the night began to thrown its black mantle over a scene fraught with more than the usual amount of horrors that characterize a contest in which men strive with each other in all the bitterness of a deadly struggle, when the Federals broke and took to the shelter of the woods, leaving the Confederates in possession of the sanguinary field of Cedar Mountain, upon which were nearly two thousand Federal dead and wounded and six hundred of the Confederates. But the Confederates also had in their possession five hundred prisoners, one thousand five hundred stands of arms, one dozen wagon-loads of ammunition, two Napoleon guns, and a large amount of excellent new clothing.

The Federal Government now felt that there was

an imperative demand upon them to do something extraordinary, if possible, to retrieve those disasters that had come in such rapid succession around Richmond; consequently they proceeded at once to carry out the design of uniting the two large armies of Pope and MacClellan. Getting knowledge of these designs, General Lee rapidly changed the position of his forces, and on the 17th of August held them in front of Pope to prevent his crossing the Rapidan.

In the meanwhile, by a rapid march of two days over the mountains, the brilliant Jackson, completely misleading the enemy, had succeeded in occupying Bristow and Manassas Stations, on Wednesday, August 27, where he captured many thousands of dollars' worth of supplies. On the same day an attack was made by the enemy upon both positions. General Taylor's Brigade of Slocum's Division of the Army of the Potomac attacked Manassas, but was hurled back in a disgraceful and thoroughly disorganized retreat toward Centerville. At three o'clock Hooker's Division moved against General Ewell at Bristow, forcing him back across the Muddy Run. By a masterly movement, on the night of the next day, General Jackson succeeded in getting an advantageous position on the old battle-field of Manassas— so inspiring from its memories of that former great victory, which was soon to be repeated with increased glory to Southern arms. Early Friday morning General Stuart dispersed the enemy's cavalry near Gainesville, on the Warrenton Pike, and later in the day General Jackson threw his forces in front of the enemy, who were evidently advancing to attack him, near the village of Groveton. General Longstreet, in the meantime, in order to join his division with Jackson's, had to force his passage through a wild and precipitous mountain pass known as Thoroughfare Gap. This would have been an impossible feat to any but Southern soldiers, for it was held by a force of two thousand of the enemy, and from aid which nature gave, with the rough and steep sides and narrow pass-way, this gap would seem completely impregnable, with even half the number which the enemy had concentrated there. But the Confederates forced their way and accomplished this daring undertaking with less than half a dozen men wounded.

The enemy began the fight by advancing in a column heavily supported by artillery. They were received by Ewell's Division, who reserved their fire until the enemy were close upon them, when they opened with terrible effect, creating a panic in the ranks of the Federals, which was further increased by the artillery, which was turned upon them as they ran. Toward evening Jackson, re-enforced by Hood's Division, fought with renewed energy, gradually driving the enemy from the field, until by nine o'clock the latter fell back, having sustained a loss of eight thousand in killed and wounded. These attacks by the Federals were upon the wings of the Confederates, and the dawn of Saturday, August 30, saw Pope gathering his energies for a still greater effort, by which he hoped to crush the ill-fed, badly-clothed soldiers of Jackson—foot-sore and weary from the forced marches and incessant fighting. But the result of the contest will show that the Federal general underestimated the heroic hearts that beat under dust-covered gray jackets and those knightly souls that looked out from eyes set in powder-stained faces.

Jackson was now re-enforced by almost all of Longstreet's entire corps, which occupied a position on the right, with Jackson himself holding the left wing—the whole line forming a crescent five miles long. Opposed to these, on the side of the enemy were Generals Sigel, Fitz John Porter, and Reno in the center, and Heintzleman and McDowell on the left and right respectively. The Confederate batteries in the center, under General S. D. Lee, opening upon the rapidly forming squadrons of the enemy, which fire was returned by their batteries. Then the Federals moved forward in three successive columns against Jackson's infantry. Desperately and boldly did they try to maintain themselves against these veterans whose exploits have made them co-heirs in the immortal glory of their commander. All to no purpose did this elect corps of the Federal army sacrifice their best blood in their efforts to redeem the trust their commanders had put in them. They staggered and reeled like the Old Guard at Waterloo, until General Lee turned the awful fire of his batteries upon them, when they turned and fled, with Jackson's men pursuing like so many incarnate spirits of the genius of battle. General Sickles's Excelsior Brigade met even a worse fate at the hands of General Hood, who charged them and left few to survive the impetuosity and effectiveness of his attack. The order was now given for a general charge along the whole Confederate line. Never did the soldiery of any age or any land respond more nobly or gallantly to a command. Grandly and superbly these gray masses moved forward, with those characteristic cheers which sounded their clarion peals of victory above the din of the artillery and the rattle of the musketry. Nothing could withstand them. The spirit of the cause itself for which they fought seemed to be personified in them, enthusing them with a courage that sent the enemy flying toward Centerville, forgetful of every thing except the desire to save life. Like a senseless mob they ran, obeying no commands until they were checked at Centerville by the arrival of General Franklin with thirty thousand fresh troops. With these Pope restored partial order to his disorganized army, and continued his retreat toward the trenches at Washington, leaving upon the field of battle a large amount of the munitions of war, and something approaching thirty thousand men, in killed and wounded. Thus, in all the fights of this memorable week, it has been estimated that the total Federal loss was thirty-eight thousand.

"On September 4 General Lee—leaving to his right Arlington Heights, to which Pope had retreated with his shattered army—crossed the Potomac into Maryland. This was only a feint; the main object was to seize Harper's Ferry, and to test the spirit of Marylanders. He then threw Pennsylvania into a state of consternation from Hagerstown." With the presence of the Confederate army at Frederick, and fearing an invasion of their territory, the North was filled with anxiety and terror. To carry on certain important movements, General Lee- having divided his forces into three corps commanded by Generals Jackson, Longstreet, and Hill—ordered General Jackson to recross the Potomac at Williamsport and to get behind Harper's Ferry, in order to take the garrison and the stores known to be there. Generals Longstreet and Hill were placed in position so as to check General MacClellan's forces, who were moving toward Harper's Ferry, with the purpose of preventing its capture. General MacClellan had resumed command of the Federals September 14, General Pope, to use the expression of the soldiers, "having lost his head."

The Battle of Boonsboro.

Jackson had separated his own division from the main body of the army in order to make his attack upon Harper's Ferry, while General Longstreet proceeded on to Hagerstown. General Miles, the Federal commander, with twelve thousand men, occupied Harper's Ferry. To thwart the Confederates in their designs upon this place, the enemy had moved their entire force to the gap in the mountain. As a counter-movement General Lee had placed General D. H. Hill on the other side of the gap, with part of his forces occupying the top. He was given imperative instructions to hold his position until Jackson's success was assured. To understand the relative position of the armies and the nature of the battle that followed, a description of this pass is necessary. "The road is winding, narrow, rocky, and rugged, with either a deep ravine on one side and the steep sides of the mountain on the other, or like a huge channel cut through a solid rock. Near the crest are three houses which overlook the valley, but elsewhere the face of the mountain is unbroken by a solitary habitation."

Beginning just after day-dawn, an artillery duel of two hours' duration opened the battle, which was then taken up generally along the whole line. Our vigorous attacks seemed to make no impression on the overpowering numbers of the enemy, and retreat seemed inevitable, when the rallying cry of Longstreet's fresh legion's from Hagerstown, wheeling themselves gallantly into action, put a new phase upon the battle. But even to these fresh re-enforcements the enemy would not yield, and with a determination equal in its tenacity to that of the Confederates, whom, however, they outnumbered by five times their number, they held their position until the darkness of the night brought a needed rest to man and beast. But the purpose of the Confederates was accomplished. Jackson had done his work.

Surrender of Harper's Ferry.

Having placed his artillery in position on the night of September 14, early next morning Jackson hurled such volleys of death upon the whole line of Federal fortifications that by half-past seven they flung out the white flag of truce, surrendering eleven thousand troops, seventy-three pieces of artillery, and two hundred wagons. Their commander, General Miles, had his left thigh shot away by a fragment of a shell. Once again had Jackson's ragged veterans forced upon the eyes of the North the thoroughly humiliating spectacle of the surrender of a magnificently equipped division of their so-called " Grand Army." One can imagine how intensely painful it must have been to these Federal soldiers, blessed with every thing that was necessary to the complete equipment

Harper's Ferry.

of soldiers, to march out as prisoners before these heroes of a hundred battle-fields in their tattered and war-stained garments.

Battle of Sharpsburg.

General Lee had now determined to confront the advancing force of MacClellan in possession of Crampton's Gap, on the road from Frederick City to Sharpsburg, the latter place being about ten miles from Harper's Ferry, resting in a deep valley in the midst of a rugged and broken country. By September 17 he had settled his forty-five thousand men in a strong position, when he was attacked by a force of one hundred and fifty thousand finely trained soldiers. General MacClellan commanded in person, with the following subordinates present with their divisions: Generals Burnside, McDowell, Hooker, Sumner, Franklin, Williams, and Sykes. The line of battle of this great army extended over a space of five miles. A preliminary fire from the Federal batteries late Tuesday evening (16th) prepared the Confederates for an early renewal the next morning. Consequently by day-break the battle was opened and continued by the pickets until it merged into a general engagement. "The enemy advanced between Antietam and the Sharpsburg and Hagerstown turnpike, and were met by General D. H. Hill and General Longstreet, where the conflict raged, extending to our entire left."

The mortality among the Federals was terrible, for they were in a position where our guns were used against them with such telling effect that they fell as grain falls before the blade of the reaper; consequently after a stubborn contest they were forced to fall back at this point. But that portion of our line nearest where the enemy crossed the Potomac was on the point of being overwhelmed, when the divisions of McLaws, Anderson, and Walker came to its assistance. With these new troops the ranks were restored, and they held their position.

Of how heroically and nobly the Confederates fought it is perhaps well to give the testimony of a Federal officer: "It is beyond all comprehension how men such as the rebel troops are can fight as they do. That those ragged wretches—sick, hungry, and in all ways miserable—should prove such heroes in fight is past explanation. Men never fought better. There was one regiment that stood up before the fire of two or three of our long-range batteries and two regiments of infantry, and though the air around them was vocal with the whistle of the bullets and the scream of the shells, there they stood and delivered their fire in perfect order."

In the afternoon the enemy made a vain attack upon our right, which was held by General Jones, but they met with better success in forcing General Tombs from his position at the bridge over Antietam

Creek. At four o'clock in the afternoon General A. P. Hill's Division came to the support of the Confederate right, thus augmenting their whole number to seventy thousand. But even with these they could not hope to gain a decisive victory over an enemy who were superior to them by twice their own number, and who had the advantage of position. Consequently, at night-fall, after superhuman efforts, with ammunition exhausted, they had to content themselves with a drawn battle, each side virtually retaining the same position in which it had begun the conflict. On both sides the loss was about the same — variously estimated between five and nine thousand. Though the Federals claimed the victory, they disappeared from the Confederate front during the night, while General Lee took a position at Shepherdstown. On the 20th the Federals made a pretense of attacking him at this point, but were repulsed by General A. P. Hill's Division.

At this time the *London Times* furnished the following tribute to the character of the Southern people:

The people of the Confederate States have made themselves famous. If the renown of brilliant courage, stern devotion to a cause, and military achievements almost without a parallel can compensate men for the toil and privations of the hour, then the countrymen of Lee and Jackson may be consoled amid their sufferings. From all parts of Europe, from their enemies as well as their friends, from those who condemn their acts as well as those who sympathize with them, comes the tribute of admiration. When the history of this war is written the admiration will doubtless become deeper and stronger, for the veil which has covered the South will be drawn away, and disclose a picture of patriotism, of unanimous self-sacrifice, of wise and firm administration, which we can now only see indistinctly. The details of extraordinary national effort, which has led to the repulse and almost to the destruction of an invading force of more than half a million men, will then become known to the world, and whatever may be the fate of the new nationality or its subsequent claims to the respect of mankind, it will assuredly begin its career with a reputation for genius and valor which the most famous nations may envy.

CHAPTER XII.

Movements in the West Again.

THE North had arranged a programme of operations in the country west of the Alleghanies. These preparations surpassed in magnitude all military movements which had been designed or attempted since the beginning of the war, the main object being the expulsion of all Confederates from Kentucky, Tennessee, and the States west of the Mississippi River, and also the penetration through the Gulf States. The enemy were at this time on their way into all these places, while another army was operating in Missouri and Arkansas. Also there was on the waters of the Mississippi a fleet of gun-boats which was considered impregnable in strength.

Nothing was now left for the South to do but to make a forward, aggressive movement, by which North Alabama and Middle and East Tennessee should be relieved, and the enemy forced to fall back, and assistance given to General Buell, who was at this time in Kentucky. The brief retirement of the favorite General Beauregard, on account of ill health, was a misfortune to the Confederates. General Bragg was appointed to take his place. The first steps of the aggressive movement was the ordering of General Kirby Smith to advance into Kentucky and threaten Cincinnati, the main object being to force the enemy across the Ohio River.

Early in the month of August General McCown moved his division from Loudon to Knoxville; thence our troops moved to the gap in the Cumberland Mountains, being joined by General Cleburne at the lower gap, when the whole force—with baggage, trains, and artillery—were ordered through. They then made a forced march until they reached Barboursville. Halting there a few hours to rest their wearied limbs, they pushed on to Cumberland Ford, and were there given several days of rest.

General Kirby Smith found the enemy in force on the morning of August 29, near Richmond, Ky., and determined to march against them. The leading division, under General Cleburne, after advancing two or three miles, encountered the enemy drawn up in line of battle in a fine position near Mount Zion Church, six miles from Richmond, Ky. Without waiting for Churchill's troops, he at once commenced action, and by half-past seven o'clock firing was very brisk. General Churchill, on his arrival, was sent with his division to turn the enemy's right, which he accomplished admirably. At the same time an attempt was being made by the enemy to flank General Cleburne's right, but it was thwarted by the gallantry of Colonel Preston Smith's Brigade, which repulsed the enemy with great slaughter. General Smith then ordered the cavalry to proceed to the north of Richmond in order to cut off the retreat of the enemy. Our artillerymen having ceased their firing, and the Federals consequently thinking that the silence of the guns meant a retreat, made an attack upon the Texas and Arkansas troops under McCray, who met them and fought the battle alone, and by courageous charging upon their advancing lines put them to flight, though they numbered three to one. In the wildest confusion they fled, "leaving knapsacks, swords, pistols, hats, and canteens scattered along the road they traveled, where their dead and dying too plainly showed the way."

General Smith received information that General Nelson had arrived with re-enforcements for the enemy, and had determined to make a stand on a commanding ridge. Generals Churchill and Preston Smith, at double-quick, formed in front of the enemy's center and left. Without waiting for the command of the officers, these brave Confederates advanced under the destructive fire of twice their number, and drove the Federals from the field with great slaughter. The worn-out, exhausted condition of our soldiers and the darkness of the night prevented pursuit of the enemy. The results of the day added new glories to Confederate arms.

On the 4th of September General Preston Smith, with forces consisting of a Texas and an Arkansas brigade, under command of General Churchill, and Generals Cleburne's and Heath's Divisions—all being under the command of General Kirby Smith—was welcomed into the beautiful city of Lexington, Ky. "The entrance of our troops into Lexington was the occasion of the most inspiring and touching scenes. Streets, windows, and gardens were filled with ladies and little girls with streams of red and blue ribbon and flags with stars and bars upon them. Beautiful women seized the hard, brown hands of our rough and ragged soldiers, and, with tears and smiles, thanked them again and again for coming into Kentucky, and freeing them from the presence and insults of the hated and insolent Yankees. For hours the enthusiasm of the people was unbounded. At every street-corner baskets of provisions and buckets of cold water were placed for the refreshment of our weary soldiers; and hundreds of our men were presented with shoes and hats and coats and tobacco from a grateful people. Private residences were turned into public houses of entertainment free to all who could be persuaded to go and eat. But if the reception of the infantry was enthusiastic, the tears, the smiles, the cheers of wild delight which greeted General John Morgan's cavalry as they came dashing through the streets amid clouds of dust was without a parallel. The wildest joy ruled the hour. The bells of the city pealed forth their joyous welcome, while the waving of thousands of white handkerchiefs and tiny Confederate flags attested the gladness and delight of every heart."

With the laurels of grand exploits in Kentucky still fresh upon him, many were hopeful that General Smith would attempt the capture of the city of Cincinnati; but his orders were to menace, not attack. Consequently he was ordered to fall back into the interior to co-operate with the army under General Bragg, who had entered the State by the eastern route, crossing the Cumberland River at Gainesboro, with the design of flanking General Buell. General Smith's movements, however, were soon understood by the enemy. On September 17 General Bragg captured five thousand of the enemy at Munfordville, with a very small loss on our side; and on October 4 joined General Smith at Frankfort.

Battle of Perryville, October 8.

By harassing his rear near Perryville the enemy showed that they were desirous of an engagement with General Bragg; and the latter, though having but fifteen thousand men against forty-five thousand of the Federals, arranged his forces for battle with General Hardee commanding Buckner's and Anderson's Divisions on the left and General Polk with

Cheatham's and Withers's Divisions on the right. About midday the battle opened. Colonel Powell's Brigade, on the extreme left, succeeded in pushing back for over a mile the largely superior numbers opposed to him; but General Adams's Brigade, after holding its position gallantly until six o'clock in the afternoon, was forced to retreat, which they accomplished in perfect order, though at the loss of a large number of men. When night put an end to this hotly contested engagement it was found that the Confederates had forced the enemy two miles from their original position, with a loss of four thousand killed and wounded, seven thousand prisoners, and fifteen pieces of artillery; while their own loss in killed, wounded, and missing was two thousand five hundred.

Inability on the part of the Confederates to reap the fruits of their victory at Perryville, just as at Shiloh, was again due to a lack of numbers; for the history of the world's battle-fields furnishes no nobler example of man's devotion to principle and the courage to stand by that principle with life itself. All day they fought in a manner worthy of their cause, though tired and worn out by their long marches over the mountains. General Cheatham's brave Tennesseeans deserve great credit for the courage with which they bore the brunt of the contest. In this day's fight the Confederates proved true to a glorious past that had made the record of noble and manly achievements richer and brighter by many a gallant deed.

The large numbers of the enemy, and the fact, too, that they were increasing daily, made a retreat absolutely necessary. Realizing this, General Bragg began his march out of Kentucky October 12, Major Adrian's Cavalry leading the van. Arriving at Bryantsville, the management of the retreat was turned over to General Polk, which was accomplished successfully by General Wheeler's skillful defense of the rear, from which he warded off frequent and strong attacks of the enemy. In many respects this retreat was unfortunate. It produced a tremendous backset to the Confederate cause in Kentucky; for the citizens, who had welcomed the army with such enthusiasm, either had to absolve themselves from allegiance to the Confederacy or else to abandon their property and possessions to the enemy. Consequently the greatest confusion resulted throughout the State, producing a large exodus of citizens toward the South in order to get within the protection of the Confederate lines.

In the South-west.

Events in this section brought little credit upon Southern arms. Disasters followed one another in a depressingly quick succession, which were begun by General Breckinridge's attack August 5, with only three thousand men, upon five thousand of the enemy strongly fortified at Baton Rouge, La. Though the attack was gallantly conducted, and though the troops fought as nobly as men well could under the circumstances, they were forced to fall back with considerable loss. This misfortune was followed by the forced destruction of the magnificent ram "Arkansas," which had made herself famous by successfully running through the Federal fleet at Vicksburg, and in which the Confederate Government entertained great hopes of future use. Her machinery refused to work, and consequently, in order to avoid capture at the hands of the enemy, she was burned near Bayou Sara.

At Iuka, Miss., September 20, General Price, in an attack against an enemy largely superior in numbers, met a similar fate to that which our troops had suffered at Baton Rouge. It was the same old story of a magnificent and splendid courage striving against sheer force of numbers. To illustrate how stubbornly and bravely the Confederates contested with the enemy, it is related that "the battle was almost hand to hand. One Ohio battery was taken four times by our men, and as often retaken by a greatly superior force. Several of our men endeavored to tear the colors from the hands of the Yankees by main force, and either perished in the attempt or were made prisoners. In one spot the next morning there were counted seventeen Confederate soldiers lying dead around one of their officers. Sixteen feet square would have covered the whole space."

Battle of Corinth.

Having united the forces of General Price with his own, on Friday, October 3, General Van Dorn prepared to attack the enemy fortified at Corinth. His own forces, consisting of only one division commanded by General Lovell, held the right, with General Price's forces of two divisions holding the left, the extreme positions on the left and right being occupied by Generals Herbert and Maury respectively. The battle was begun at half-past seven o'clock by General Villipigue's Battery opening a severe fire upon the enemy, which forced them to make a gradual retreat for two hours. Here, within half a mile of their line of fortifications, the Federals made a stubborn stand. The whole Confederate line now moved grandly forward to the attack. In the midst of the concentrated fire of the enemy's heavy batteries, they advanced superbly in a double-quick charge, driving the Federals from their first line of intrenchments to the protection of the second.

Here the battle ended for the day, and General Van Dorn, overconfident and ignorant of the strength of the enemy, telegraphed to Richmond the news of a great victory. Early next morning the conflict was renewed with a terrific artillery fire upon the enemy's works, which was kept up until ten o'clock, when the whole line again advanced to the attack. Nothing could withstand them. But the very enthusiasm of victory cost them dear. Inspired by the spirit of battle itself, the individual soldier forgot order and discipline, and in the greatest and the wildest confusion they cut through the ranks of the enemy and broke into the village of Corinth. Here the Federals turned loose their batteries upon them, and either a retreat was inevitable or the taking of the enemy's strongest battery, on College Hill, was necessary. The latter course was ordered. Eight deep, in a grim and determined silence, the representatives of Southern hopes and aspirations advanced to the charge into the very jaws of death. On they went in the face of bullets as thick as rain-drops in a summer storm. Still advancing, and falling by the hundreds, they reached the top of the hill. Twice were they beaten back; but the third time they seemed to succeed. A cheer was raised above the din of battle, and the Southern cross with its stars of heaven floated from the enemy's works; but it was immediately torn away by a shot. Again it was set up, but only to be shot away. Physical nature inspired by divine courage could do no more. The bleeding, shattered ranks, after having given an exhibition of fortitude which glorifies the human race, fell back, followed by an increased fire of the enemy at close range, and the day was lost. But even then they were unwilling to give up the contest without another struggle, and only retired to the shelter of the woods to await the expected attack of the enemy. But the latter seemed contented with the day's fighting. Consequently General Van Dorn began to withdraw his forces. About half-past eight o'clock next morning he was again attacked by the enemy, which at first produced a temporary confusion. But order was soon restored, and an artillery fire was kept up all day, which enabled General Van Dorn to gradually lead his troops across the Hatchie River, and take a position near Ripley. In killed, wounded, and prisoners General Van Dorn had lost forty-five hundred men, while it is conjectured that the Federal loss was perhaps about half that number.

Guerrilla Warfare in Missouri.

The State of Missouri had much to complain of at the hands of the enemy. From one end of her borders to the other she had been overrun with the full license of war—robbery, murder, and pillage being the order of the day. Consequently, as a matter of self-defense and to protect themselves against the unrestrained oppression of the enemy, the citizens began to organize themselves into irregular bands, known as "guerrillas." Troops of this character, however, did not disdain to try conclusions with the enemy even in open battle. On the 6th of August Porter's band was attacked by a large force of the Federals under Colonel McNeil, at Kirksville, and only retreated after killing fully one thousand of the enemy and losing five hundred themselves. This was followed on the 15th of the same month by a total defeat and rout of the Federals, near Lone Jack, by Hughes's and Quantrell's bands, the arrival of re-enforcements only saving the enemy from destruction.

To illustrate the terrible vindictiveness of the Federals, one has only to mention briefly what was known as the "Palmyra massacre," which occurred in October. A Federal spy had been captured, and Colonel McNeil issued orders that unless he were returned ten Confederate prisoners should pay the penalty with their lives. Being a legitimate prisoner of war, the man was not returned. The Federal commander, true to his word, carried out his cruel edict to the very letter.

CHAPTER XIII.
Campaign in Northern Virginia.

NOT satisfied with the dilatory policy of General MacClellan, as indicated in the previous chapter, the Federal Government had superseded him with General Burnside. With this change the North again took up their old cry, "On to Richmond!" which had been so often turned to one of grief by the prowess of Southern arms.

General Burnside began operations by massing his forces at Fredericksburg, Va., with the determination of crossing the Rappahannock. Consequently on the night of December 10 he began to construct three bridges over the Rappahannock—"two at Fredericksburg and a third about a mile and a quarter below at Deep Run. In the prosecution of this work the enemy were defended by their artillery on the hills of Stafford, which completely commanded the plain upon which Fredericksburg stands." During the process of construction the Seventeenth Mississippi Regiment of Barksdale's Brigade, posted on the bluffs on the opposite side of the river, opened fire upon the enemy, which was replied to with a storm of shells. Though the Confederates harassed the enemy persistently and incessantly all through the night, yet they succeeded in finishing their bridges by the morning of the 11th. The Confederates retreated through the streets of Fredericksburg, followed by the fire of the enemy, which forced the citizens to evacuate the town and to flee to the surrounding country for protection. By the 13th the Confederates had taken a strong position upon the bluffs on the south bank of the river, presenting a front to the enemy six miles in length. About twelve o'clock in the day the latter moved forward across the valley intervening between our forces and theirs. They were received with a terrible cannonading from General Stuart's Horse Artillery, but managed to keep on across the valley until they came within the protection of the woods, from which position they were driven by Generals Hill's and Early's troops, and pursued until they reached the shelter of their batteries. While this portion of the Confederate line, which consisted of Jackson's Corps, was thus engaged, the enemy also advanced against General Longstreet's position on the left, and directed their principal attack against Mayre's Hill, upon which was stationed the Washington Artillery and a part of McLaw's Division. Right gallantly did they press forward to the charge, facing the awful fire of shot and shell turned upon them with such effectiveness as to make the ground over which they passed literally a ghastly field of dead men. Broken and shattered, they reeled back, pursued into the town by our troops. Night put an end to the conflict. The pale December moon gave a ghastlier appearance to a field already horrible in the extreme. That terrible tenacity and doggedness with which each fought was shown in the number of the killed, for the field is said to have been "literally packed with dead. At the foot of Mayre's Hill was a frightful spectacle of carnage." The victory was indeed a costly one to the Confederates. Not having the whole world to draw from, the number of killed and wounded signified much to them: it meant a vacant place in their ranks that could not be filled, a gap which, when closed up, brought the wings nearer together. Consequently the fruits of the victory at Fredericksburg hardly compensated them for the loss they had sustained, which was about eighteen hundred, among whom were Generals Cobb, of Georgia, and Gregg, of South Carolina; while the enemy are said to have lost something near ten thousand men in killed, wounded, and missing. Although the battle was decisive enough, very little advantage was reaped from it by allowing General Burnside to safely cross the Rappahannock with his shattered and thoroughly whipped army.

While detailing the story of man's stern devotion to duty on the bloody field of carnage, woman's quieter though none the less noble devotion cannot be consistently passed over. Therefore, in quoting the language of an historian in regard to the heroism of the women of Fredericksburg during this time one but describes the qualities that characterized the women of the whole South during the shifting and trying scenes of the civil war:

> The romance of the story of Fredericksburg is written no less in the quiet heroism of her women than in deeds of arms. The verses of a poet rather than the cold language of a mere chronicler of events are more befitting to describe the beautiful courage and the noble sacrifices of these brave daughters of Virginia. . . . . In all the terrible scenes of Fredericksburg there were no weaknesses and tears of women. Mothers, exiles from home, met their sons in the ranks, embraced them, told them to do their duty, and, with a self-negation most touching to witness, concealed their wants, sometimes their hunger, telling their brave boys that they were comfortable and happy, that they might not be troubled with domestic anxieties. At Hamilton's Crossing many of the women had the opportunity of meeting their relations in the army. In the haste of flight mothers had brought a few garments or perhaps the last loaf of bread for the soldier boy, and the lesson of duty whispered in the ear gave the young heart the pure and brave inspiration to sustain it in battle. No more touching and noble evidence could be offered of the heroism of the women of Fredericksburg than the gratitude of our army; for afterward, when subscriptions for their relief came to be added up, it was found that thousands of dollars had been contributed by ragged soldiers out of their pittance of pay to the fund of the refugees. There could be no more eloquent tribute offered than this—a beautiful and immortal souvenir of their sufferings and virtues.

The Federals in North Carolina.

During the month of December the Federals were actively engaged in overrunning the State of North Carolina. Near Kinston General Evans, with only two thousand men, succeeded in holding them in check for three days, from the 13th to the 16th. The number of the enemy was fifteen thousand, commanded by General Foster. They then moved against General Robertson at Whitehall Bridge, over the Neuse River, eighteen miles below Goldsboro, but were repulsed with great loss. This was followed by an attack of the whole Confederate force—under Generals Evans, Clingman, and Pettigrew—upon the Federal position along the river (Neuse). The latter were driven back to the shelter of their fortifications and gun-boats. Thus, with a loss of only about three hundred in killed and wounded, the Confederates had held the enemy in check, and had prevented them from accomplishing any thing of special importance.

General Hindman's Success in Arkansas.

Before closing the record of the year 1862 General Hindman's encounter with the enemy on the 27th of November, at Prairie Grove, Ark., must be noticed. With only about nine thousand men General Hindman sustained himself against a much larger force. All day the battle waged, with the enemy making persistent and stubborn charges upon his lines, but all to no purpose, for when the day ended he had thoroughly and completely pushed the enemy back, with a loss of one thousand in killed and wounded, three hundred prisoners, and a large amount of stores, for which the Confederates paid with a total loss of three hundred.

Cavalry Exploits.

On the other side of the Mississippi River the last movements of the year were signalized by the daring raids of the Confederate cavalry under Generals Forrest, Morgan, and Clarkson, by which the Federals were continually harassed, for they never knew where or when these hard riders would strike them a blow, and then vanish like a shadow. On the 7th day of December General John Morgan, around whose name the glamour of romantic story has spread itself, succeeded in taking the town of Hartsville, on the Cumberland River, with two thousand stands of arms, a large quantity of provisions, two pieces of artillery, and eighteen hundred prisoners. This exploit was followed by Colonel Clarkson with like success, taking the town of Piketon, Ky.

On the whole the year 1862 had been a brilliant one to the South, though it was overshadowed by some signal disasters. Relying solely upon the virtue, integrity, and patriotism of her people, she had successfully resisted each of the magnificent armies that the enemy, with inexhaustible resources behind them, had hurled against her. The story of the successive battles has given to the world a clear and positive proof of the valor of her troops, and their devotion to principle under the most trying and adverse circumstances. Consequently, with such a record as this, she was prepared to enter upon the next year with comparative confidence and few misgivings as to the results. Therefore, preliminary to the important events which were to follow, General Pemberton was appointed to supersede General Van Dorn at Holly Springs, Miss.; General Joseph E. Johnston was put in command of all the armies between the mountains and the great river; and General Beauregard was ordered to defend the cities of Charleston and Savannah against the fleet being prepared on a large scale by the enemy.

CHAPTER XIV.

Murfreesboro—Galveston—Arkansas.

AT Murfreesboro, Tenn., General Bragg had concentrated as gallant an army as ever followed the flag of any country into battle. It was thirty thousand in number, coming principally from the extreme Southern States—Louisiana, Florida, South Carolina, Alabama, Georgia, Kentucky, and Tennessee. The horrors of battle were not new to them, for they were the same troops who had given evidence of such magnificent and superb courage at Shiloh and Perryville and other scarcely less memorable fields. They were now resting from the dread alarms of war, and had entered with all a soldier's zest into the full enjoyment of the festivities of Christmas, when, on Friday, December 26, word was brought that Rosecrans was marching against them from Nashville with over forty thousand troops. The scene changes from the delights and pleasures of the ball-room to the sterner duties of war and death.

"The grounds in front of Murfreesboro had been surveyed and examined a month before in order to select a position for battle in case of a surprise, and our troops were thrown forward to prevent such a misfortune. Polk's Corps, with Cheatham's Division, occupied our center, Maney's Brigade being thrown forward toward La Vergne, where Wheeler's Cavalry was annoying the enemy. A portion of Kirby Smith's Corps, McCown's Division, occupied Readyville on our right, and Hardee's Corps occupied Triune on our left, with Wharton's Cavalry thrown out in the vicinity of Franklin." The advance of the enemy drove in Hardee's Corps from Triune, and made the call of McCown's Division from Readyville necessary. By the 28th the Confederates had arranged themselves in line of battle, with Polk's command, Cheatham's and Withers's Divisions, on the west bank of Stone's River, presenting a front six miles in length from wing to wing, which rested respectively on the Nashville and Salem pikes; Hardee's Corps, Breckinridge's and Cleburne's Divisions, held a position on the east bank of the river, stretching over a distance of three miles, thus making the whole line "nine miles in length, in the shape of an obtuse angle." McCown's Division and Jackson's Brigade were held as reserves for the center and right flank respectively. After preliminary skirmishing and cannonading on the 29th and the morning of the 30th, at three o'clock in the afternoon of the latter day the enemy massed their forces and attacked the Confederate left, charging Robinson's Battery no less than three times; but each time they were driven back by those courageous

Tennesseeans, the One Hundred and Fifty-fourth Regiment. Perceiving that the intention of the Federals was to concentrate their efforts against the left, McCown's and Cleburne's Divisions were moved to that part of the line. In the meantime Wheeler's Cavalry had surprised the enemy in the rear, and had captured a wagon-train, together with some prisoners. All through that December night the Confederates lay around the camp-fires, chilled by a bitter winter rain. But this did not damp their ardor for the grand charge which they, in the cold, gray dawn of the next morning (31st), made. The charge was begun by Cleburne's and McCown's Divisions, and took the enemy completely by surprise. The bright sun broke through the clouds just at the time, and shed a ray of splendor upon that grand gray column as it moved irresistibly forward, sweeping the enemy before it, and driving them back six miles. Withers's and Cheatham's Divisions had also made the enemy feel the weight of their awful blows in the number of dead which they left upon the field and the batteries which they abandoned to the possession of the Confederates. A splendid and magnificent charge had been conducted, "driving the enemy before it like the hurricane scatters leaves upon its course, and literally blackening the ground with the dead. For miles, through fields and forests, over ditches, fences, and ravines, they had swept. Brigade after brigade, battery after battery were thrown forward to stay their onward course, but another volley of musketry, another gleaming of the bayonet, and, like their predecessors, they were crushed into one common ruin." The Confederates had taken nearly five thousand prisoners, thirty pieces of artillery, five thousand stands of arms, and a large amount of ammunition.

General Rosecrans had refused to aid his defeated right by weakening his left or center, for he knew that the forces in front of him were ready and waiting to strike these points when any signs of weakness might appear. Consequently, unperceived by the Confederates, he moved his center forward and took a strong position on a hill. This the latter gallantly charged; but it was simply impossible to withstand the awful fire of the enemy, and they were forced to fall back, though not without capturing two batteries. The Confederates camped for the night upon one of the most sanguinary fields of the war, and New-year's-eve was passed in the midst of the dead and wounded and all the horrible scenes of the day's fighting.

On the following day (January 1, 1863) General Bragg presented a glorious victory to the authorities at Richmond as a New-year's gift; but unfortunately he allowed the enemy to restore order among their disorganized forces, and did not attack until three o'clock in the afternoon of January 3. In the meantime the Federals had arranged themselves in a strong position in the bend of the river, which General Breckinridge was ordered to take. At four o'clock the signal was given, and the fated band moved forward like the very embodiment of courage to that awful charge, in the face of such a storm of artillery and musketry fire as any battle-field had rarely witnessed. With a bravery that seemed nothing short of sheer madness they drove the enemy from the ridge to the river, the Twentieth Tennessee Regiment capturing two hundred prisoners. They next turned their attention to the enemy on the other side of the river, and with the of his command; consequently, in the approaching same never-faltering courage they crossed it in the midst of such a fire that in a short space of time, measured only by a few brief moments, two thousand vacant places were made in the home life of the South. But the sacrifice was fruitless save only as an example of a grand courage that causes one to honor his race more and more as he reads the story of the "bloody crossing of Stone's River." To continue against such a fire meant the total annihilation darkness, Breckinridge fell back. Among his dead were the brave Captain Wright and the noble and gallant Hanson, whose last words were: "I am willing to die with such a wound, received in so glorious a cause." With these heroic words he joined the grand army of warriors on the other shore, who have died battling for the right.

On the next day (the 3d) General Bragg withdrew with his army to Tullahoma, while the Federal forces occupied Murfreesboro. While the battle may be accounted a Federal success in that the Confederates fell back from their position, yet when the enemy's terrible defeat in the first day's fight is considered, together with the number of their loss in killed and prisoners, and also the fact that Bragg was holding a position which virtually held them in check, then it will be seen that their claims to a complete victory might be well questioned.

Capture of Galveston.

As an offset to the apparent disaster at Murfreesboro, the Confederates also began the new year with a victory at Galveston, Tex. At three o'clock on the morning of December 31st General Magruder, with seven regiments of infantry and twenty-two guns, proceeded to retake the city, which, as has been noticed in a previous chapter, had been captured by the enemy. Only a few of the latter occupied the city, but out in the harbor, not three hundred yards from the shore, lay five of the enemy's boats, with their guns ready and frowning threateningly upon the city. Silently Magruder's little band moved through the streets and took a position on Strand Street near the wharves; and before daylight he astonished the citizens with a roar of his guns directed against the ships, which replied to their fire so effectively that it soon became evident that the small Confederate battery was no match for their heavy guns. Meanwhile an unsuccessful attack was made upon three companies of the Forty-second Massachusetts Regiment, which were fortified at one end of the wharfs.

Assistance now came to the Confederates from the water. The "Bayou City," the "Neptune," the "John F. Can," and the "Lucy Gwinn" steamed toward the Federal vessels, directing their attention especially to the "Harriet Lane," which the "Neptune" struck amidships, and having cleared her decks by fire from small-arms, the crew of the latter were preparing to board the "Lane" when it was discovered that their own vessel was damaged to such an extent as to be sinking; consequently they steamed off and sunk her. The "Bayou City" next attacked the Federal vessel, and boarded her and forced a surrender. The other ships of the enemy managed to escape out of the harbor, with the exception of the "Westfield," which was burned.

Surrender of Arkansas Post.

On the 11th of January, after two days' attack with both water and land forces, the enemy, under General MacClernand, succeeded in forcing the surrender of Arkansas Post, on the Arkansas River, which was held by General Churchill with over three thousand troops. This victory was important to the Federals, in that it gave them control of the commerce of the Arkansas River.

Confederate Rams Attack the Federals in Charleston Harbor.

In Charleston Harbor, on the 30th of January, the Confederate rams moved out against the Federal fleet, which had held a position off the mouth of the harbor for over a month. The result of this attack was the serious disabling of the "Mercedita" and the "Key-stone State," the latter vessel losing twenty-one men.

The Federal gun-boat, "Queen of the West," had managed to pass the Confederate batteries at Vicksburg, and was committing depredations on Red River, where she had also taken a small Confederate boat, the "Era." The commander of the "Queen of the West," had forced the pilot of the "Era," George Wood, to take the helm of the "Queen of the West" and direct her toward the capture of a Confederate fort on the river. Wood drove her ashore just opposite the fort, however, and turned her side to the batteries, and, in the confusion which followed from this movement, succeeded in making his escape. Part of the crew of the "Queen of the West," and her commander, jumped upon cotton-bales and floated down the river; but the remainder, thirteen in number, remained on board all night, and the next morning the

Confederates took possession. In like manner another Federal vessel, the "Indianola," had succeeded in passing our batteries, and for some time had been a source of great annoyance in the damage which she was doing to Confederate transportation. Consequently the "Queen of the West," the "Webb," the "Era," and the "Dr. Batey," under the command of Major Walker, went in quest of the enemy's boat, and came up with her about thirty miles below Vicksburg at nine o'clock on the night of February 24. The Confederate boats at once moved to the attack, and after a terrible contest of over an hour's duration it was found that the "Indianola" was in a sinking condition. Consequently her officers surrendered their boat with the crew, which numbered one hundred and twenty men.

While the Confederates were thus gaining these successes on the inland waters they also had a few privateers upon the Atlantic, which were doing much damage to the Federal shipping, and the exploits of the "Alabama" and the "Florida" were such as even to call forth from the North a merited tribute to their efficiency.

Destruction of the "Hatteras" by the Confederate Steamer, "Alabama," Admiral Semmes Commanding.

CHAPTER XV.

Impressment—Batteries and Gun-boats.

BEFORE again taking up the thread of military operations it is important to notice briefly the "Law of Impressment," which the Confederate Congress was forced to enact on account of a scarcity of provisions. The great grain-producing districts had all felt the iron heel of war, and the State of Kentucky, which had heretofore furnished the principal supply of meat to the army, was now in the hands of the Federals. Moreover, the paper money of the Confederacy, with no assurance back of it save a promise to pay six months after the close of the war, had been turned loose upon the country to such an extent that in the beginning of the year 1863 there was $300,000,000 in circulation. Consequently it had so decreased in value that one dollar in silver was worth four dollars in paper. Furthermore, with the scarcity of food and the depreciated value of the currency, the South was cursed with the misfortune of speculation. Foreigners flooded the country, and traded and speculated in the very necessities of life, inflating the prices to a very high figure even for times of want and scarcity. Therefore, without discussing the nature and condition of such matters any further, it is very evident what the ultimate results and effects should be. And the armies of the South fighting so gloriously in the face of such circumstances but adds another evergreen leaf to their laurel crown of honor.

FEDERALS ATTACK FORT MCALLISTER.

On the 3d of March the enemy made an attack with five vessels upon Fort McAllister, on the Ogeechee River, near Savannah, Ga. All day they bombarded the fort, but at night they withdrew with one of their iron-clads considerably damaged, while the fort had only one gun dismounted, and within its walls not a single life was lost.

THE FEDERALS IN FRONT OF VICKSBURG.

"The enemy had three distinct projects for compassing the capture of Vicksburg. First, the canal across the isthmus opposite the city; secondly, the project of getting through the Yazoo Pass; thirdly, the Lake Providence canal project. It had been all the time their principal aim to get in the rear or below Vicksburg. Their present plan was to get through the Yazoo Pass in the hope of getting in our rear and cutting off our supplies. Their idea was to flank Vicksburg, capture Jackson, cut off Grenada, and destroy all possibility of our getting supplies throughout that rich country by one bold stroke."

On the 13th of March they began active operations by an attack with their gun-boats on that part of the Confederate works known as Fort Pemberton, situated in a bend of the Tallahatchie River. After four hours of heavy fighting they were repulsed, which thwarted their project of getting to the lower Yazoo by this route. This unexpected defeat produced a lull in the operations of the enemy in the immediate vicinity of Vicksburg. However, they next turned their attention to Port Hudson, "a strongly fortified position on the lower Mississippi, about sixteen miles above Baton Rouge, and three hundred below Vicksburg." Accordingly, six magnificent ships were fitted out, and on the night of March 15, under the command of Admiral Farragut, they attempted to pass the batteries, which were located upon a high bluff. Silently these mighty war monsters passed on, with each man waiting intently at his gun; but they were discovered when just opposite the batteries, and the alarm was given. Immediately the ships opened the thunders of their artillery upon the Confederates, who endured the fire in silence until they all got within easy range, when they let loose such a storm of shot and shell upon the enemy that it soon became evident that it meant destruction for the ships to pass. Therefore all except the "Hartford" turned around and began to steam back in the midst of a fire that furnished a grand scene as shell after shell cut its bright way through the darkness of the night. All managed to escape, more or less injured, except the "Mississippi," whose rudder was broken and machinery so damaged that she floated aimlessly to the opposite shore, giving the batteries a good opportunity to tear her literally to pieces. Most of her crew succeeded in escaping, but the wounded were left on board the doomed vessel, which floated off down the river, and when near Baton Rouge her magazine exploded, sending to the bottom of the river one of the most magnificent ships of the United States Navy.

During the time of these engagements in the West the armies both in Virginia and in Tennessee only watched each other, without any offensive movements being made on either side. But the monotony was somewhat broken by a force of the enemy three thousand strong crossing the Rappahannock River at Kelly's Ford on the morning of March 17. They continued their march until within six miles of Culpepper Court-house, when they were attacked by General Fitzhugh Lee's Brigade, and after several hours of hard fighting they were routed and driven back. The Confederates lost in killed and wounded about one hundred men, among whom was the youthful and gallant Major Pelham, of Alabama, who, although but twenty-two years of age, had been through all the battles in Virginia, and had won that enduring fame and honor which only comes to men after long experience and service of many years. Peace be to the ashes of this "boy major!" and may the roses of immortality ever bloom over his grave, inasmuch as he typified in his own person and death all of that fresh, glorious, young manhood of the South that went down in the awful struggle, even though they wore not upon their shoulders the straps of rank, and lie in nameless graves!

The Federals Repulsed from Charleston.

To the minds of the Federals Charleston, S. C., was the "cradle of the rebellion." Therefore its capture was to them a matter of supreme importance. With this in view, for many months they had been bending their energies toward a signal and decisive attack upon this city. The known purpose and designs of the enemy had kept the citizens of Charleston in a state of suspense until three o'clock in the afternoon of April 7, when a part of the enemy's fleet, which consisted of more than seventy vessels, moved to attack Fort Sumter. The joy of an anticipated victory took the place of doubt and suspense when, in the midst of the strains of "Dixie," the iron throats of our cannon spoke forth their volleys of death and destruction. The fleet advanced in two divisions, lead respectively by the iron-clads, "Ironsides" and "Keokuk," which delivered a tremendous fire upon the walls of both Forts Sumter and Morris, and in return they received a crushing tempest of iron hail from the heavy guns of the two forts, so that they were forced to withdraw out of range. So effective, indeed, was the fire of the Confederates under the skillful Beauregard that it was discovered on the next day that the "Keokuk" had been sunk near Morris Island. Thus the enemy had been brilliantly repulsed from Charleston, with a loss on the part of the defenders of only one man killed and five wounded.

CHAPTER XVI.

Chancellorsville—Vicksburg—Gettysburg.

AS the different attempts upon Richmond failed, it was the custom of the Federal Government to take each unsuccessful general from command, and to supply his place with a new one. It now became General Hooker's turn to try the fortunes of war with the sagacious Lee. Accordingly, with an army behind him which he himself said was "the finest on the planet," on Monday, April 26, he began the crossing of the Rappahannock in three large divisions. One was to cross at Kelly's Ford; another at Deep Run, three miles below Fredericksburg; and a third at United States Ford, "just below the confluence of the Rappahannock and Rapidan." By Thursday, April 29, Hooker had successfully accomplished all of these movements, and had fortified himself in a strong position "across the turnpike and plank road at Chancellorsville, eleven miles from Fredericksburg, in order to cut off our anticipated retreat in the direction of Gordonsville." These arrangements and plans on the part of the Federals did not escape the watchful eye of General Lee, and as soon as it was discovered that the enemy had crossed the river at Kelly's and Ellis's Fords Wright's Brigade was ordered to the support of the Confederate forces, eight thousand in number, under Generals Anderson, Posey, and Mahone, who "had been for several weeks stationed in the neighborhood of Ely's Ford, on the Rapidan, and the United States Ford, on the Rappahannock, guarding the approaches to Fredericksburg in that direction." During the night of Thursday, April 29, General Lee himself, with Anderson's and McLaw's Divisions, took a position in front of the enemy, while he sent General Jackson around to gain their rear. This skillful movement was successfully accomplished by the afternoon of May 2, when Jackson hurled his veterans against the enemy's right and rear. Sigel's Corps of Germans was the unfortunate portion of the Federal army that received Jackson's characteristic charge, which threw them in confusion upon the guns of Anderson's and McLaw's Divisions, through whose lines they attempted to break, but only to be sent back in a panic-stricken retreat toward the river. There was now a lull in the battle until nine o'clock, when General Stuart took command, Generals Jackson and Hill both having been wounded. In accordance with instructions from the former, General Stuart continued to batter the right wing of the enemy until he had driven it in upon the center. At daylight Sunday morning the battle was renewed by the Confederates making a gallant charge upon the fortifications and rifle-pits of the Federals. With that same grand courage that had always marked them, they swept the enemy before them in rout and confusion. The Confederates now seemed to be on the point of a great and decisive victory, and General Lee moved his forces to the plank-road above Chancellorsville.

But while thus successful in this part of their lines the Confederates were defeated at Fredericksburg, where Barksdale's Brigade and Early's Division held a position extending from Mayre's Hill to Hamilton's Crossing. With two thousand troops, the Washington Artillery, and Read's Battery, stationed on a hill, General Barksdale occupied the left wing. Against these small numbers the enemy hurled Gibbins's Division and Sedgewick's Corps, twenty thousand strong. Three times did they throw the weight of their immense numbers upon the brave little band on the heights, and each time they were sent back broken in ranks, with their dead lying thick on the hill-side. About nine o'clock in the day, under the pretense of carrying back their wounded, the enemy sent a flag of truce, and by that means learned how very few were the defenders of the heights. They at once, therefore, with Gibbins's entire command, attacked the left, which was held by Colonel Humphreys with the Twenty-first Mississippi Regiment. After a heroic resistance on the side of the Confederates the overwhelming numbers of the enemy prevailed.

Hearing of this reverse, General Lee turned his attention for the time from Hooker, and sent Anderson's and McLaw's Divisions to put a stop upon the progress of Sedgewick, which they succeeded in doing, when night put an end to the contest. The next day the enemy prepared to renew the battle by concentrating their forces against the left flank of McLaw's Division. In doing this, however, they weakened their own left, of which General Lee at once proceeded to take advantage by massing Early's and Anderson's Divisions at this point, and as the red glow of the setting sun colored the western sky the boys in gray once more charged the enemy and sent them shattered and broken to Banks's Ford, thus brilliantly putting an end to this series of conflicts on the 4th of May.

But it was the purpose of General Lee not to let the contest end here, and accordingly he began the disposition of his troops so as to completely destroy the army of Hooker. Fortunately, however, for the latter a violent storm set in, which caused a lull in General Lee's operations, and allowed the Federals to escape across the river.

To sum up the fruits of the victory, an army of fifty thousand men had met and put to rout an army "variously estimated at from one hundred thousand to one hundred and fifty thousand." Besides, the Confederates had taken large amounts of supplies, seven thousand prisoners, four thousand stands of arms, and had punished the enemy to the extent of twenty-five thousand in killed and wounded. But the sun of victory was clouded. To the Confederate soldiers the laurels of Chancellorsville will ever be draped in the sable hue of mourning for their ideal leader—great even among the greatest of earth's great captains—who laid down his command to enlist in that immortal army where battles and wars are not known.

Death of General Jackson.

About eight o'clock Saturday night, May 2, as "Stonewall" Jackson was returning into his line, accompanied by his staff, being mistaken for a cavalry detachment of the enemy, they were fired into by the first line of Confederate skirmishers. General Jackson received three balls—two in the left arm and one through the palm of the right hand. He was borne from the field much exhausted from loss of blood. He rallied, however, and his arm was amputated. This operation was successfully accomplished, and it was thought that the soldier would live to fight other battles in behalf of the cause which to him was almost as sacred as the religion that shaped and directed every action of his life. But unfortunately, in a few days pneumonia set in, and by the eighth day from the time he had received his wounds it was seen that he was dying. With the wife of his heart by his bedside, and filled with that ever abiding faith in the great God of battles as the disposer of all things for the best, Thomas J. Jackson, the grandest soldier in the greatest war of modern times, laid aside the earthly part of himself, and entered into that inheritance prepared for those who live pure and undefiled before God and man. "His last thoughts vibrated between religious subjects and the battle-field: now asking some question about the Bible or Church history; and then giving an order—'Pass the infantry to the front;' 'Tell Major Hawks to send forward provisions to the men;' 'Let us cross over the river, and rest under the shade of the trees'—until at last the gallant spirit gently passed over the dark river, and entered into its rest."

Loss of Vicksburg.

It now becomes necessary to again return to the progress of events on the Mississippi River. Beginning on the 1st of May, the enemy had successively defeated the Confederates at Port Gibson, Bayou Pierre, captured Jackson, the capital of the State of Mississippi, fought and driven back the Confederates at Baker's Creek and Big Black Bridge, and by the 18th had succeeded in investing Vicksburg. On the 21st General Grant made a general attack upon the Confederate fortifications, but was repulsed with great loss. He then settled himself down for a long siege, which the defenders of the city felt perfectly confident they could endure. The siege was continued until July 4, when the whole country was horrified by the announcement that Vicksburg had surrendered, throwing into the hands of the Federals twenty thousand prisoners. The causes that led to the giving up of this the key to the whole lower Mississippi region have been much discussed; but it will be sufficient here to say that the garrison were worn out and exhausted, and General Pemberton, learning that the enemy were contemplating a general assault, rather than expose his weakened troops to the horrors of a slaughter that must necessarily follow from their condition, turned the city over to the Federals.

Invasion of Pennsylvania.

Returning again to Virginia, General Ewell had followed up the success at Chancellorsville by falling upon General Milroy at Winchester and Martinsburg. Of this Federal defeat the *New York Herald* gave the following account:

> Not a thing was saved except that which was worn upon the persons of the troops. Three entire batteries of field artillery and one battery of siege guns—in fact, all the artillery of the command—about two hundred and eighty wagons, over one thousand two hundred horses and mules, all the commissary and quartermaster's stores and ammunition of all kinds, over six

thousand muskets and small-arms without stint, the private baggage of officers and men—all fell into the hands of the enemy. Of the seven thousand men of the command, but from sixteen hundred to two thousand have as yet arrived here, leaving to be accounted for five thousand men.

From this position Ewell moved rapidly up the Potomac River, followed by Longstreet and Hill. These movements threw the North into the greatest confusion, for they feared that the Confederates meant a prompt attack upon Washington. But General Lee contented himself with the invasion of Pennsylvania, though not after the manner of the Federal troops, who had pillaged and robbed every Southern State through which they had passed. In keeping with the magnanimity of his great heart, General Lee protected the lives and the property of the citizens of Pennsylvania, when he might have retaliated for the burned homes, the desolated fields that had been left in the track of the enemy through a land which had been blessed by the lavish hand of nature and the skillful hand of art, but which now seemed like one of the earth's waste places.

Battle of Gettysburg.

General Lee's line of march was brought to a stop on the 1st of July by the enemy confronting him at Gettysburg, with General Meade in command. The Federals immediately began with an attack upon A. P. Hill's and a part of Ewell's Corps, but they were driven back to the mountains south of the town. With this the first day's fight ended. On the following day (Thursday) each army seemed to wait for the other to attack, until late in the afternoon, when Longstreet took the initiative by hurling his corps against the Federal left on Round Top Hill. For four long hours the awful storm of battle raged, and when night came it was found that both sides had sustained a frightful loss of life, with nothing decisive gained by either. Each army was now straining every nerve to the utmost tension for the memorable struggle of Friday. The Federal position was an almost impregnable one on the heights south of Gettysburg. "All the heights and every advantageous position along the entire line where artillery could be massed or a battery planted frowned down upon the Confederates through brows of brass and iron. On the slopes of this mountain occurred one of the most terrific contests of modern times, in which three hundred cannon were belching forth their thunders at one time, and nearly two hundred thousand muskets were being discharged as rapidly as men hurried with excitement and passion could load them." Early in the morning this grand spectacle began, continuing all day, with only an intermission of a few hours from about ten o'clock to about one o'clock. The principal attack of the Confederates was directed against the enemy's center. Pickett's Division of Virginians, supported by Heth's Division, under the command of General Pettigrew on the left, and Wilson's Brigade on the right, charged this position, and that charge made "Pickett's Virginians" a synonym for all those qualities of knightly courage and superb endurance which put a nimbus of divine glory around the soldiers' conduct upon the battle-field. On these devoted sons of the "Old Dominion" pressed in the face of a fire which was so rapid and continuous that it seemed but one solid, unbroken sheet of flame that was scorching to the earth line after line, like the grass on the Western prairie is consumed. But they never faltered until they set their battle-stained flag upon the Federal fortifications. All in vain was their sacrifice, for the enemy moved heavy columns toward their rear, and, having victory in their grasp, unsupported, they were compelled to fall back. But there was no confusion in the retreat, even though the mortality in their lines was greater than it was during the charge. They reached their own lines; and the dead with which they strewed the field is a noble testimony to their valor. "Every brigadier in the division was killed or wounded. Out of twenty regimental officers only two escaped unhurt. The colonels of five Virginia regiments were killed. The Ninth Virginia went in two hundred and fifty strong, and came out with only thirty-eight men."

The Federal loss in killed, wounded, and missing

is given at twenty-three thousand, while the Confederate loss, though terrible enough, was hardly this much.

After the battle of Gettysburg General Lee left in the hands of the enemy the palm of a doubtful victory, and conducted an orderly retreat back into Virginia.

CHAPTER XVII.

Siege of Charleston—Morgan's Raid.

NOT satisfied with the repulse of their fleet from Charleston April 7, the enemy, under General Gilmore, now determined upon vigorous operations by putting the city in a state of siege. Immediately after their reverse the Federals in large force occupied Folly Island, constructing in secret works which would enable them to drive the Confederate batteries from Morris Island. Not anticipating the movements of the enemy which were to follow, so many troops had been drawn from General Beauregard to strengthen other positions that he was left with a force inadequate for the defense and maintenance of all his batteries in the harbor. Having finished on the morning of August 10, under cover of darkness, the erection of their fort, the enemy opened with their batteries upon Fort Morris, and sent a detachment on foot to attack Fort Wagner. This latter expedition came to grief, for when the fire of the heavy guns of the fort was turned upon them they broke and ran in confusion, with a considerable loss of life. This reverse, however, did not thwart the purposes of the enemy, for, gaining a foot-hold on Morris Island, they constructed a battery at a distance of a little over a mile and a half from Fort Wagner. From this position and the one on Black Island, together with their fleet of monitors and gun-boats, at the dawn of day, August 18, they turned the thunders of their guns upon the Confederate fort. All day the bombardment was kept up, old Fort Sumter and Battery Gregg, at Cummings's Point, contributing their share of the awful din of the cannonading. But when the shadows of evening began to fall the Federals moved an infantry column, with a negro regiment in front, to attack the fort. With a destructive fire thinning their ranks, they pushed their way with signal gallantry to the walls of the fort, and began to clamber over the breastworks. Here a desperate and bloody hand-to-hand encounter took place. As fast as the Confederates would beat back one line of their assailants another fresh line would take their place. But finally, after lining the parapet walls with their dead, the enemy gave way, and beat a full retreat across the beach in the darkness. However, the Federals were not yet prepared to give up the fort without another struggle. Consequently in less than half an hour the defenders of the fort found themselves again battling with a fresh column of the enemy; but the latter were repulsed even more disastrously than those who had participated in the first attack, for they left behind between two and three hundred prisoners. In both of these attacks the enemy gave their mortality at fifteen hundred and fifty, while the Confederates only suffered to the extent of a little over one hundred in killed and wounded.

Despairing of taking the forts by attack and bombardment, the Federal general resorted to other means hardly in keeping with the most approved methods of civilized warfare. On the 21st of August he informed General Beauregard in an unsigned note that unless Fort Sumter and Morris Island were evacuated within four hours he would turn his guns upon the city of Charleston. Without giving the necessary time for a reply, General Gilmore carried out his threat by actually sending his missiles of death into the midst of the defenseless city. Beauregard's reply to the act is worthy to be recorded here:

It would appear, sir, that, despairing of reducing these works, you now resort to the novel means of turning your guns against the old men, the women and the children, and the hospitals of the sleeping city. . . . And your omission to attach your signature to such a grave paper (the demand for the evacuation of the forts) must show the recklessness of the course upon which you have ventured, while the fact that you knowingly fixed a limit for receiving an answer to your demand, which made it almost beyond the possibility of receiving an answer in that time, and that you actually did open fire and throw a number of the most destructive missiles ever used in war into the midst of a city taken unawares and filled with sleeping women and children, will give you a bad eminence in history, even in the history of this war.

For three days (August 21, 22, and 23) the enemy kept up a continuous fire upon the walls of Fort Sumter, doing considerable damage. Meanwhile they not only did not cease their efforts against Fort Wagner, but on the 5th of September they also turned their attention to Fort Moultrie and Battery Gregg. Upon the latter they made an especially vigorous attack by trying to get in the rear of the fortifications; but they were repulsed by the effective fire from the fort, and were forced to give up their attempt. But both Morris Island and Battery Gregg had suffered so much from this continuous bombardment of over fifty days that, perceiving that they were no longer tenable, on the night of September 6 General Beauregard accomplished a successful evacuation, leaving these two positions, which had been so long coveted, in the hands of the Federals. Two days later Admiral Dahlgreen, the commander of the Federal fleet, sent a demand to General Beauregard for the immediate surrender of Fort Sumter, to which the reply was given that they could have it when they took it. With this, at one o'clock on the morning of September 9 the enemy began to assail the walls of the old fort that had so long stood between them and their much longed for prize. The Charleston Battalion, under Major Elliot, were watching and waiting, and they reserved their fire until their assailants were close upon them, when they opened upon them with such volleys that this "ruin" (as the Federal commanders had reported to the Government at Washington) seemed fairly vocal with the thunder of weapons that meant death to the Federals. However, the latter managed to land, and for half an hour engaged the Confederates in a stubborn hand-to-hand contest, when they were forced to surrender. The Federal reserve line, which had been left in the boat, pulled off and escaped, though followed by the shells that Fort Moultrie sent whistling after them. With not the loss of a single life, the Confederates found in their possession as the fruits of the conflict one hundred and twenty men, including twelve officers, with five stands of colors.

General Morgan's Raid.

Leaving for a time the city of Charleston to the fruitless attacks of the enemy, on the other side of the mountains General John Morgan was preparing to set out from Sparta, Tenn., with only two thousand troops, for that romantic raid of his into Ohio and Indiana. He began his exploits by attacking the enemy at Green River Bridge on July 4; but their fortifications were too strong, and he had to content himself with the capture of Lebanon on the next day, in which he took six hundred men and many stores and arms. In the gallant charge which he made upon this place his brother, Lieutenant Thomas

Morgan, fell mortally wounded with these words on his lips: "Brother Cally, they have killed me."

Thence Morgan proceeded through Central Kentucky to Bardstown, taking a company of cavalry as prisoners. There is a peculiar and striking feature connected with the Confederate advance through this portion of Kentucky, in that they were in the midst of their own homes and were forced to carry war upon friends and neighbors, or even father, brother, or other kinsmen who may have espoused the Federal cause, while they themselves were following the banner of the "Southern Cross." These divisions of family in Kentucky even marred the relation of husband and wife, for the narrator of these events knew personally of a case where the husband was a gallant soldier of the Confederacy and the wife was an efficient and valued *spy* in the service of the Federal army. Under such circumstances many a Kentucky mother has mourned a soldier-boy whose heart's best blood stained a gray jacket at Shiloh, and another perhaps lay upon the same dread field with his body wrapped in blue for his winding sheet.

But General Morgan continued his march, threatening Louisville, and crossing the Ohio River at Brandenburg. On the 8th of July he captured the Indiana town of Corydon, with six hundred prisoners. Thence, destroying railroads, telegraph communications, and all manner of Government stores, he advanced into the interior of the State, creating the greatest amount of consternation and terror among the astonished Federals.

Learning that the enemy were concentrating large forces at Indianapolis, New Albany, and Mitchell, Morgan left Indiana, and entered the borders of Ohio, throwing Cincinnati into a spasm of fear. He proceeded to harass the enemy as he had done in the former State, until at Pomeroy he encountered the Federals several thousand strong. Leaving part of his forces to hold these in check, with the main body he attempted to cross the river at Buffington Island early on the morning of July 18. Prevented from accomplishing this undertaking by the gun-boats of the enemy, he again tried farther up the river at Bellville, but only succeeded in getting about two hundred of his command across. These latter managed to make their escape back to the Confederate lines, but most of the others who had been left on the other side of the river fell into the hands of the enemy, among whom was the gallant Morgan himself, who was captured after an exciting chase near West Point, and confined in the Ohio penitentiary until the 20th of November, when, with six of his officers, he effected his escape by digging out with knives.

Though the end of this expedition is to be accounted a failure, yet, relatively, the two thousand prisoners which fell to the Federals were more than compensated for by the loss which this intrepid cavalryman inflicted upon them; for he had overrun two large, rich States, throwing them into a state of complete demoralization, stopping all trade, business, farming, , destroying railroads, bridges, public property, steamboats, and telegraph systems, all of which in the aggregate will amount to many millions of dollars. Consequently the capture of General Morgan and his men by the Federals is deprived of most of its glory in that it came too late, for the purposes of the invasion were virtually accomplished.

CHAPTER XVIII.

Chickamauga—Martial Law in Kentucky.

THE preceding chapters in regard to military events in the West seem to furnish a striking contrast to the brilliant successes in Virginia. After the battle of Murfreesboro General Bragg had fallen back to Tullahoma. Thence he proceeded to Wartrace and Shelbyville, with his army much weakened by the forces which had been drawn from it to strengthen the South-west. By a flank movement on the 27th of June the enemy forced the Confederates to fall back to Chattanooga. General Rosecrans slowly followed with his army of seventy thousand men, arriving at Stevenson and Bridgeport by August 20.

At the same time another movement was in progress against the Confederates. General Burnside, with an army of at least twenty-five thousand men, moved from Kentucky against Knoxville, Tenn., which was held by General Buckner with five thousand troops. Feeling his inability to cope with such large numbers, the latter evacuated the city, and moved to join General Bragg at Chattanooga, leaving, however, at Cumberland Gap General Frazier with two thousand troops. Against this position the Federals turned their attention, and on the 9th of September General Frazier, without firing a single gun, surrendered the garrison into the hands of the enemy. This movement was a painful surprise to the whole country, and even to the garrison themselves; for it was thought that the position could have been held against the force with which the enemy were investing it.

Battle of Chickamauga.

While General Burnside was pressing General Buckner in front, General Rosecrans had sent a corps up the Sequatchie Valley to give him a blow in his rear. Though somewhat re-enforced, General Buckner's command was not yet large enough to meet the enemy, so he retreated to Hiwassee. The purpose of the Federals seemed to be to threaten the Confederate rear; but the latter, though having at the highest estimate but thirty-five thousand men, determined to offer battle at the first opportunity. Therefore, on the 7th of September General D. H. Hill moved with his corps to La Fayette, and General Buckner, with the Army of East Tennessee, and General Walker, with a division of the Army of Mississippi, took a position at Anderson, while General Polk concentrated his forces at Lee & Gordon's Mills. Meanwhile the enemy's left, under General Crittenden, swung around in the direction of Chattanooga, with General Thomas's Corps moving toward La Fayette, and by the 9th they had crossed Lookout Mountain into McLemore's Cove. Appreciating at once the error of the Federals in allowing Thomas's Corps to become thus separated from the main army, General Bragg ordered General Hindman to attack the enemy, and General Hill to co-operate; but the latter, believing it to be impossible to get his command through the gaps in the mountains on account of obstructions, failed to unite his forces with those of Hindman on the morning of the 10th. In hot haste General Buckner was ordered to fill the command which had been given to General Hill, and by evening he succeeded in joining General Hindman at Davis's Cross Roads; but it was too late. The Federals, perceiving their almost fatal mistake, by a series of rapid marches managed to restore their scattered divisions, and by Saturday, September 19, they held a position in the Chickamauga Valley, with a creek of the same name separating them from the Confederates, who had been re-enforced by General Johnston with two brigades from Mississippi and five brigades from General Longstreet's Corps of Virginians. The enemy opened the battle by hurling a large force upon General Walker's Corps, which held a position on General Buckner's extreme right. The Confederates repulsed the enemy and drove them some distance, but were themselves being forced back, when they were re-enforced by General Cheatham's Division, which had been held in reserve. The battle became general along the whole line. Generals Stewart, Cleburne, and Hood had each driven the enemy before him, and in some cases had penetrated far into their lines. With this auspicious beginning the Confederates gathered their energies together for a grand victory on the next day. The following was the disposition of the troops: The right wing, under General Polk, consisted of General Hill's Corps, composed of Cleburne's, Breckinridge's, Cheatham's, and Walker's Divisions; the left wing, under General Longstreet, consisted of Generals Johnston, Preston, and Buckner's Corps, General Hindman's Division, Bennings's, Lane's, Robertson's, Kershaw's, and Humphries's Brigades. At ten o'clock Breckinridge and Cleburne moved forward against the rude fortifications which the Federals had erected during the night. Magnificently did they make the attack, and they were on the point of overwhelming General Thomas, who held the left, when re-enforcements arrived in time to save him. All along the line the battle raged with terrible fury, the enemy gradually giving way before the enthusiastic Confederates. Late in the afternoon the latter in one solid column swept forward against the enemy. With a cheer which seemed to shake the mountains, inspired by the memories of their forced retreat from

Murfreesboro before this same army which now confronted them, they began their victorious advance. Like a storm-cloud ready to let loose its torrents, the Federals saw these gray masses rushing toward them. Men of Mississippi, Louisiana, South Carolina, Alabama, and Tennessee stood side by side in an unbroken, unfaltering line, and, like a swollen torrent of the mountains upon which they fought, they literally hurled the enemy before them, and sent them in rout and confusion toward Missionary Ridge. Never was a victory more complete. That bright September moon looked down upon the shattered wreck of Rosecrans's thoroughly beaten army and the Confederates tenting upon the well-won field, full of the enthusiasm that comes from a contest nobly fought and gained. It is said that "General Forrest had climbed a tree, and from his lofty perch watched the retreating enemy. He saw the blue uniforms swarming over the fields, and the disorganized masses of the enemy choked with flight and struggling with mortal panic as sounds of feeble pursuit followed on their heels. He shouted to a staff officer: 'Tell General Bragg to advance the whole army; the enemy is ours.'" The Federals left in the hands of the conquering Confederates "eight thousand prisoners, fifty-one pieces of artillery, fifteen thousand stands of small-arms, and quantities of ammunition, with wagons, ambulances, teams, medicines, hospital stores, etc., in large quantities." Among the dead on the Confederate side were Generals Helm, Preston Smith, and James Deshler, and the gallant Hood was so severely wounded as to make the amputation of his thigh necessary.

On the 23d of September General Bragg moved his army from Chattanooga, crossing over Missionary Ridge, where he rested several weeks, leaving the enemy in possession of Chattanooga, where they reorganized their army and fortified themselves.

Martial Law in Kentucky.

The State of Kentucky at all times seemed to have more than her share of the evils and misfortunes incident to the war. Her people, being equally divided between Southern and Northern sympathies, were kept in a continued state of disturbance. Failing to oppress the Southern sympathizers, such influence was brought to bear upon Governor McGoffin that in August, 1862, he resigned his position. When the elections came round for the following year General Burnside had taken matters into his own hands, and declared the State under martial law. The following are some examples of the orders which he issued:

1. By way of precaution the people are informed that whenever any property is needed for the use of the United States army it will be taken from rebel sympathizers, and receipts given for the same marked "disloyal," and to be paid for at the end of the war on proof that the holder is a loyal man.

2. Rebel sympathizers are defined to be not only those who are in favor of secession, but also those who are not in favor of a vigorous prosecution of the war, and of furnishing men and money unconditionally for that purpose. "Loyalty" is to be proved by the vote given at the election.

3. County judges are required to appoint none but "loyal" men as judges of election, notwithstanding the provisions of our laws which require officers of election to be taken equally from each political party.

4. Persons offering to vote, whose votes may be rejected by the judges, are notified that they will be immediately arrested by the military.

5. Judges of election are notified that they will be arrested and held responsible by the military should they permit any disloyal man to vote.

These orders are here quoted at greater length and are given more attention perhaps than they deserve, but they serve to show the line of procedure to which the Federal Government had at this time committed itself in the management of any free and sovereign State over which it might gain the power. They show that the life, liberty, freedom, and the possession of one's goods and property were put in strange jeopardy, even for war times. Therefore, with such pressure as this brought to bear upon the citizens of Kentucky, the candidate who was elected (Mr. Bramlette) was virtually an appointee of the Federal Government forced into the executive office by the strong arm of the military. With such a fate as this which befell the noble State of the "dark and bloody ground" staring them in the face, one ceases to wonder at that almost superhuman endurance with which the South so repeatedly hurled back from her borders the vast and inexhaustible numbers which the enemy were sending against her in one constant stream; and that she only ended her efforts when completely worn out, like the best-tempered steel, which from long usage and the continued action of the elements finally loses its strength and breaks.

But not only did the Confederacy have to contend with the North itself, but also indirectly with the powers of Europe; for they, especially England, made invidious distinctions between the two Governments. In fact, while allowing the Federals to recruit their armies from her dominions and to get ammunition and supplies, the British Government seized upon two ships which were in course of construction at Birkenhead for the Confederacy. Thus it can be seen how much the more is that struggle remarkable which the South, unaided and alone, maintained against one of the strongest powers of modern times that marshalled its forces at her very doors.

CHAPTER XIX.

Rappahannock—Missionary Ridge.

AT the beginning of this chapter, before again taking up the thread of active military operations on the land, a brief account of the navy of the Confederate States, which has heretofore been playing such an important part, would not be out of place. At the beginning of the war the South was not only virtually without a fleet, but also the means of constructing one. But at once recognizing the importance of ships for coast and river defenses, she had directed her energies in this direction, and now had succeeded in floating about seventy-two vessels, with twenty-nine in process of construction. This enumeration includes ships of every description. With this navy, since the beginning of the war, the Confederacy had succeeded in capturing over one hundred and fifty Federal ships, which, with their cargoes, will aggregate a total damage of many millions of dollars.

SKIRMISHES ON THE RAPPAHANNOCK.

Retreating from Pennsylvania, General Lee had taken a position on the Rapidan, from which place he moved on the 9th of October with the purpose of engaging the enemy who were in the vicinity of Culpepper Court-house, and on the 10th his right, under General Stuart, met the advance line of the enemy at James City and drove them back in the direction of their main body at Culpepper Court-house. On reaching the latter place on the 11th, General Lee found that the enemy had withdrawn toward the Rappahannock. However, General Stuart did not relax his pursuit, and continued to harass their rear. General Fitzhugh Lee, who had been left to guard the Rapidan, met a detachment of the enemy who had crossed the river, and drove them as far as Brandy Station, where, on the evening of the 11th, he was joined by General Stuart. With their united commands they pushed the cavalry of the Federals to the other side of the Rappahannock. Continuing his march with the main army, General Lee reached the Rappahannock at Warrenton Springs on the afternoon of the 12th. Here the enemy made a spasmodic resistance, but were soon put to flight by the Confederate cavalry. This pursuit was kept up for three or four days, and was marked by frequent and severe skirmishes, especially at Bristoe's Station, where General Hill, with two brigades, was repulsed by a superior force of the enemy behind a railroad embankment. Besides a considerable loss in killed and wounded, General Hill left in the hands of the enemy quite a number of prisoners. Finding that he had failed in his purpose to flank General Meade, and that the latter was so near the intrenchments at Washington that it would be utterly impossible to get between him and them, General Lee, on the 18th, again withdrew his army to the Rappahannock.

When the army first set upon the movements just related General Imboden had been sent down the valley to protect General Lee's left against any probable attacks of the enemy from that direction. With a brilliancy and dispatch he carried out these plans, and while the main body of the army was on the retreat on the 18th, he surrounded the town of Charlestown, where a force of the enemy were fortified in the court-house and jail. To General Imboden's summons to surrender, Colonel Simpson, the Federal commander, replied: "Take me if you can." A few shells, however, from the Confederate batteries, showed the utter vanity of this boastful response by forcing the enemy from these positions. The latter fled in the direction of Harper's Ferry, but were checked by the Eighteenth Cavalry and a detachment of infantry. After a short conflict, the Federals surrendered themselves to the number of over four hundred. Re-enforcements from Harper's Ferry now came to their support, but too late to be of service. The gallant Imboden retired before their largely superior numbers, but kept possession of his spoils and prisoners.

General Lee's army now held a position "on both sides of the Orange and Alexandria railroad, General Ewell's Corps on the right and General Hill's on the left, with cavalry on each flank." Above the railroad bridge the Confederate general had fortified two hills on each side of the Rappahannock in order to prevent any flank movement on the part of the Federals. In the meantime the latter continued to rebuild the railroad which the Confederates had destroyed, and by the 6th it was discovered that they were approaching the river with the intention of fighting their way across. They fell upon General Rodes with the Second and Thirtieth North Carolina Regiments, stationed at Kelley's Ford, and drove the latter regiment to some buildings near the river, where they captured them. The enemy were also directing their attention to the Confederate rifle-pits at the bridge on the north bank, which was occupied by Colonel Godwin with one brigade, and General Hayes, also with one brigade. Anticipating an attack, the artillery was moved to the front, and General A. P. Hill's Corps, with Anderson's and Early's Divisions, were kept on the alert. The enemy, however, had planned a surprise, and under the cover of darkness they hurled their overwhelming numbers against the troops stationed on the north bank of the river. In a triple line they made their attack. Their first column melted away before the destructive fire of the Confederates, but had every bullet that sped from that little band defending the pits found a lodgment in a human breast, they could not even then have maintained themselves against such a force of numbers, that by their very weight pushed them from their position and surrounded them on all sides. Right gallantly, however, did they fight, with a courage that comes of desperation. Many were captured and a few cut their way through the almost solid lines which surrounded them, swam the river, and made their escape. This reverse caused General Lee to withdraw his forces to the south side of the Rapidan, where, on the 27th of November, that portion of his army drawn up at Germania Ford was attacked by a large force of the enemy under General French. In this contest the Federals again attempted a surprise; but they did not meet with that success which had crowned their efforts in the former attack on the Rappahannock, for they were driven back with great loss—perhaps double that of the Confederates, which was four hundred and fifty in killed and wounded. This repulse seemed to put an end to General Meade's designs of engaging General Lee in a decisive battle.

MISSIONARY RIDGE.

The defeat at Chickamauga cost General Rosecrans his command, for on the 18th of October he was superseded by General U. S. Grant, who at once proceeded to Chattanooga, where the Federal forces were practically invested by General Bragg. Moreover, the Confederate cavalry were keeping the enemy in a continued state of alarm by their continuous and constant raids—especially that one of General Wheeler in the direction of McMinnville and Shelbyville, in which he captured a large number of prisoners, destroyed many bridges, and took much stores and supplies which the enemy could ill spare at this time.

On reaching Chattanooga General Grant immediately put new life into the dispirited Federals, and on the 28th of October he sent General Hooker into the Lookout Valley with the Eleventh Corps and one division of the Twelfth Corps; and he also succeeded in getting possession of the range of hills at the entrance to this valley. The Confederates, however, did not permit these movements to proceed entirely in peace, for on the night of the 29th six regiments of troops fell upon the enemy, but after a gallant attack they were forced to retire on finding that they were engaged with the entire Twelfth Corps, under General Slocum. In the early part of November General Bragg sent General Longstreet with his forces to attack General Burnside at Knoxville. Immediately upon hearing of this movement General Grant determined to attack the Confederates at once in their weakened condition. General Bragg had taken up a position on the top of Missionary Ridge, which was between four and six hundred feet in height, and had posted his troops "along the crest of the ridge from McFarland's Gap almost to the mouth of the Chickamauga, a distance of six miles or more." Re-enforced by General Sherman, the Federals consumed the 23d and 24th of November in getting their forces in position for a general attack, and on the 25th, with a magnificent army of eighty-five thousand men, they moved against the Confederates, who numbered less than one-half that amount. At ten o'clock the enemy hurled their heavy double columns, supported by large reserves, against the left under General Hardee, which consisted of Generals Cleburne's, Walker's (commanded by General Gist), Cheatham's, and Stevenson's Divisions. As became the veterans of Shiloh and Chickamauga, did these tried divisions maintain themselves against two successive assaults of the enemy, gallantly holding their position. But the left, commanded by General Breckinridge, did not fare so well when the Federals fell upon them about twelve o'clock. At first it seemed as if the latter were going to be served in the same manner as the brave Hardee had served them on the right; but somehow a brigade in the center gave way, allowing the enemy to get a foot-hold upon the crest of the ridge and to turn their fire upon our flanks. Soon the whole left broke and retreated, and the day was lost and the victory at Chickamauga rendered fruitless save as an exhibition of grand courage. Though General Hardee had been decisively victorious in his encounter with the Federals, the complete disaster on the left made his success vain and fruitless, so the night of the 25th found General Bragg in retreat in the direction of Dalton, Ga., with Cleburne and his division guarding the rear. The latter's remarkably skillful, brave, and successful performance of this duty casts a brilliancy over an otherwise gloomy and disastrous movement. To make their victory more complete, the enemy had sent a picked division of ten thousand men in pursuit, which the Confederates managed to repulse at every point, and especially at Taylor's Ridge did General Thomas's advance come to grief. Here General Cleburne concealed his artillery and planted his infantry on both sides of the road and when the enemy came very close upon them, with both heavy guns and muskets the Confederates turned loose such a fire that it fairly cut them to pieces and caused them to break and flee in confusion, leaving scattered upon the bloody road one thousand five hundred killed and wounded as an evidence that they had entered literally into the very jaws of death. Moreover, the brave Cleburne had in his possession two hundred and fifty prisoners and three battle-flags belonging to the enemy; and the latter showed their appreciation of this sanguinary lesson by ceasing at once from any further pursuit.

General Longstreet had been sent against Knoxville with hardly eleven thousand men, and with but an insufficient amount of supplies and means of transportation for even these. However, this did not daunt the hero of so many Virginia battles; but, by taking large amounts of booty at Lenoir and Bean's Stations and in the Clinch Valley, he succeeded in forcing the enemy to assist him in the maintenance of his army. By the 18th of November he had driven the advance line of the Federals into the shelter of their works, and thus had Knoxville completely invested, with every probability of an early surrender, when the news of the fatal field of Missionary Ridge made it either necessary for him to make an immediate assault or to retreat. The former course was decided upon; and accordingly, at the break of day on the morning of the 29th of November, three brigades of McLaw's Division moved against that part of the Federal works known as Fort Sanders. Over a ground obstructed with stumps and wires ingeniously prepared by the enemy to throw the assaulting column into confusion, the gallant fellows moved in the midst of a hail-storm of death, which put in mourning many a home in Mississippi, Georgia, and South Carolina, from which the men who made up this division were drawn. However, with their comrades falling around them like the leaves of the forest when swept by an autumn gale, they pressed upon the fortifications and planted their own banner side by side with the flag of the enemy. But unavailing was this superb and unsurpassed courage, and, leaving their dead and wounded to the number of one thousand, they fell back. Upon this failure General Longstreet took up his line of march in the direction of Rogersville, with the enemy following as far as Bean's Station, where the Confederates halted long enough to repulse them, driving them back a distance of twelve miles, and reminding them that the veterans of Fredericksburg and Manassas were still in a condition to punish them with a severe defeat. General Longstreet then proceeded to overrun all the extreme North-east of the State, maintaining his army upon the spoils of the country.

CHAPTER XX.

Minor Operations in the West.

THOUGH the operations in the extreme Southwest were upon a small scale, when compared with the scenes that were being enacted upon the great theaters of war in the East, yet the record of how the Southern soldier fought—the story of his noble struggle for four long years against an enemy so many times his superior in point of numbers—would be strangely lacking should one omit to weave into the chronicle of events how, on the 8th of September, the little garrison at Sabine Pass, between Louisiana and Texas, won their victory. This fort, though only mounting three guns, was attacked by a fleet of five gun-boats. However, they directed their fire so well that in a short time they had disabled one of the gun-boats and forced two others to surrender. Thus, with not the loss of a single man, they had gained a victory the fruits of which were, besides the two boats, two hundred men and fifteen cannons.

Many volumes might be written of those gallant but irregular bands that swept up and down this whole Western country, too few in number to risk a general and open encounter with the enemy. About all of their actions, their manner of life, their hair-breadth escapes, their heroic refusal to bow to the iron heel of oppression, preferring the long ride, the midnight surprise, choosing to be houseless and homeless, wanderers and outcasts from the lands they loved, hunted like the beasts of the forest, as mercilessly slain when found, there is the atmosphere of romantic fiction rather than the sober, uncolored record of history. Therefore one will have to content himself only with this passing tribute to their devotion to the cause they loved, with relating only one characteristic incident which took place near Fort Smith, Ark. While Quantrell and his band of "guerrillas" were in the neighborhood of the fort, General Blount, accompanied by two hundred cavalrymen, rode out to meet them, thinking that they were Federal soldiers. Too late did they discover their fatal mistake. With the fierce swoop of an eagle these defenders of individual rights and the independence of the separate States in the far West were upon them, and soon had almost swept the entire command from the face of the earth.

Virginia and Tennessee Border.

Near the dividing line between East Tennessee and Virginia the Confederate forces of General Jones and the Federals under General Averill were battling for supremacy in that region. On the 26th of August these two commands met near Dublin, and the first day's fight ended without either gaining any decisive advantage. However, the enemy renewed the contest on the next day, but after two unsuccessful attacks they were forced to retreat toward Warm Springs, with the Confederates following. The latter lost between two and three hundred in killed and wounded, but took one hundred and fifty prisoners and one piece of artillery. On the 6th of the following month the Confederates gained a still more decisive victory by surprising the Federals near Rogersville, and taking—besides wagons, artillery, and cattle—eight hundred and fifty prisoners. While General Ransom was performing this brilliant achievement the enemy, seven thousand five hundred strong, were surrounding Colonel W. L. Jackson at Droop Mountain, who had under his command only fifteen hundred men. But even with this small number he kept the enemy at bay for seven hours, marked by a stubborn and heroic resistance, when he was forced to retreat in the direction of Lewisburg, which retreat he successfully accomplished without the loss of either his stores or artillery. The Federal general then made a rapid raid into Virginia, destroying many supplies, especially at Salem. On his return, however, he was met near Covington by Colonel Jackson, who succeeded in capturing two hundred of his command, though General Averill himself managed to escape.

Lincoln's "Peace Proclamation."

About this time President Lincoln issued what is known as the "Peace Proclamation," only a few features of which need to be given to show how very insulting it was to every feeling of honor, and how thoroughly humiliating and degrading it would have been had the South accepted it:

> Whereas in and by the Constitution of the United States it is provided that the President shall have power to give reprieves and pardons for offenses against the United States, except in cases of impeachment; and whereas a rebellion exists, whereby the loyal State Governments of several States have for a long time been subverted, and many persons have committed and are now guilty of *treason* against the Government of the United States, etc.

In this document the complete independence of the slaves was further guaranteed, and the following exceptions from its provisions were made:

> All who are or shall have been civil or diplomatic officers or agents of the so-called Confederate Government; all who have left judicial stations under the United States to aid in the rebellion; all who are or shall have been naval or military officers of the said so-called Confederate Government above the rank of colonel in the army or of lieutenant in the navy; all who left seats in the United States Congress to aid in the rebellion, etc.

Such were the general characteristics of this remarkable document. One need not read far to see that it was a strange "peace," a peculiar "peace" that was offered to the "said so-called Confederate

Government." One feels that the generous glow of an earnest, magnanimous desire for a cessation of hostilities which had caused the crimson tide of human life to flow out upon many a bloody field was so far wanting that one would not be wrong in designating it as the "Proclamation of Humiliation" rather than of "Peace," for it was like acid to the bleeding wound. It meant a confession of treason, of offense against civil and moral law. Its acceptation would have been at the time like one taking a burning brand and stamping upon his own forehead an ineffaceable acknowledgment of a crime which he had not committed. Moreover, the soldiers who had followed the glorious fortunes of their commanders through the varying scenes of the war were hardly willing to give them over to the uncertain fate threatened in this proclamation. Consequently this document, couched more in the language of flippant boast and vain triumph than in the sober and dignified terms of a great State paper, only served to make the South nerve herself for the last grand heroic struggles which only sheer exhaustion can conquer.

Under such circumstances as these, and upon such terms, the South never for a moment considered the question of peace; therefore, with the heroic purpose to die for the principles they had espoused, with a steadfast resolve not to willingly submit to a settlement which would place upon them chains of everlasting disgrace, the people resumed the third year of their struggle with a foe which was so numerous that it would seem that the Federal armies were like the mythical warriors in the Valley of the Walhalla, who fought all day, slaying and being slain; but who, being restored to life and strength during the night by some magical power, renewed their endless battles the next morning.

The year 1864 was opened in Virginia with General Early's proposed attack upon the Federals fortified at Petersburg in the latter part of January. General Rosser, with his brigade, was sent on ahead of the main body, and near Petersburg he found a wagon-train—ninety-six in number—loaded with a vast quantity of important stores of every description and guarded by a force of one thousand two hundred men, who had taken a position behind a rail fence. The prize was too valuable to let slip without a struggle; so the Confederates charged the enemy, and in less than half an hour had them completely routed and were in possession of the wagons and their coveted and needed contents. Thence General Rosser turned toward Petersburg, with the intention of assisting General Early in the attack which they had planned upon that city. But the Federals, though well fortified, did not have the temerity to risk an encounter with the Confederates, and therefore they abandoned the city, and, aided by the darkness, escaped. This expedition of General Rosser was quite profitable, in that he captured, besides the wagon-train, nearly three hundred prisoners and over one thousand five hundred cattle.

Attack upon New Berne, N. C.

Immediately following these exploits of the Confederates in the valley was General Pickett's expedition against the Federals at New Berne, N. C., which resulted hardly less brilliantly than the former. With only two brigades, he charged the enemy's outposts on Bachelor's Creek, in the vicinity of New Berne, and with an impetuous rush he pushed the Federals before him, driving them to the shelter of their fortifications. During the night a small detachment surprised and captured one of the finest of the enemy's gun-boats moored in the Neuse River. After a brilliant hand-to-hand combat they forced the crew to surrender, but were unable to hold the vessel on account of the fire from the batteries on the banks; therefore, rather than allow her to fall back into the hands of the enemy, they gave her over to the flames, and she was soon burned to the water's edge. The result of this enterprise was three hundred prisoners with their arms, two fine cannons, and quite a goodly quantity of provisions, clothing, camp supplies, and a number of horses and cattle.

This series of small victories was continued in another quarter on the 10th and 11th of February. The enemy made an attack on the Confederates on John's Island, near Charleston, S. C. Being somewhat successful on the 10th, they renewed their efforts on the following day, but the Confederates having been reenforced, they were beaten back in confusion.

Battle of Ocean Pond.

The month of February was rendered still more conspicuous by a victory farther south in the pine woods of Florida, and near the clear waters of one of her picturesque lakes. General Finnegan, the Confederate commander, had with him a force much too small to cope with the Federals, fully eight thousand in number, who had come under General Seymour from Charleston harbor; therefore the former was forced to retreat before the enemy until he was reenforced by General Colquitt, with his brigade and other troops, which aggregated his command to fully five thousand, with which he took a position near Ocean Pond and awaited the approach of the enemy. They did not have to wait long, for on the afternoon of the 20th the latter made their expected attack, which was but a repetition of the results which usually followed whenever the forces of the two armies were approximately equal. The Federals sustained themselves for a time, but when the Confederates made that furious onslaught so peculiar to them in all their battles from the Potomac to the Rio Grande, the Federals fled in rout and confusion in the direction of Jacksonville; nor did they make a halt until they had put twenty miles between themselves and the battle-field upon which they left over three hundred dead and wounded, two thousand stands of arms, five cannons, and five hundred prisoners. The Confederates suffered to the extent of eighty killed, and between six and seven hundred wounded.

CHAPTER XXI.
Invasion of Mississippi and Alabama.

GENERAL GRANT now conceived the design of carrying the war more thoroughly into the interior of the extreme Southern States, thus destroying the great source of Confederate supplies. This plan was put into active operation February 1, 1864, by General Sherman marching out of Vicksburg with a column thirty-five thousand strong, and Generals Grierson and Smith proceeding through the northern part of the State of Mississippi at the head of ten thousand cavalry and mounted infantry. The objective point of both of these expeditions was the city of Mobile, which place was at the same time anticipating an attack from the water by the gunboats of the enemy. General Polk was in command of the Confederate interests in this quarter, with a force not at all adequate to contend with the large numbers of the enemy. However, sending General Forrest to observe the course of Generals Grierson and Smith, he succeeded in holding General Sherman in check long enough to save his supplies and to evacuate Meridian, Miss., in good order, and to retreat safely to Demopolis, Ala.

In contending with the other column General Forrest added new laurels to his fame as a cavalry leader. With only a force of less than twenty-five hundred men it was imperatively necessary for him to crush this magnificently equipped cavalry of the enemy, nearly thrice his own in numbers. Near West Point this undaunted Tennesseean made a stand, and, having posted his men irregularly in the bushes, he awaited the rush and onslaught of the enemy. As the Federals rode to the attack the Confederate rifles began to crack, and with these whip-like reports the enemy were seen to fall in such alarming rapidity as to produce confusion and to check their advance. However, they reformed and charged again, but the empty saddles still continued to increase to such an extent as to spread a contagious terror among them, and they gave up the contest and fled.

Again, at Okolona, on the evening of February 21, the Federals made a disastrous attempt to crush Forrest's small force. In this conflict the rout of the enemy was even more complete than in the first, and they turned and fled precipitately in the direction of Memphis, with General Gholson pursuing with only six hundred men.

These brilliant successes on the part of the Confederates prevented General Sherman from reaping any of the fruits of his invasion of the State. Therefore he was forced to withdraw to Vicksburg his heavy column, with which he had expected to accomplish so much, with very barren laurels resting upon their banners. General Polk issued the following account of the results of the campaign:

> The concentration of our cavalry on the enemy's column of cavalry from West Tennessee formed the turning-point of the campaign. That concentration broke down his only means of subsisting his infantry. His column was defeated and routed, and his whole force compelled to make a hasty retreat. Never did a grand campaign, inaugurated with such pretension, terminate more ingloriously. With a force three times that which was opposed to its advance, they have been defeated, and forced to leave the field with a loss of men, small-arms, and artillery.

On the 25th of February the Federals followed this expedition by an attempt on the part of General Thomas to push through the Confederate lines upon Atlanta. But this movement was checked, and the enemy were forced to fall back to Chickamauga.

Legal Enactments.

Besides this auspicious beginning in the field, the year 1864 was characterized by the enforcement of a few important acts of legislation: first, the funding of the currency; second, the stopping of further issues of paper money; third, a provision for greater revenues by an increase in taxation; and fourth, the sale of six per cent. bonds to the amount of $500,000,000. In addition to these financial measures the "Conscript Law" was revised and more rigorously enforced, thus putting the army on a better basis.

Federal Cavalry Raids.

In Virginia operations were continued by a plan of the enemy with a picked body of men to surprise and take the city of Richmond. To consummate this design, on the 28th of February there were three expeditions, under the command of Generals Kilpatrick and Custer and Colonel Ulric Dahlgreen, respectively, having Richmond for their objective point. Each in turn came to grief after having signalized themselves by certain notorious acts of rapine and pillage which the true soldier, fighting under any civilized flag, would hardly feel himself honored in doing. First, General Custer collided with a detachment of Stuart's Horse Artillery, under Major Beckham, near Rio Mills, and the result was that the enemy were sent back across the Rivanna River. General Kilpatrick, however, managed to get within sight of the spires of Richmond; but he retreated before getting in range of the batteries of the outer fortifications. The fate of Dahlgreen was rather worse than the other two; for, on his way to Richmond, he was confronted by a local battery and a force of clerks and boys, whose first fire scattered his command in confusion, with a loss of fifty in killed and wounded. He continued his retreat, harassed at every point by irregular bands of Confederates, until near Walkerton, where he was attacked by Lieutenant Pollard with a company of rangers, together with a few cavalry under Captain Cox. At the first fire Colonel Dahlgreen himself was slain, and his band without any order scattered in flight through the woods, where most of them were captured by the Confederates. Papers found upon the body of the dead Federal commander showed how well-laid his plans were, and how very atrocious they were in respect to murder and destruction.

Federal Expeditions from New Orleans and Vicksburg.

Transferring the scene of operations to the Southwest, we find the Federals engaged in the preparation of an extensive movement in that quarter, which had for its purpose the complete subjugation of the country west of the Mississippi River. Accordingly, two large forces—one from New Orleans, under General Franklin; the other from Vicksburg, under General A. J. Smith—moved westward on the 1st and 10th of March respectively. The latter, under General Smith, proceeded up Red River, and on the 14th captured Fort De Russy, with nearly three hundred prisoners. Thence they advanced up through that rich cotton section, destroying and confiscating many thousands of dollars' worth of this valuable commodity, and on the 16th took possession of Alexandria.

All three divisions of the Federal forces now turned their attention to Shreveport as the most important point in all the South-west region, and were endeavoring to form a junction there. However, the Confederates, appreciating the value of this position, were determined not to give it up without a struggle. Accordingly, on the 8th of April, near the town of Mansfield, General Banks was confronted by the Confederates under General Kirby Smith. The contest raged stubbornly for several hours; but finally, outflanked and being unable to sustain themselves against the furious attacks of the Confederates, the enemy began to retreat, which soon degenerated into a thorough panic, and was continued until re-enforced by General Franklin, who had meantime arrived. This battle cost the Federals, in killed, wounded, and missing, fifteen hundred men, eighteen cannon, and wagon-trains containing large quantities of supplies. On the following day General Banks re-organized his forces, and having been further re-enforced by the arrival of General A. J. Smith with his division, he awaited the on-coming Confederates in an open field in which was a small hill, which gave the name to the battle—Pleasant Hill. After preliminary skirmishing all day, the real engagement was begun by a magnificent charge of the Confederates in a triple line. After pushing the enemy back for some distance and capturing one battery, General Kirby Smith withdrew his forces to their original position, and awaited further developments from the

Federals. But the latter had suffered too much—perhaps two thousand in killed and wounded—to try the results of another conflict, and therefore retreated to Grand Ecore without having accomplished the great purpose of their expedition. Moreover, the gallant Kirby Smith, who had made such a signal and conspicuous defense, had in his possession as the spoils of victory over one thousand wagons, thirty-five cannon, and six thousand prisoners. His opponent, General Banks, occupied himself during nearly all of the month of May in getting his shattered army back behind the guns of New Orleans, thus bringing to a disastrous conclusion an expedition that had promised so much in the beginning.

General Forrest in Kentucky.

The Confederates seemed determined to have an unbroken line of victories in the West. General Forrest, with his band of tireless riders, swept up through Kentucky, and on the 12th of April, after a refusal of the commander, Major Booth, to surrender, he stormed Fort Pillow, and in half an hour's time had slain five hundred of the garrison and captured the remainder, together with a large amount of stores. This attack upon Fort Pillow the Federals have been ever willing to designate as a "massacre." It is true that the mortality of the enemy was fearful, yet when one considers that they failed to take down their flag, and that the Confederates found opposed to them as a part of the garrison a large number of negroes—their former slaves, whom they had reared and cared for, and who now turned to bite the hand that fed them—then one can appreciate the determination and thorough exasperation with which they fought. The ever restless, enterprising Forrest did not stop here, but at once moved against Paducah, which place he reached on the morning of the 25th. Driving the Federal force, over two thousand strong, back beyond the town, he took possession, capturing and destroying vast quantities of stores of every description, and then retiring.

Confederates Retake Plymouth, N. C.

Across the mountains in the "Old North State" the Confederates were preparing to place yet another star in their brilliant constellation of victories. The Federals had strongly fortified Plymouth, situated on the south bank of the Roanoke River. Against this place General Hoke organized an expedition, which consisted of three brigades, commanded by General Ransom and Colonels Mercer and Terry respectively, one regiment of cavalry, under Colonel Dearing, and seven batteries of artillery, commanded by Major Reid and Colonel Branch. After a forced march of seventy-five miles, on the 17th of April the expedition arrived in the vicinity of the town, and began operations by turning their artillery upon Warren Neck, about a mile above. The result of the bombardment was considerable damage to the fort and the destruction of one of the gun-boats, which had come to its help. This was followed by an attack upon Fort Wessell the next day, which surrendered after a brave resistance. In this assault the noble and gallant Colonel Mercer lost his life. At two o'clock the next morning the Confederate iron-clad, "Albemarle," steamed past the Federal batteries, and attacked two of their gun-boats. One of these the Confederate vessel sunk, but the other escaped, though she sustained much damage. Early on the morning of the 28th a general attack with infantry, cavalry, and artillery was made. With cheers the Confederates rushed on to victory, taking battery after battery until they had driven the enemy from the town and were in complete possession of all the forts, together with sixteen hundred prisoners, immense quantities of stores and supplies, and twenty-five cannon. Such was the brilliant and successful ending of this expedition against Plymouth.

CHAPTER XXII.

In Virginia Again.

ATTENTION is now once more turned to the grand old "Mother State," upon whose bosom is soon to take place the final struggles which are to decide the fate of the new Government which has been battling so nobly, so superbly for her independence. The Federal Government had transferred General Grant to the East with the hope and expectation that he would repeat in this new field that characteristic success which had marked his career in the West, and had put under him as magnificently equipped an army as had ever stepped to the sound of martial music. Each side somehow had a premonition that this was to be the final and decisive campaign; that there was going to be a mighty struggle in which one cause or the other was going to die. The victories that the gray lines had been gaining in the South made the Southern heart throb with a new hope, into which no element of despair or doubt entered; therefore it was with buoyant and confident step that the veterans of Lee's army marched out to meet the two huge columns which General Grant set in motion on the 4th of May. On the following day they had crossed the Rapidan and were making an attempt to turn General Lee's right flank, which consisted of General Edward Johnson's Division holding a position along a turnpike. The attack of the enemy was made with vigor, and for a time it seemed as if it would be successful. But their apparent good fortune was only temporary, for the break they had made in the Confederate lines was soon closed up, while at the same time Gordon's Brigade struck them a severe blow in front that sent them reeling back in confusion. The Federals made a second attack upon another part of General Johnson's line—the left— but were warmly received by Pegram's and Hayes's Brigades, and hurled back after the manner of their first attack. Not satisfied with these advances, the enemy made a still more determined effort against Heth's and Wilcox's Divisions, which lasted from three o'clock until dark. But they made no impression upon that unbroken line of gray, and it was confessed from their own stand-point "that no cheer of victory swelled through the wilderness that night." The next day was consumed in assaults by Generals Hill and Longstreet upon Hancock's Corps; but though the line of the enemy was broken in several places by the effective blows of these two tried corps, yet they managed in the main to hold their position. Toward evening, however, the Confederates succeeded in capturing a large part of General Seymour's Brigade, and this action created among the forces of the enemy such consternation that at one time it seemed that their whole army was on the point of a panic. On the following day (the 7th) General Grant moved his army in the direction of Fredericksburg, with the intention, it seems, of taking this route to Richmond. On the 8th, at Spottsylvania Court-house, General Warren's Corps received two severe repulses at the hands of General Longstreet's Corps, which was now under the command of General Anderson, for the former had been wounded in the battle two days before. This ended matters until Thursday, the 12th, when the Federals moved against the Confederate fortifications, and before the latter could recover themselves they had surrounded and captured nearly all of Johnson's Division. It was a critical point. The fate of the Confederacy almost hung in the balance. The Federals seemed now to be on the point of a decisive victory that would throw open the gates of Richmond. General Lee rode forward in front of the lines he had so often led to conquest and success. The scene was dramatic in its subdued intensity. He took a position "opposite at the time to the colors of the Forty-ninth Regiment of Pegram's Brigade. Not a word did he say. He simply took off his hat 'as he sat on his charger.' An eye-witness says of him: 'I never saw a man look so noble or witnessed a spectacle so impressive.' At this interesting mo-

General Lee before the "Battle of the Wilderness."

ment General Gordon, spurring his foaming charger to the front, seized the reins of General Lee's horse, and turning him around, said: 'General, these are Virginians! They have never failed! They never will; will you, boys?' Amid loud cries of 'No, no! General Lee, to the rear!' 'Go back, go back! General Lee, to the rear!' General Gordon gave the command, 'Forward, charge!'" With this the inspiration of the battle was upon them. The heroes of Jackson were again themselves, and grandly did they fight through all that terrible day in a manner fully worthy of that grim warrior under whom they had swept so gloriously up the valley. The shadows of night dropped their dark curtain on a theater upon whose stage had been played in awful reality one of the fiercest of all the acts in the dread tragedy of this war. Ewell, Longstreet, and Hill had flung column after column of the enemy back, each time piling the ground thick with dead and dying, for the outflow of the crimson tide of human life stained between eighteen and twenty-five thousand blue uniforms, and perhaps seven thousand of the gray. But the enemy also had in their possession the three thousand prisoners of Johnson's Division and the twenty pieces of artillery captured at the same time.

While General Grant was thus trying to break General Lee's front, General Sheridan was sent to coöperate with General Butler, who was to move against

Richmond from the south. On his route to Turkey Island on the 10th, at Mud Tavern, he was opposed by General J. E. B. Stuart with his cavalry. In this encounter the gallant Stuart, the very soul of Virginia chivalry, laid down his life for the country for which he had done so much and at whose hands he deserves a high rank in the calendar of heroic names in remembrance of which the South has planted an evergreen of immortality.

On the 5th of May General Butler advanced, with a large force and fleet of gun-boats, up the James River, and landed and proceeded to intrench himself around Drury's Bluff; but he was forced to abandon this position when General Beauregard struck him such a forcible blow on the right as to crush it, inflicting a loss upon the enemy to the extent of several thousand in killed, wounded, and prisoners.

There was still another feature of the enemy's extensive operations in Virginia by which they hoped to effect a speedy destruction of the Confederacy. General Sigel, with twelve thousand troops, was sent up the Shenandoah against Staunton, General Crook with six thousand against Dublin, and General Averill with two thousand five hundred cavalry against Wytheville. The first, under General Sigel, felt the might of General Breckinridge's army at Newmarket when the latter punished him to the extent of a large number in killed and wounded, six cannons, and nearly one thousand stands of arms. At Dublin General Crook was sent back in full retreat by General McCausland with only a force of one thousand five hundred. Besides a severe loss in killed and wounded, the enemy left in the hands of the Confederates nearly seven hundred prisoners. General Averill's attack upon Wytheville was no more successful, for he was repulsed by General Morgan with a heavy loss. Thus it will be seen that the plans of the enemy were thoroughly and completely baffled at every point and brought to naught.

Cold Harbor.

On the 18th the guns were again thundering along the lines holding the approaches toward Richmond, for the tenacity of the Federal commander expressed itself in another fruitless assault upon General Ewell's position. General Grant changed his position again and again, but each time the ever-watchful Lee threw his insuperable wall of gray between him and the devoted city. The former, however, kept testing the strength of this wall by attacks on the 23d and 25th, and at the same time continued to swing his line around until by the 28th he had his army across the Pamunky River, and by the 1st of June was near Cold Harbor, with the object for which they had struggled so long almost in sight. But the fruition of their hopes was yet to be deferred, and the successful consummation of their plans, which seemed now at hand, to be shattered like a crystal fabric of frail glass by the blow which they received at Cold Harbor. On the morning of Friday, June 3, the enemy massed their forces against the Confederates intrenched along the Chickahominy. Assault after assault was made, and each time the enemy were hurled back, the Confederates retaining every position and giving no evidence of weakness at any point of their line save in one instance on the left, which was quickly repaired. Thus the enemy were again made to feel the effectiveness of those blows that had so completely held at bay each successive "On to Richmond" expedition. The enemy paid the penalty for their attack upon the Confederate lines with ten thousand men.

It seemed now that this leader, whom the North had chosen to lead them to a decisive victory, was to fare at the hands of General Lee just as his predecessors had fared, for from a Federal historian his loss so far in this campaign was sixty thousand men, while the same authority gives the Confederate loss at a little over half that number.

THE WESTERN PART OF VIRGINIA.

The Federals were not satisfied with the repulses which they had met in the western part of Virginia. Accordingly they prepared a large force and put it under command of General Hunter. To oppose this force the Confederates could only bring three small divisions—neither large enough to be called an army—commanded respectively by Breckinridge, McCausland, and William E. Jones. By the 5th of June the enemy had accomplished the capture of Staunton, in defense of which the brave and eccentric General Jones lost his life. Several days later General Hunter united to his own command those of Generals Cook and Averill, and moved in the direction of Lynchburg.

Attack upon Petersburg.

General Grant now determined to put forth a greater effort for the capture of the city of Petersburg, which had already on the 9th of June repulsed an attack from General Butler. Active preparations were begun on the 14th by General Smith with his forces assaulting and getting possession of the first line of Confederate fortifications on the north-east. This was followed on the 16th by an attack of three corps of the Federal army on the front, which were not only repulsed, but the Confederates themselves became the attacking party and drove the enemy before them and captured some of their artillery, together with a large portion of an entire regiment. The next day the enemy repeated these tactics with the same results, but on the 18th they made one more effort to get possession of the city, which, as Governor Wise said in the beginning, "is to be and shall be defended on her outer walls, on her inner lines, at her corporation bounds, in every street and around every temple of God and altar of man." Three times during the day did the enemy hurl their heavy columns against the fortifications, but all to no purpose. The Confederates still held possession, having inflicted upon their opponents a loss of ten thousand in killed and wounded.

Other Reverses of the Enemy.

The enemy seemed now to be meeting with reverses all along their lines. At Port Walthall Junction Pickett's Division had struck Gilmore's command a blow that put him to flight, while Hampton's Cavalry had served Sheridan in a similar manner on June 10 at Trevillian Station, and on the 18th Hunter was sent back to the mountains, having been repulsed from his anticipated attack upon Lynchburg, with a loss of thirteen pieces of artillery. South-west Virginia was also saved by General Morgan's bold advance into Kentucky, which forced the enemy to follow him in order to protect that State.

While these offshoots, so to speak, from the main stem of General Grant's purposes were being nipped in the bud, he himself was made to suffer when the Confederates under General Anderson fell upon the Second and Sixth Corps, penetrated their line, and took one battery and one whole brigade. Still another Federal expedition, commanded by Wilson and

Kautz, came to grief a score of miles south of Petersburg. At the hands of Generals Hampton, Mahone, and Finnegan they lost sixteen hundred prisoners, together with artillery, wagons, stores, and small-arms.

General Grant now determined that he must do something to retrieve the disasters which were falling upon him thick and fast. Therefore he resorted to the method of undermining and blowing up the principal fortifications around Petersburg. The mine was constructed under Cemetery Hill, and at half-past four o'clock on the morning of July 30 the match was applied, and a mighty gap was rent in the earth by the explosion. Simultaneous with this the thunders of a hundred guns were opened upon the city, which was a signal for a general attack on the part of the enemy, hoping to take the Confederates unawares. But they discovered how completely they had mistaken the latter when they found themselves beaten back in rout and confusion, many falling into the crater, making with their own dead and dying the chasm which they themselves had constructed a pit of horrors. This experiment cost General Grant over five thousand men, while the loss of the Confederates was comparatively light—about one thousand men.

THE LOSS OF THE "ALABAMA."

The ardor of the Confederates, however, was somewhat chilled by the loss of their most formidable ship of war, the "Alabama," under the command of Captain Semmes. On the 19th of June, in the harbor of Cherbourg, France, Captain Semmes offered battle to the Federal ship, "Kearsarge." The latter was so well protected by iron plating and chains that the shot of the "Alabama" made little impression upon her, while her own shot were so effective that in a short time it was discovered that the Confederate vessel was in a sinking condition, and Captain Semmes was forced to haul down his colors.

CHAPTER XXIII.

General Sherman in the South.

WHILE General Grant was moving against Richmond, General Sherman was preparing for an invasion of the South with an army of ninety-eight thousand men divided into three great divisions, under Generals Thomas, Schofield, and McPherson. To oppose these mighty columns General Johnston could only bring in the field an active army of not over forty thousand men.

General Sherman now moved in the direction of Dalton, Ga., and met his first check on the 14th of May in the Resaca Valley, when he attempted to carry the Confederate works. The enemy were driven back with a loss of two thousand men. General Johnston gradually fell back before the advancing legions of the enemy, but all the time waiting and watching for an opportunity to strike a blow, if the enemy should expose any weak point or commit a blunder. By the 20th he had crossed the Etowah River, and on the 25th he encountered the fortifications of the enemy near Dallas. The latter assumed the offensive by hurling Hooker's Corps against Stewart's Division at New Hope Church; but after struggling for two hours to drive the Confederates from their position, the Federals were repulsed. All day during the 26th and until five o'clock in the afternoon of the 27th was consumed in skirmishes between the two armies, when the enemy again essayed an assault upon the Confederates. Cleburne's brave division received their attack this time at the hands of Howard's Corps. The latter were again beaten back with an estimated loss of perhaps three thousand men, while the Confederates only suffered to the extent of four hundred and fifty.

General Johnston still kept up his brilliantly conducted retreat, striking the enemy now and then some severe blows, until he reached Kennesaw Mountain, where he made a stand. The huge column of the enemy made a strong attack on the 27th of May, but they were met by the veteran troops of Cheatham's and Cleburne's Divisions of Hardee's Corps, together with French's and Featherstone's Divisions of Loring's Corps, and the result was that they were repulsed with a frightful loss of fully three thousand men, according to their own reports. Thence General Johnston was forced to withdraw to the fortifications of Atlanta, which the enemy began at once to besiege.

The wise and cautious Johnston was superseded by the rash, lion-hearted, but unfortunate Hood, who would not patiently endure a siege, but suddenly hurled a column, led by Walker's and Bate's Divisions of Hardee's Corps, against the enemy's right at Peach Tree Creek. Grandly they charged with that cheer which had been the sound to which they had rushed to many a glorious victory; but with marvelous rapidity the enemy managed to mass their artillery upon them, and they were forced to withdraw. Two days later, July 22, by a second attack with Hardee's Corps the enemy were driven from their fortifications, leaving in the hands of the Confederates nearly two thousand prisoners, twenty-two pieces of artillery, and five stands of colors.

This was followed by an attempt of the enemy to destroy the railroads around Atlanta. For this purpose two forces of cavalry, under Generals Stoneman and McCook, were to meet near Lovejoy, and fall upon the Confederate cavalry under General Wheeler. Both of these expeditions proved to be hardly adequate for their task; for General Stoneman was encountered near Macon, and he and one thousand of his men were captured, while General McCook managed to escape with a loss of five hundred men captured by the Confederates.

On the 28th of July General Hood made a vigorous assault upon the Fifteenth Corps; but he was repulsed with a loss of fifteen hundred men. How grandly the Confederates moved to this attack forced from General Sherman the remark: "His [Hood's] advance was magnificent." For several weeks the enemy kept up an almost ceaseless bombardment upon the city, until on the 18th of August Sherman moved his line upon the road toward Macon in order to cut off General Hood's supplies. The latter sent his cavalry, under General Wheeler, to harass the Federals.

Meantime a part of the Confederates, under General Hardee, had intrenched themselves at Jonesboro, a distance of twenty-two miles from that portion under General Hood at Atlanta. Quickly perceiving this unfortunate position of the Confederates, General Sherman threw his army between the two positions. By the 30th of August the enemy had succeeded in crossing Flint River, and had taken up a position near Jonesboro, where they were subjected to a fruitless attack from General Hardee. This was followed on the 1st of September by an assault from the Federals themselves, with a largely superior force, and the Confederates found it necessary to retreat in the night, and leave the position in the hands of the enemy. On the same day General Hood also evacuated Atlanta, and allowed the enemy the possession of the prize for which they had been struggling for more than three months, but kept at bay by an army much less than half their own. The enemy now heaped upon the citizens of Atlanta all the misfortunes, all the indignities, all the hardships incident to war; and to the protests coming from both General Hood and the mayor of Atlanta the Federal general would reply that "war is cruelty, and you cannot refine it," forgetting that modern, civilized warfare had for its arena the battle-field, where either the one side or the other prevailed through superiority in courage and skill, and not the oppression of the women and the children in the cities which chance or conquest might throw into its hands.

General Forrest at Guntown.

A Federal expedition, under General Sturgis, had been sent out from Memphis for the purpose of following in the rear of General Sherman and co-operating with him. This force assumed the title of the "Avengers of Fort Pillow," and they took this as a pretext for robbery, pillage, and murder. But these acts were not destined to go on long, for by a singular coincidence on the 13th of June they came in contact at Guntown with the terrible Forrest and his band, who had perpetrated the so-called "massacre" at Fort Pillow. Short, sharp, and effective were the blows which this redoubtable cavalryman struck, and the result was that two thousand of Sturgis's force were taken prisoners, and almost as many were killed and wounded.

General Early's Raid.

In Virginia the Confederates assumed the offensive by General Early's raid into Maryland. On the 3d of July he moved forward near Harper's Ferry, frightening Sigel so badly at Martinsburg that he retreated to Sharpsburg, leaving in the hands of the Confederates a quantity of valuable stores. After two severe engagements the enemy were again forced to fall back to Maryland Heights, where they were re-enforced by Generals Max Weber and Lew Wallace; thence they took a position at Monocacy Bridge, four miles from Frederick City. Here intrenched they were attacked by General Early, and after a contest of two hours' duration they were completely routed, with a loss of over one thousand in killed and wounded and seven hundred prisoners, while the Confederates won their victory at the cost of five hundred in killed and wounded.

Thence General Early advanced toward Washington, throwing the city into a state of complete consternation and terror, for his attack was hourly expected. But the Confederates contented themselves with withdrawing across the Potomac, with a vast quantity of booty as the fruits of their expedition, among which were "five thousand horses and twenty-five hundred beef cattle." However, the enemy did not allow him to depart in peace, but a force fifteen thousand strong, under General Crook, followed him, which General Early turned upon, about five miles from Winchester, and thoroughly routed, with a loss of over one thousand, while he himself hardly suffered to the extent of sixty men.

General John Morgan Invades Kentucky.

Coincident with General Early's expedition was General Morgan's second invasion of the State of Kentucky. In rapid succession the Confederates captured Paris, Georgetown, Cynthia, Williamstown, and Mount Sterling. At the latter place on the 9th of June General Morgan encountered General Burbridge. The Federals had been in pursuit since the Confederates left Pound Gap. This engagement was barren of decisive results to either side, and General Morgan continued his work of destruction - burning the enemy's cars and depots, and capturing two regiments of prisoners at the town of Cynthia, which was also destroyed. However, while at breakfast at this place on the morning of June 12, the Confederates were surprised by the enemy, under General Burbridge, and, though the former fought nobly for an hour, they were defeated, losing six hundred in killed and wounded and nearly four hundred prisoners.

General Price in Missouri.

General Price's raid into Missouri in the latter part of the month of September was equally wanting in any material benefit. He attacked the enemy, who were strongly fortified at Pilot Knob, eighty-six miles south of St. Louis, and forced them to evacuate the place. The Confederates pursued the Federals as far as Rolla and then desisted, and without further operations went into winter-quarters.

The "Peace" Question.

About this time the question of peace between the two sections was again agitated. So much blood was being spilled, and so much money spent, that at the North, as was made clearly evident from the tone of the leading newspapers, was growing a strong sentiment toward the establishment of peace on terms honorable to both sides. To show what the South had done in the effort to put a stop to a war that was drawing from the peaceful walks of life over three million men, it would be well to quote from a letter of President Davis on the subject:

We have made three distinct efforts to communicate with the authorities at Washington, and have been invariably unsuccessful. Commissioners were sent before hostilities were begun, and the Washington Government refused to receive them or hear what they had to say. A second time I sent a military officer with a communication addressed by myself to President Lincoln. The letter was received by General Scott, who did not permit the officer to see Mr. Lincoln, but promised that an answer would be sent. No answer has been received. The third time, a few months ago, a gentleman was sent whose position, character, and reputation were such as to insure his reception were not the enemy determined to receive no proposals whatever from the Government. Vice-president Stephens made a patriotic tender of his services in the hope of being able to promote the cause of humanity; and although little belief was entertained of his success, I cheerfully yielded to his suggestion that the experiment should be tried. The enemy refused to let him pass through their lines or to hold any conference with them. He was stopped before he reached Fortress Monroe on his way to Washington. To attempt again (in the face of these repeated rejections of all conference with us) to send commissioners or agents to propose peace is to invite insult and contumely, and to subject ourselves to indignities without the slightest chance of being listened to.

This letter is given to show the nature of opinion at the South. The people of this section were battling for a principle which was, in their eyes, very essential to the freedom and prosperity of Republican institutions; but, however firm and tenacious their belief in the righteousness of this principle, even in the moment of victory they ever showed themselves willing and ready to stop the ceaseless flow of blood upon a fair and equitable basis. But on the other hand, that party represented by the Government at Washington, inasmuch as it had come into power with the tide of a war, showed no disposition to treat with the Southern States on any but the most humiliating terms, and would accept no proposition coming from them which looked toward an amicable and honorable settlement; therefore in regard to the character and purpose of this administration words were not minced when the Democratic party met in Chicago on the 29th of August. Mr. Augustus Belmont, from New York, said: "Four years of misrule by a sectional, fanatical, and corrupt party have brought our country to the verge of ruin." Senator Bigler, of Pennsylvania, expressed the opinion that "the termination of Democratic rule in this country was the end of the peaceful relations between the States and the people. The men now in authority through a feud which they have long maintained with violent and unwise men at the South, because of a blind fanaticism about an institution in some of the States, in relation to which they have no duties to perform and no responsibilities to bear, are utterly incapable of adopting the proper means to rescue our country from its present lamentable condition." Governor Seymour, of New York, made the following arraignment of the character of the Government: "They were animated by intolerance and fanaticism, and blinded by ignorance of the spirit of our institutions, the character of our people, and the condition of our land. . . . They will not have the Union restored unless upon conditions unknown to the Constitution. . . . We are shackled with no hates, no prejudices, no passions. We wish for fraternal relations with the people of the South. We demand for them what we demand for ourselves: the full recognition of the rights of the States."

Thus it will be seen that the crime of loving liberty

and hating fanaticism was not confined to the section south of the Mason and Dixon line, and that the latter only differed from those at the North in that they had that courage which has made all individual freedom possible, and that they resisted a practical subversion of their rights with the might of arms.

CHAPTER XXIV.

Naval Operations—General Grant in Virginia.

THE port of Mobile, Ala., was a very important naval station to the Confederacy. Therefore the enemy proceeded to invest it by land with a force under General Canby, while Admiral Farragut was to make the attack by water. The enemy's fleet numbered eighteen vessels, with an armament of over two hundred guns and nearly three thousand men. To meet this large squadron, the Confederates could only bring three gun-boats and one iron-clad, the "Tennessee." On the morning of the 5th of August the Federals steamed into the harbor, and their entire fleet fell upon the "Tennessee," which gallantly reristed with no hopes of success against such numbers until she was forced to surrender when completely surrounded by the enemy. But the latter did not accomplish their victory without the loss of one of their best iron-clads, the "Tecumseh," which was sunk by a torpedo, carrying down beneath the waters of the gulf her commander, with the most of his crew. On the following day the enemy turned their guns upon Fort Gaines, Fort Powell having already been taken on the 5th. In a short time Fort Gaines capitulated,

The "Sumter" Running the Blockade, and Chased by the Federal Ship, "Iroquois."

repulsed with great slaughter. They followed this with another attack on Market Heights, with results equally disastrous. Another column of the enemy succeeded in getting possession of Fort Harrison before assistance could reach it, and then they advanced upon Fort Gilmer, but the gallant Confederates repulsed them and sent them back with great loss. This action closed the day's fighting, and it was found that the enemy had lost over four thousand in killed and wounded, with six flags and five hundred prisoners. On the next day (the 30th) General Field made an unsuccessful attempt to retake Fort Harrison, but owing to a failure of support just at the proper time, he was repulsed.

The dawn of October 6 saw the Confederates with General Geary's Brigade of cavalry make a brilliant attack upon the enemy's right on the Charles City Road, about five miles from Richmond. The latter were driven back to their works, but the Confederates did not stop, but in their enthusiasm they rushed over the works, pushing the Federals out, and capturing seven hundred prisoners, nine guns, and one hundred horses. Again the enemy made another stand at their second line of intrenchments; but they melted away before the impetuous onslaught of the Confederates, and fled to the shelter of the guns of Fort Harrison. Re-enforced, they returned to retake the works from which they had been beaten; but the Confederates sent them back shattered and broken with terrible loss, and night put an end to the contest.

On the 27th General Grant made an effort to turn General Lee's left flank, and was advancing his columns by the Williamsburg and Nine Mile roads. The works on the latter position had been taken by three brigades of negro troops; but they could not maintain themselves long, for Hampton's Legion and the Twenty-fourth Virginia drove them back with terrible slaughter. On the other road (the Williamsburg) the enemy had stationed their batteries, and were pouring shots and shells into the Confederate works. The latter endured this cannonading in silence, and thus misled the enemy into making a charge. Having reserved their fire until the Federals were close upon them, they made the ground tremble with the terrific thunder of their artillery and musketry, and the enemy broke and fled in confusion, with a loss, besides a considerable number in killed and wounded, of five hundred prisoners. Again, the attack upon the gray lines on the Boydton road proved no less disastrous to the enemy, for General Mahone received them so valiantly that he soon had them in full retreat, leaving with the Confederates as their spoils of victory over four hundred prisoners.

Thus this human wall was still between the capital of the Confederacy and the enemy. With unbroken front the latter were met at every point, and in this autumn of 1864 they seemed as far from gaining their object as in the fall of 1861. But still the Federal general persisted, and made up in tenacity for any lack of military genius. Surely he must have had a certain premonition that one day these gray veterans who flung themselves so often between him and the goal of his struggles must inevitably succumb to the solid and almost innumerable lines which he was throwing around them, however heroically they might fight.

Sheridan's Raid in the Valley.

Coincident with his operations in the immediate vicinity of the city, the Federal commander adopted another plan, which, if successfully consummated, would deprive General Lee of his source of supplies from the rich, productive valley of the Shenandoah. For this purpose General Hunter was superseded on the 8th of August by General Sheridan, who had under his command no less than three corps, together with the divisions of Cook, Averill, and Kelly. With this large force he proceeded to take possession of Martinsburg, Williamsport, and Winchester, General Early falling gradually back before his advance. Near Winchester, however, on the 19th of September, though outnumbered nearly four to one, the Confederates made a stand. The enemy moved to the attack, and the engagement was stubbornly and hotly contested. One division of the enemy was broken and thrown into confusion, which the Confederates took advantage of and charged. A glorious victory seemed almost in their hands. The impetuous rush of Early's men was carrying every thing before it, and the enemy were obliged to call in their reserves to the rescue in order to restore their shattered lines. Unfortunately, the enemy fell upon the Confederate cavalry on the left and threw it into confusion, which made a retreat necessary. General Early then took up a strong position at Fisher's Hill, whither the enemy followed, and on the 22d moved to attack him. With their large numbers the enemy managed to literally surround General Early's command and to force them from their intrenchments, driving them beyond Port Republic with a loss of over seven hundred prisoners. This victory left the Federals in complete possession of the rich valley, and they at once turned themselves loose in it, pillaging and destroying every thing of worth and value, so that along their track were ruin and desolation. Farm and manufactory were leveled to the earth as if by the breath of a hurricane, and the beautiful and picturesque valley, that fairly blossomed like a garden, became as a desert and a waste place.

Battle of Cedar Creek.

The undaunted Early, in spite of his two defeats, was not yet prepared to allow the enemy to rest on their laurels without another struggle; therefore we find him again at Fisher's Hill on the 18th of October, "with two corps of Sheridan's army in his front on the north side of Cedar Creek. Another corps, the Sixth, was between Middletown and Newtown. Sheridan himself was at Winchester with his cavalry a little withdrawn from the front." By a toilsome, arduous night march through a mountainous country, with the Shenandoah to be crossed twice, General Early placed himself in front of the enemy. With a gallant, sweeping charge, he struck terror to them, taking them completely by surprise, and soon had Sheridan's magnificent army of three corps in a confused, panic-stricken retreat, leaving in the hands of the victorious Confederates their camps with one thousand five hundred prisoners; but the fatal mistake was made of stopping to plunder the abandoned booty of the Federals. This gave them time to reorganize their demoralized divisions and to renew the battle. Misfortune followed misfortune. In one of those inexplainable moments that come to men whose courage has been tested upon a hundred battle-fields, the followers of Early, that had made illustrious the Army of Virginia, gave way in a disordered retreat, sustaining a total loss of three thousand while the glory of one of the grandest victories of the war was just in their grasp. With this reverse the larger portion of his army was transferred to assist General Lee around Richmond.

General Breckinridge in East Tennessee.

While these important battles were taking place in Northern Virginia General Breckinridge had administered two severe defeats upon the enemy in the South-west—one on the Holston River on the 2d of October, and one at Morristown, Tenn., on the 18th of November. On the 20th of the following month the enemy made a raid into Virginia, capturing the salt-works at Saltville, and, forcing Colonel Preston to evacuate Fort Breckinridge, they sacked the town of Abingdon.

CHAPTER XXV.

Operations of Generals Sherman and Hood.

IT now becomes necessary to resume the narrative of General Hood's movements after the evacuation of Atlanta. In reviewing these forces on the 18th of September President Davis had told Cheatham's Division to be of good cheer, for within a short while their faces would be turned homeward, and their feet pressing Tennessee soil.

Ten days later General Hood took up his line of march toward Tennessee, with Sherman following on the 3d of October. On the 12th the Confederates took Dalton; thence they proceeded to La Fayette; and from that place they moved across to Gadsden, Ala., pursued by General Sherman as far as Gaylesville. The latter cut himself loose from all communication with the North, and took up his celebrated movement to the sea, while General Hood advanced into Tennessee, driving the enemy constantly before him, and forcing General Schofield to fall back from Columbia on the 26th of November, with the loss of a large quantity of stores. "The retreat to Franklin was one of constant fighting. Skirmishing of the very heaviest and deadliest character was maintained all the way. Forrest hung like a raging tiger upon the rear. . . . The Confederates pressed on—Forrest leading, Stewart next, and Cheatham following. Lee was still in the rear, but coming up. The enemy were closely pushed, retreated rapidly, and left evidences of their haste on every side." In this way the march was continued until on the evening of November 30, when General Hood found himself before the frowning breastworks of the town of Franklin. The troops under him were now upon the soil of their native State, which had long been in the possession of the enemy. They could look around them and see the homes that had been denied them for many a long day, and for which now at their very thresholds they were to do battle. With such incentives as these urging them to action, at five o'clock in the afternoon they began one of the grandest attacks of the war, an attack illuminated by as sublime an exhibition of personal courage from field-officer to the humblest private in the ranks as has ever blazoned the records of human bravery. In the face of a fire that tore ghastly gashes in their unfaltering column they stormed and drove the enemy from the first line of works. Onward they advanced, stopping not nor halting however obstinately the enemy might resist and however thick might be that awful, bloody field of carnage with their own dead. On that crimson battle-ground many a knightly soul went out while within sight of the firesides where their wives and little ones were praying and watching for the absent soldiers' return. This was the last battle of gallant Pat Cleburne, "the bravest of the brave." The gallant Gist fell in this conflict, as also did Brown, Strahl, Johnson, and Manigault; and though the gray dawn of the next day saw the Federal army shattered and flying toward Nashville, the victory had been dearly bought, and the sacrifice that these Tennesseeans offered upon the altars of their country was great.

BATTLE OF NASHVILLE.

General Hood followed the enemy to Nashville, and on the 2d of December proceeded to invest the city, where General Thomas was strongly fortified with a largely superior force. Therefore, with his own numbers largely in excess of those of General Hood, General Thomas felt no hesitation in assuming the offensive. Accordingly, on the 15th he moved out his heavy columns against both flanks of the Confederates, but they were beaten off with severe losses. Not discouraged by these reverses, they renewed the contest on the next day by attacking the entire Confederate line. All day the latter resisted grandly the overwhelming numbers that were being thrown against them, and until late in the afternoon it seemed that the story of Franklin was to be more gloriously repeated. But just at the crisis of the

Col. John Overton's Residence, General Hood's Head-quarters at the Battle of Nashville.

battle, when it was almost evident that the "stars and bars" were once more going to be graced with the laurels of victory, a weak, unsupported point in the center was crushed by the heavy mass of the enemy. This misfortune for the Confederates was a signal for a general retreat of the whole army, with the loss of fifty cannon and most of the ordnance wagons. With this disaster General Hood crossed the Tennessee River and entered Mississippi; and at Tupelo, on the 23d of January, 1865, he resigned the command of the army.

GENERAL SHERMAN'S MARCH.

From this reverse of the Confederates at Nashville we again turn to General Sherman, whom we left beginning his march through Georgia, which the Federals regarded as one of the greatest achievements of the war. It will not be necessary to go into this movement in detail. Its record is written in the ruthless desolation of a great State, the pillaging of its citizens, and the destruction of their property.

With almost no opposition the enemy swept completely across the State, and by the 10th of December they were before the fortifications of Savannah, which were held by General Hardee with fifteen thousand men. Between four and five o'clock on the morning of the 13th the enemy stormed and captured the important position of Fort McAllister. Until the 16th

General Sherman kept up a bombardment from all sides, both by land and water, when he demanded the surrender of the city. This demand General Hardee refused to accede to, and on the night of the 20th he escaped with his troops, retreating toward Charleston, and on the following day the enemy took formal possession, signalizing the closing days of the year 1864 with this crushing disaster to the Confederate cause.

ATTEMPTS UPON WILMINGTON.

The next objective point of the enemy was Wilmington, N. C., especially defended by Fort Fisher. Therefore on the 23d of December we find Admiral Porter before Fort Fisher, with the largest fleet under his command the Federals had ever yet assembled. Operations were begun on the same night by the explosion of a "powder" vessel close under the walls of the fort, which was expected to destroy it. But this ingenious contrivance totally failed of its purpose, and the next day was consumed in a heavy bombardment, to which the brave garrison responded vigorously and warmly. Meantime General Butler came up with a land force six thousand five hundred strong, which was to attack the fort in conjunction with the fleet. All the next day the fleet kept up a terrific cannonading, so that the earth trembled as if in the throes of an earthquake. But still the defenders of the fort worked their guns in a magnificent fashion.

The land force did not risk an attack, and this expedition proved such a complete failure as to cost General Butler his command.

However, the enemy were not content with their reverse from such an important point, and by January 13, 1865, they had another force stronger by two thousand men before the walls of Fort Fisher. During the night they had succeeded in landing and throwing up such a strong line of intrenchments that General Bragg decided not to attempt to dislodge them, but to re-enforce the fort. The continuous bombardment from the fleet never ceased, and, with their attention thus engaged toward defending themselves from the water, on the night of the 15th the garrison were attacked by an assaulting column four thousand strong. In spite of the fact that they were worn out and exhausted with the hard and arduous labor of manning the guns, for three long hours they resisted with a courage born of desperation, until the force of numbers compelled them to surrender, though indeed not until eight hundred of the enemy lay dead and wounded.

From this victory the Federals did not get immediate possession of the town of Wilmington, for it was not abandoned by General Bragg until the latter part of February, when he retreated into the interior of the State, and left it in their hands without resistance.

Fall of Charleston and Columbia.

Almost one month from his success at Savannah General Sherman again set his column in motion toward the north, with Charleston as the objective point. General Hardee, perceiving that his forces were much too small to offer any thing like a successful resistance, and appreciating the importance of making a juncture with Generals Beauregard and Cheatham, after burning all Government buildings and stores, abandoned to the rapacity of the enemy the historic, noble old city, which place they entered February 18. The indentations of shells, the marks of fire, the ruins on every side stood like grand though somber and sorrowful monuments to the heroism of a people who had endured so bravely and so patiently all the horrors and misfortunes that come in the train of war — siege and bombardment, rapine and murder yet so noble and eloquent in her ruins, so very typical of the whole South, whose very scars were a glory and honor to her, telling a grand story of how she had fought and toiled and struggled and labored in the face of adverse circumstances.

Leaving Charleston, General Sherman still continued his devastating march. Columbia met even a more terrible fate than Charleston. A large portion of the town was given to the devouring flames, while *no part* of it escaped the thirst for robbery and plunder which had taken complete possession of the Federal army. Citizens were rendered houseless and homeless, and whatever valuables they had the enemy appropriated to their own use.

On this band of invaders advanced; nor did they abate those tactics that had first characterized their entrance into the State of Georgia. On the 6th of March they crossed the Great Pedee River, against the towns of Laurel Hill and Montpelier, N. C., meeting with no resistance until March 10, when General Kilpatrick's forces received a severe blow at the hands of General Wade Hampton. On the 16th the enemy came up with General Hardee, who was fortified between Cape Fear River and Black Creek. The latter gallantly sustained three assaults from two corps under General Slocum, and then retreated. The severity of this engagement is showed by the fact that the enemy lost thirty-three hundred men, while the Confederates lost only four hundred and fifty.

Again, three days later, General Johnston made another blow for the cause of the State. Right bravely was this blow struck upon Slocum, at Bentonville. Generals Bate's and Cleburne's Divisions swept the enemy from two lines of fortifications on the right, while Generals Hill and Loring accomplished the same thing on the left. At evening the Federals were heavily re-enforced, and, when it was found on the next morning that they had intrenched themselves, General Johnston declined to renew the battle, and retreated in the direction of Raleigh. General Sherman then took up his head-quarters at Goldsboro.

CHAPTER XXVI.
The End.

THUS now one needs no prophetic eye to see that the final act in the great drama is near at hand, that the catastrophe is approaching. The North, with her mighty hosts, is tightening and drawing in the lines. The South, though she had gained victory after victory, never had a force adequate to consummate the war in a complete victory for the Confederacy. Therefore, from the beginning it was merely a question of time when those very first victories themselves, as paradoxical as it may seem, hastened defeat; for they cost many lives, and the Confederate dead that lay upon the battle-fields of Murfreesboro, Shiloh, Gettysburg, Chancellorsville, and other places could not be replaced with the living; whereas the North was rich in men and resources, and her armies stretched in an almost unbroken line from the Potomac to the Rio Grande. What could a Confederate victory avail against such a power, with the whole world for a recruiting-ground? The South had worn herself literally out with the victories won from the enemy; and now, with a depleted army and an exhausted commissary, one only wonders in admiration that divine courage could so triumph over the weakness of human physical nature as to enable those veterans of the Army of Virginia and of the Army of Tennessee to resist so long and so bravely. Grand indeed must have been the motives that actuated those hearts and caused those arms to strike the superior forces of the enemy so effectively and terribly for four long years of civil warfare.

Peace Conference.

Early in the year 1865 a conference took place between President Lincoln, Mr. Seward, and three commissioners appointed by President Davis—Messrs. Stephens, Campbell, and Hunter. The meeting was held on board a steamer anchored in Hampton Roads; but the Government at Washington still insisted upon terms which the Confederacy would not accept, and nothing tangible resulted from the conference.

Consequently hostilities in Northern Virginia were again resumed by Sheridan once more raiding up the Shenandoah Valley. Near Waynesboro, toward the end of February, he fell upon the weakened remnants of General Early's Division, defeated them, and took as many as thirteen hundred prisoners. Thence the Federals proceeded on their course of destruction, and finally joined General Meade near Petersburg.

Closing Conflicts.

The enemy still continued to batter with their huge forces the weakened, poorly fed, and ill-clothed lines in the immediate vicinity of Richmond. On the 6th of February they flung themselves against Pegram's Division, and were on the point of overpowering it when General Evans arrived with General Gordon's Division. Charge after charge was made, but still the enemy managed to maintain themselves until the Confederates were further re-enforced by General Mahone. With their former enthusiasm and spirit they swept the Federals before them in confusion to the shelter of their fortifications at Hatcher's Run.

This was followed by a well-planned attack upon the enemy's position at Hare's Hill, near Appomattox. Here again was a glimmer of the glory of the former days of the war. Early on the morning of March 25 General Gordon surprised and captured a considerable portion of the Federal works, repulsing brilliantly two successive attacks of their infantry to regain them. But the Confederates were forced by the artillery which the enemy massed against them to abandon the position which they had taken, carrying back with them, however, seventeen pieces of artillery and six hundred prisoners.

This partial, spasmodic success was more than counterbalanced on the 1st and 2d of April by the blows which the enemy struck against the gray wall around Petersburg, now grown so thin that it would seem sheer madness for them to attempt to offer resistance to the heavy, unbroken columns of the Federals. However, they fought in the face of despair itself, and were pierced by the numerous hosts of the enemy. Here in the closing scenes General A. P. Hill, another of the South's great leaders, laid down his life for the Confederate cause, and was placed in the muster-roll of immortals as one of the heroes in the struggle. But yet a greater loss was in store for the South. The clouds were gathering to cast their shadows over the brightness of that spring day. The city of their love, for the defense of which their best, their truest blood had been poured out—in front of whose fortifications lay the bones of those whose return was watched for in the Carolinas, in Tennessee, in Georgia, in Louisiana, in Mississippi, in Alabama, and in far-off Texas—was soon to be given over into the hands of the foeman.

While President Davis was attending church on the 2d of April a notice was brought to him from General Lee, telling him of the disaster at Petersburg, which made the evacuation of Richmond necessary on that very night. As President Davis retired the services were put to an end and the dread news soon spread all over the city, causing many a cheek to blanch and many a strong heart to throb in unspeakable sorrow over the loss of this the last stronghold and the only hope of the young Government that had lived its life in the midst of the troublous times of war. Night came, and Richmond was without defenders, and to add to the gloom of the situation many large warehouses had been burned by the retreating Confederates, that their contents might not fall into the hands of the victors. In this conflagration it would seem that the hopes which in the moments of victory promised a glorious consummation in the formation of a free, happy, contented union of individual States, into which jealousy, passion, and prejudice could find no place, were being consumed and only the dead ashes of despair were left them.

Early on the morning following the evacuation a detachment of cavalry from General Weitzel's Division planted the United States flag upon the dome of the capitol, and later in the day General Weitzel himself entered the city and put it under martial law.

THE SURRENDER.

The fortunes of the little band under General Lee need not be pressed much farther. They were now on the north side of the Appomattox River, with the enemy pressing and harassing them on all sides, and gradually capturing squad after squad of his worn and exhausted troops. Against such a force as that of the enemy it would be utterly useless for him to hurl his decimated columns. Moreover, many of his men, foreseeing the inevitable result, had left the ranks, and were seeking to escape to their homes in order to avoid subjecting themselves to the humiliation of a surrender. The Federal commander himself clearly perceived the sure doom that awaited the once glorious army of Northern Virginia—still grand even in the midst of its misfortunes—and on the 7th of April sent a demand for the surrender of the troops that had made themselves the admiration of the world. After a correspondence lasting through two days, the following terms were proposed by General Grant, and agreed to by General Lee on the 9th:

Roll of all officers and men to be made in duplicate, and one copy to be given to an officer to be designated by me and the other to be retained by such officers as you may designate; the officers to give their individual parole not to take up arms against the Government of the United States until properly exchanged, and each company or regimental commander to sign a like parole for the men of their commands. The arms, artillery, and public property to be packed and stacked and turned over by me to officers appointed to receive them. This will not embrace the side-arms of the officers, nor their private horses or baggage.

This done, each officer and man will be allowed to return to their homes, not to be disturbed by United States authority so long as they observe their parole and the laws in force where they may reside.

The conference between General Lee and General Grant was held in the residence of Mr. Wilmer McLean, at Appomattox Court-house. The meeting was

Mr. Wilmer McLean's Residence, Where General Lee Surrendered.

(242)

of the simplest character. Each conducted himself with dignity and courtesy, the Federal Commander displaying a magnanimity worthy of recording in that he subjected General Lee to no humiliating forms and conditions. The result was that General Lee issued the following order to his troops:

General Order No. 9.

After four years of arduous service, marked by unsurpassed courage and fortitude, the Army of Northern Virginia has been compelled to yield to overwhelming numbers and resources.

I need not tell the brave survivors of so many hard-fought battles who have remained steadfast to the last that I have consented to this result from no distrust of them; but feeling that valor and devotion could accomplish nothing that would compensate for the loss that must have attended the continuation of the contest, I determined to avoid the sacrifice of those whose past services have endeared them to their countrymen.

By the terms of agreement, officers and men can return to their homes and remain until exchanged. You will take with you the satisfaction that proceeds from the consciousness of duty faithfully performed; and I earnestly pray that a merciful God will extend to you his blessings and protection.

With an unceasing admiration of your constancy and devotion to your country and a grateful remembrance of your kind and generous consideration of myself, I bid you an affectionate farewell. R. E. Lee, *General.*

April 10, 1865.

With this ends the story of the Army of Northern Virginia. A glorious story it is, too. They had fought a good fight, and had kept the faith with the country and the principles which they had espoused. They did their duty nobly, and have left to the keeping of the land for which they battled the record of their sublime devotion and incomparable courage. Taking leave of their leader, in whom they ever had a steadfast faith, whether in victory or defeat, they turned their weary steps to their desolated homes, where fond hearts were waiting to welcome the battle-scarred soldier; and with the same grand courage with which they had brightened the pages of human history they went to work to rehabilitate the wasted farm and the deserted workshop.

The surrender of the other divisions of the Confederates necessarily followed that of General Lee in rapid succession. On the 18th of April General Joseph E. Johnston surrendered at Durham, N. C.; General Dick Taylor to General Canby at Citronelle, Ala., May 4; and General Kirby Smith to the same general at Baton Rouge, La., on the 26th. Thus ended the long and arduous struggle which the South made for the rights which she had under the Constitution, and in this struggle those who wore the gray and stepped to the inspiring strains of "Dixie" under the banner of the Southern cross decked with its stars, have made their uniform a symbol of the sublimest courage of the soldier and the truest devotion of the patriot.

APPENDIX.

THE SOUTH JUSTIFIED.

The agitation of the slavery question, in its several aspects, with centralization for its great purpose, was a main cause of trouble and separation.

The words of the Constitution were: "No person held to service or labor in one State, under the laws thereof, escaping into another, shall, in consequence of any law or regulation therein, be discharged from such service or labor, but shall be delivered up on claim of the party to whom such service or labor may be due."

Of this clause Judge Story, in delivering the opinion of the Supreme Court in Prigg *vs.* Pennsylvania, said: "It cannot be doubted that it constituted a fundamental article, without the adoption of which the Union *could not* have been formed." (16 Peters.) It must, therefore, of course have been a condition of the Union's continuance.

We will see how this provision of the Constitution was observed and treated by the abolition or free States. Between the years 1810 and 1850, the losses to the South in fugitive slaves amounted to $22,000,000, an annual loss for that period of $550,000. The ratio of loss increased as the slave population increased. To what it amounted at the date of secession I am unable to state just now; the curious, however, may readily ascertain. The census for 1810 gave a slave population of 1,191,400; that of 1820, 1,538,100; that of 1830, 2,009,030; that of 1840, 2,480,500; that of 1850, 3,205,300; that of 1860, 3,979,700. Estimating the average value at $300, the South lost by emancipation $1,193,910,000, exclusive of at least $6,500,000 in fugitives between the years 1850 and 1861.

The claim of the party of coercion that morality justified the infliction of that loss on the South is met and fully answered by their head, President Lincoln, who said in the Hampton Roads conference that " the people of the North were as responsible for slavery as the people of the South." History shows the North to be equally responsible at the least, and I undertake to say more so, and I feel sure that I am able to prove it should it ever become necessary.

About the 1st of May, 1850, the New York State Vigilance Antislavery Committee, of which the famous Gerritt Smith was chairman, held its anniversary meeting in public in the city of New York. I give a single passage from its official report: "The committee have, within the year since the 1st of May, 1849, assisted one hundred and fifty-one fugitives (for that, you know, is our business) in escaping from servitude." I cite this as one of many specimens of the respect the antislavery people had for constitutional guarantees and protection.

In speaking upon the clause of the Constitution just cited, Mr. Seward, of New York, said in the Senate of the United States, on March 11, 1850: "The law of nations disavows such compacts; the law of nature, written on the hearts and consciences of freemen, repudiates them. I know that there are laws of various sorts which regulate the conduct of men; there are constitutions and statutes, codes mercantile and codes civil; but when we are legislating for States, especially when we are founding States, all these laws must be brought to the standard of the law of God; must be tried by that standard, and must stand or fall by it. To conclude on this point, we are not slave-holders; we cannot, in our judgment, be true Christians or real freemen if we impose on others a chain that we defy all human power to fasten on ourselves." He also said: "Wherein do the strength and security of slavery lie? You answer that they lie in the Constitution of the United States and the Constitutions and laws of the slave-holding States. Not at all. It is in the erroneous sentiments of the American people. Constitutions and laws can no more rise above the virtue of the people than the limpid stream can rise above its spring. Inculcate the love of freedom, and the equal rights of man under the paternal roof; see to it that they are taught in the schools and in the churches; reform your code; extend a cordial welcome to the fugitive who lays his weary limbs at your door, and defend him as you would your paternal god; correct your error that slavery has any constitutional guaranty which may not be released and ought not to be relinquished; say to slavery, when it shows its bond and demands the pound of flesh, that if it draws one drop of blood, its life shall pay the forfeit; inculcate that free States can maintain the rights of hospitality and humanity; that executive authority can forbear to favor slavery." Thus it was urged and attempted to be taught that the Constitution was the embodiment of crime, and oaths to support it of no effect or binding force; that we must regard such obligations as baubles, as things to deceive, as snares to entrap. We were asked to make such doctrines a part of our education and a controlling feature of our religion; to make perjury a pillar of Church and State, and the crime of larceny a commendable virtue. The seeds so sown bore fruit.

Article IV., Section 2, of the United States Constitution ordains: "A person charged in any State with treason, felony, or other crime, who shall flee from justice and be found in another State, shall, on demand of the executive authority of the State from which he fled, be delivered up to be removed to the State having jurisdiction of the crime."

In two instances, Kent and Fairfield, governors of Maine, refused to comply with this provision on requisitions by the governor of Georgia for negro thieves. Governor Seward (afterward Senator), of New York, made a similar refusal to the same State, saying it was not against the laws of New York to *steal* a negro. He made a similar refusal to Virginia. These governors were sworn to support the Constitution of the United States, and certainly understood its plain command.

In 1793, while Washington was President, an act was passed to carry out the provision for the return of fugitive slaves. It was adopted unanimously in the Senate, and nearly so in the House. The Federal and State Courts held it to be constitutional, and yet these governors refused to execute it.

On January 7, 1861, more than two weeks after South Carolina had passed her ordinance of secession, Mr. Toombs, of Georgia, in a speech in the Senate, said: "The Supreme Court has decided that by the Constitution we have a right to go to the Territories and be protected with our property. Mr. Lincoln says he does not care what the Supreme Court decides, he will turn us out anyhow. He says this in his debate with the honorable Senator from Illinois (Mr. Douglas); I have it before me. He says he would vote against the decision of the Supreme Court." This charge upon Mr. Lincoln was never denied by himself or friends.

Instances of disregard of the Constitution by those sworn to observe it might be readily multiplied; but I only want to make prominent the principles moving the South to its course.

Having seen our rights under and by the Constitution, I will turn attention to that course. The Southern States claimed they were sovereign, having all powers except such as were specially delegated to Congress. They demanded that property in slaves should be entitled to the same protection from the Government of the United States, in all its departments everywhere, which the Constitution confers upon it; the power to extend to any other property, provided nothing shall be construed to limit or restrain the right now belonging to every State to prohibit, abolish, or establish and protect slavery within its limits; that persons committing crimes against slave property in one State and fleeing to another shall be delivered up in the same manner as persons committing crimes against other property, and that the laws of the State from which such persons fled shall be the test of criminality; that Congress should pass efficient laws for the punishment of all persons, in any of the States, who shall in any manner aid and abet invasion or insurrection in any other State, or commit any other act against the laws of nations tending to disturb the tranquillity of the people or government of any other State; that the people of the United States should have an equal right to emigrate to and settle in the present or any future acquired Territories with whatever property they might possess, and be protected in its peaceable enjoyment until such territory may be admitted into the Union with or without slavery, as she may determine, on an equality with all existing States, as the Supreme Court had decided, and as the "originally small party" now decides in principle, when in its June platform of 1888 it declares: "The government by Congress of the Territories is based upon necessity, only to the end that they become States in the Union; therefore, whenever the conditions of population, material resources, public intelligence, and morality are such as to insure a stable government therein, the people of such territories should be permitted to form for themselves Constitutions on State government, and be admitted into the Union." Time and circumstances work wonderful changes. What howls were raised by that party over such doctrines a few decades back! and now with what deafening cheers it greets them! How many of you, my friends, ever hoped to live to see the day when the party of coercion would not only indorse, but actually adopt, a chief article of your faith in the right and act of secession? I answer, not one; nevertheless, you have seen it. Wonder of wonders!

All our demands were reasonable and conformable to the Constitution; still they were stubbornly refused by those high in authority, who had sworn to support the Constitution, and who were followed in their course by the people they represented.

After all this, and after South Carolina had seceded, the other States of the South were so anxious to continue the Union under the Constitution, and to stand by and perpetuate its principles, that a peace congress was called. Virginia, taking the lead, called that congress, which met in Washington City in February, 1861. Judge Chase, a teacher of the anti-slavery movement, afterward Mr. Lincoln's Secretary of State, and later Chief-justice of the United States, was a delegate to that congress. As such delegate he, on March 6th, made a speech in which he said: "The result of the national canvass which recently terminated in the election of Mr. Lincoln has been spoken of by some as the effect of sudden impulse or of some irregular excitement of the popular mind, and it has been somewhat confidently asserted that, upon reflection and consideration, the hastily formed opinions which brought about the election will be changed. It has been said, also, that subordinate questions of local and temporary character have augmented the Republican vote and secured a majority which could not have been obtained upon the national questions involved in the respective platforms of the parties which divide the country. I cannot take this view of the presidential election. I believe, and the belief amounts to absolute conviction, that the election must be regarded as a triumph of principles cherished in the hearts of the people of the free States.

These principles, it is true, were originally asserted by a small party only. But after years of discussion they have, by their own value, their own intrinsic soundness, obtained the deliberate and unalterable sanction of the people's judgment. Chief among these principles is the restriction of slavery within State limits, not war upon slavery within those limits, but *fixed opposition* to its extension beyond them." "Mr. Lincoln was the candidate of the people opposed to the extension of slavery. We have elected him. After many years of earnest advocacy and severe trial, we have achieved the triumph of that principle. By a fair and unquestionable majority we have obtained that triumph. Do you think we who represent this majority will throw it away? Do you think the people would sustain us if we undertook to throw it away? I must speak to you plainly, gentlemen of the South. It is not in my heart to deceive you. I therefore tell you explicitly that if we of the North and West would consent to throw away all that has been gained in the recent triumph of our principles, the people would not sustain us, and so the consent would avail you nothing. And I must tell you further that under no circumstances will we consent to surrender a principle which we believe to be sound and so important as that of restricting slavery within State limits."

Here was a positive assertion that Lincoln and the party which had elected him would not respect the decision of the Supreme Court. Then if the Constitution as construed by that court, a tribunal constituted for the purpose, was to be so emphatically disregarded and ignored, what remedy was left for the South? If that organic law by the terms and assurances of which the States became parts of the Union is repudiated, was the South required in morals or good faith to fold its arms and quietly submit? I answer: No. Mr. Chase proceeds: "Aside from the territorial question, the question of slavery outside of the slave States, I know of but one serious difficulty. I refer to the question concerning fugitives from service. The clause in the Constitution concerning this class of persons is regarded by almost all men, North and South, as a stipulation for the surrender to their masters of slaves escaping into free States. The people of the free States, however, who believe that slave-holding is wrong, cannot and will not aid in the reclamation, and the stipulation therefore becomes a dead letter. . . . You, thinking slavery right, claim the fulfillment of the stipulation; we, thinking slavery wrong, cannot fulfill the stipulation without consciousness of participating in wrong."

This leaves no room to question the policy marked out by Mr. Lincoln. The speech of Mr. Chase, his chief adviser, distinctly announced that in two essentials the Constitution should not be observed and executed. He avows that the Constitution shall not be the law of the land, but that the will of the party coming into power shall be that law, a declaration in words that the Constitution is a dead letter. The course to be pursued was the usurpation of the powers and their absorption in centralization of government. It is admitted that that party understood the Constitution as we did, but that for years it had been its settled and fixed determination not to execute it; that while it would solemnly swear to execute it, it would not do so; that it had triumphed in its purpose and principle of disobedience, and it would avail itself of that triumph, and subvert and overthrow the principles of the Government and obliterate the Constitution it must swear to maintain, and by virtue of which only it could take control and management.

Try the questions by the rules laid down by Mr. Chase for his party, and who are the rebels, the traitors, the conspirators against the Government? The assertion that the Southern States are is the cap, the climax of deliberate and criminal impudence or inexcusable ignorance. The entire speech of Mr. Chase is interesting as part of the history of its time and the spirit of the party about to take control of the Government. All Southerners, especially those of Confederate blood and extraction, should read it. They will find in it much to defend us against the charges of treason, conspiracy, and rebellion, and much to shift these charges to the shoulders of others. It proves, as was said by Hon. C. J. Ingersoll, of Pennsylvania, in the House of Representatives, on June 9, 1841, that "the abolition agitation is [was] a conspiracy in the true definition of that offense. It is the combination of many to break law, which is the definition of conspiracy; none the better that the conspirators are, many of them, persons of fair character and *perhaps pious designs*."

The South was left without protection of constitutional guaranties and without hope in the decisions of the court of last resort; it must therefore resort to its only remedy, secession. It was outlawed, the Constitution denounced as "a dead letter." The evils likely and almost certain to flow from the teachings of Judge Chase's "originally small party" were seen and dreaded by the best and most patriotic minds of the North. Daniel Webster, who had no superior as a statesman, who was regarded the best constitutional lawyer in the land, and whose patriotism embraced the whole country, was alarmed, and gave the best efforts of his to check and paralyze the lawlessness of the "originally small party." In a reception speech made in New York on the 15th of March, 1837, he said: "We have slavery already amongst us. The Constitution found it in the Union, recognized it, and gave it solemn guaranties. To the full extent of these guaranties are we bound in honor, in justice, and by the Constitution. All the stipulations contained in the Constitution in favor of the slave-holding States which are already in the Union ought to be fulfilled, and, so far as depends on me, shall be fulfilled in the fullness of their spirit and to the exactness of their letter. Slavery, as it exists in the States, is beyond the reach of Congress. It is a concern of the States themselves; they have never submitted it to Congress, and Congress has no rightful power over it." I shall concur, therefore, in no act, no measure, no menace, no indication of purpose which shall interfere or threaten to interfere with the exclusive authority of the States over the subject of slavery as it exists within their respective limits. All this appears to me to be a matter of plain and imperative duty."

At Buffalo, on the 22d of May, 1851, he said: "There is but one question in this country now, or if there be others they are but secondary or so subordinate that they are all absorbed in that great and leading question, and that is nothing more nor less than this: Can we preserve the Union of States, not by coercion, not by military power, not by angry controversies, but can we of this generation, you and I, your friends and my friends, can we so preserve the Union of these States by such admission of the powers of the Constitution as shall give content and satisfaction to all who live under it, and draw us together, not by military power, but by the silken cords of mutual, fraternal, patriotic affection? That is the question, and no other. Gentlemen, I believe in party distinctions; I am a party man. There are questions belonging to party in which I take an interest, and there are opinions entertained by others which I repudiate, but what of all that? If a house be divided against itself, it will fall and crush everybody in it. We must see that we maintain the government which is over us; we must see that we uphold the Constitution, and we must do so without regard to party. The question, fellow-citizens (and I put it to you now as the real question), the question is whether you and the rest of the people of the great State of New York, and of all the States, will so adhere to the Constitution, will so enact and maintain laws to preserve that instrument, that you will not only remain in the Union yourselves, but permit your brethren to remain in it? That is the question. Will you concur in measures necessary to maintain the Union, or will you oppose such measures? That is the whole point of the case." After giving a history of the formation of the Union, Mr. Webster proceeds: "Now I am aware that all these things are well known, that they have been stated a thousand times, but in these days of perpetual discontent and misrepresentation to state things a thousand times is not enough, for there are persons whose consciences, it would seem, lead them to consider it their duty to deny, misrepresent, and cover up truths. Now these are the words of the Constitution, fellow-citizens, which I have taken the pains to transcribe therefrom, so that he who runs may read: 'No person held to service or labor in one State, under the laws thereof, escaping into another, shall, in consequence of any law or regulation therein, be discharged from such service or labor, but shall be delivered up on claim of the party to whom such service or labor may be due.' Is there any mistake about that? Is there any forty shilling attorney here to make a question of it? No, I will not disgrace my profession by supposing such a thing. There is not, in or out of an attorney's office, in the country of Erie or elsewhere, one who could raise a doubt, or a particle of doubt, about the meaning of this provision of the Constitution. He may act as witnesses do sometimes on the stand. He may wriggle and twist, and say he cannot tell or he cannot remember. I have seen many such efforts in my time on the part of witnesses to falsify and deny the truth. But there is no man who can read these words of the Constitution of the United States and say they are not clear and imperative. 'No person,' the Constitution says, 'held to labor or service in one State under the laws thereof, escaping into another, shall, in consequence of any law or regulation therein, be discharged from such service or labor, but shall be delivered up on claim of the party to whom such service or labor may be due.' Why, you may be told by forty conventions in Massachusetts, in Ohio, in New York, or elsewhere, that if a colored man comes here he comes as a freeman. That is *non sequitur*. It is not so. If he comes as a fugitive from labor, the Constitution says he is not a freeman, and that he shall be delivered up to those who are entitled to his service. Gentlemen, that is the Constitution. Do we or do we not mean to conform to it, and to execute that part of the Constitution as well as the rest of it? I believe there are before me here members of Congress. I suppose there may be here members of the State Legislature or executive officers under the State government. I suppose there may be judicial magistrates of New York, executive officers, assessors, supervisors, justices of the peace, and constables before me. Allow me to say, gentlemen, that there is not, there cannot be, any one of these officers in this assemblage, or elsewhere, who has not, according to the form of the usual obligation, bound himself by solemn oath to support the Constitution. They have taken their oaths on the holy evangelists of Almighty God, or by uplifted hands, as the case may be, or by solemn affirmation, as is the practice in some cases; but among all of them there is not a man who holds, nor is there any man who can hold, any office in the gift of the United States, or of this State, or of any other State, who does not bind himself by the solemn obligation of an oath to support the Constitution of the United States. Well, is he to tamper with that? Is he to palter? Gentlemen, our political duties are as much matters of conscience as any other duties. Our sacred domestic duties, our most endearing social relations are not more the subjects for conscientious consideration and conscientious discharge than the duties we enter upon under the Constitution of the United States. The bonds of political brotherhood, which hold us together from Maine to Georgia, rest upon the same principles of obligation as those of social and domestic life." At Capon Springs, in Virginia, June 28, 1851, Mr. Webster said: "The leading sentiment in the toast from the Chair is the Union of the States. The Union of the States! What mind can comprehend the consequences of that Union, past, present, and to come? The Union of these States is the all-absorbing topic of the day. On it all men speak, write, think, and dilate from the rising of the sun to the going down thereof. And yet, gentlemen, I fear its importance has been but insufficiently appreciated." "How absurd it is to suppose that when different parties enter into a compact for certain purposes, either can disregard any one provision and expect, nevertheless, the other to observe the rest! I intend, for one, to regard and maintain and carry out to the fullest extent the Constitution of the United States which I have sworn to support in all its parts and provisions. It is written in the Constitution: 'No person held to service or labor in one State under the laws thereof, escaping into another, shall, in consequence of any law or regulation therein, be discharged from such service or labor, but shall be delivered up on claim of the party to whom such service or labor may be due.' That is as much a part of the Constitution as any other, and equally binding and obligatory as any other on all men, public or private. And who denies this? None but the abolitionists of the North. And pray, what is it they will not deny? They have but the one idea, and it would seem that these fanatics at the North and the secessionists at the South are putting their heads together to defeat the good designs of honest and patriotic men. They act to the same end and the same object, and the Constitution has to take the fire from both sides. I have not hesitated to say, and I repeat, that if the Northern States refuse willfully and deliberately to carry into effect that part of the Constitution which respects the restoration of fugitive slaves, and Congress provides no remedy, the South would no longer be bound to observe the compact. A bargain cannot be broken on one side, and still bind the other side. I say to you, gentlemen, as I said on the shores of Lake Erie and in the city of Boston, and as I may say again in that city or elsewhere in the North, that you of the South have as much right to receive your fugitive slaves as the North has to any of its rights and privileges of navigation and commerce. I am as ready to fight and to fall for the constitutional rights of Virginia as I am for those of Massachusetts."

Now, if Daniel Webster, whose greatness of mind and nobility of soul are better and more impressively and significantly expressed by the isolated name, " Daniel Webster," than they would be by the use of any or all the adjectives of our language defining those virtues, and whose patriotism was as broad as the land, who loved the Union for its constitutional ties and guaranties, and who hated slavery in every form, and was willing to use all lawful means for its abolition—if he, with his universally known character and convictions, was ready to fight and to fall for the constitutional rights of the South, where was the wrong, or even the slightest mistake on the part of the Southern man who had been reared in the education that the institutions of the South were sound in law and in morals?

He told us we had the constitutional right to the property; that if the North disregarded the compact in any one particular, we were released from all obligations to observe the rest.

Trying the principles of the "originally small party" of Mr. Chase, Mr. Lincoln, and Mr. Seward by the plain and incontrovertible rules of constitutional law as laid down by Daniel Webster, we find they can only exist in the palpable and gross violation of the Constitution as it then was.

Mr. Webster's argument is so full, clear, and exhaustive that I will not be guilty of the folly of attempting to add to or elucidate it. I commend it to the attention and perusal of all Southern men and women. Its teachings should be transferred to our school-books to supersede and paralyze the false and poisonous manufacture of history that has found its way into so many of the books that have been introduced into the schools of the South, with the purpose to mislead and disease the minds of our children as to the purpose, policy, and good faith of our separation from the government of that "originally small party" so much condemned, if not despised, by Mr. Webster, and to which he administered such rebukes as to induce us to believe he could and would keep it in check and perhaps obliterate it.

If Daniel Webster could have been spared to the Union, there would not, in my opinion, have arisen cause for separation. His death, in October, 1852, unbridled the fanaticism of that "originally small party," and brought it into power eight years later, when it proposed to conduct the government on its peculiar sentiments of morality, regardless of the constitutional limitations and restrictions which had been upheld and enforced by the Supreme Court for more than seventy-five years.

It was "the higher law party" acting without warrant of authority and in violation of that compact of which Mr. Webster said one party could not disregard any one provision and expect the other to observe the rest. That great man loved law, system, order; had great respect for the ability, patriotism, and integrity of the Supreme Court of the United States, and would certainly, I think, have acquiesced in its decision made at the December term, 1856, that Congress had no power to exclude slavery from the Territories. His course through life warrants the conclusion that he would have urged it as a settlement of that agitation.

260 APPENDIX.

Our affairs having reached the crisis indicated, the work of secession began. The question is: Did we have that right which we exercised in the hope that war would not follow? We proposed to quit in peace.

The first authority I rely on in support of the right is a speech of Mr. Lincoln (the head and leader of coercion), made in the House of Representatives on January 12, 1848. He said: "Any people, anywhere, being inclined and having the power, have the right to rise up and shake off the existing government and form a new one that suits them better. This is a most valuable, a sacred right, a right which we hope and believe is to liberate the world. Nor is it confined to cases in which the whole people of an existing government may choose to exercise it. *Any portion* of such people that can, may revolutionize and make their own so much of the territory as they inhabit. More than this, a majority of any portion of such people may revolutionize putting down a minority, intermingled with or near them, who may oppose their movements. Such minority was precisely the case of the tories of our own Revolution. It is a quality of revolutions not to go by old lines or old laws, but to break up both and make new ones." There is no room for enlargement, expansion, or extension of this view of Mr. Lincoln on the right of revolution in any form it may take.

Mr. Rawls, of Pennsylvania, an eminent jurist, who had been United States District Attorney under President Washington, and had been offered by him the attorney-generalship of the United States, and who was a firm supporter of the administration of the elder Adams, wrote in 1825: "Having thus endeavored to delineate the general features of this peculiar and invaluable form of government, we shall conclude by adverting to the principles of its cohesion, and to the provisions it contains for its own duration and extension. The subject cannot, perhaps, be better introduced than by presenting in its own words an emphatical clause in the Constitution: 'The United States shall guaranty to every State in the Union a republican form of government, shall protect each of them against invasion, and on application of the Legislature, or the executive when the Legislature cannot be convened, against domestic violence.' The Union is an association of the people of republics; its preservation is calculated to depend on the preservation of these republics. The principle of representation, although certainly the wisest and best, is not essential to the being of a republic, but to continue a member of the Union it must be presumed, and therefore the guaranty must be so construed. It depends on the State itself to retain or abolish the principle of representation, because it depends on itself whether it will continue a member of the Union. To deny this right would be inconsistent with the principles on which our public systems are founded, which is that the people have in all cases to determine how they will be governed. This right must be considered as an ingredient in the original composition of the general Government which, though not expressed, was understood, and the doctrine heretofore presented to the reader in regard to the indefeasible nature of personal allegiance is so far qualified in respect to allegiance to the United States. It was observed that it was competent for a State to make a compact with its citizens; that the reciprocal obligations of protection and allegiance might cease on certain events; and it was further observed that allegiance would necessarily cease on the dissolution of the society to which it was due." "The secession of a State from the Union depends on the will of the people of such State. The people alone, as we have seen, hold the power to alter their Constitution. The Constitution of the United States is, to a certain extent, incorporated into the Constitutions of the several States *by the act of the people*. The State Legislatures have only to perform certain organical operations in respect to it. To withdraw from the Union comes not within the general scope of their delegated authority. There must be an expressed provision to that effect inserted in the State Constitutions. This is not at present the case with any of them, and it would, perhaps, be impolitic to confide it to them. A matter so momentous ought not to be intrusted to those who would have it in their power to exercise it lightly and precipitately, upon sudden dissatisfaction or causeless jealousy, perhaps against the interests and wishes of a majority of their constituents. In the present Constitution there is no specification of number after the first formation. It was foreseen that there would be a natural tendency to increase the number of States with the increase of population then anticipated and now so fully verified. It was also *known*, though it was not *avowed*, that a State *might withdraw itself.*" This comes from one who was an officer under the first administration and familiar with the interpretation of the Constitution by its framers.

Senator Wade, of Ohio (afterward Vice-president of the United States), in the United States Senate, on February 23, 1855, said: "Who is to be judge, in the last resort, of the violation of the Constitution of the United States by the enactment of a law? Who is the final arbiter, the general Government, or the States in their sovereignty? Why, sir, to yield that point is to yield up all the rights of the States to protect their own citizens and to consolidate this Government into a miserable despotism! Whatever you may think of it, I tell you, sir, that, if this bill pass, collision will arise between the State and Federal jurisdictions— conflicts more dangerous than all the wordy wars which are got up in Congress, conflicts in which the States will never yield; for the more you undertake to load them with acts like this the greater will be their resistance." "I said there were States in this Union whose highest tribunals had adjudged that bill to be unconstitutional, and I was one of those who believed it unconstitutional, and that, under the old resolutions of 1798 and 1799, a State must not only be the judge of that, but of the remedy in such case." There was no mincing there, no stringing together of words for sound's sake; but a solid shot, straight to the mark, from antislavery quarters.

In his address in 1839, before the Historical Society of New York, Mr. John Quincy Adams said: "With these qualifications we may admit the same right as vested in the people of every State in the Union, with reference to the general Government, which was exercised by the people of the united colonies with reference to the supreme head of the British Empire, of which they formed a part, and under these limitations have the people of each State in the Union a right to secede from the Confederate Union itself. But the indissoluble Union between the several States of this Confederate nation is, after all, not in the right, but in the heart. If the day should ever come (may heaven avert it!) when the affections of the people of these States shall be alienated from each other; when the paternal spirit shall give way to cold indifference, or collision of interest shall fester into hatred, the bonds of political asseveration will not long hold to other parties no longer attached by the magnetism of conciliated interest and kindly sympathies, and far better will it be for the people of these disunited States to part in friendship than to be held together by constraint; then will be time for reverting to the precedents which occurred at the formation and adoption of the Constitution, to form a more perfect Union by dissolving that which could no longer bind, and to leave the separated parties to be reunited by the law of political gravitation to the center."

Acting upon this principle, the Legislature of Massachusetts, the home of Mr. Adams, in 1844, resolved "that the project of the annexation of Texas, unless arrested on the threshold, may drive these States into a dissolution of the Union." On the same subject, on February 22, 1845, it resolved, ". . . and as the powers of legislation granted in the Constitution of the United States to Congress do not embrace the case of the admission of a foreign State or foreign Territory by legislation into the Union, such act of admission would have no binding force whatever on the people of Massachusetts."

Here we have the unequivocal assertion of the right to secede. In 1814, on the call of Massachusetts, several of the New England States met in convention in Hartford, and promulgated the following: "It is as much the duty of State authorities to watch over the rights reserved as of the United States to exercise the powers which are delegated." " In cases of deliberate, dangerous, and palpable infractions of the Constitution affecting the sovereignty of a State, and liberties of the people, it is not only the right, but the duty of such State to interpose its authority for their protection in the manner best calculated to secure that end. When emergencies occur, which are either beyond the reach of the judicial tribunals, or too pressing to admit of the delay incident to their forms, States which have no common umpire must be their own judges and execute their own decisions."

We of the South were watching over not only our reserved rights, but also those guaranteed to us as well. We had the deliberate, dangerous, and palpable infraction of the Constitution. Emergencies had reached beyond the cure of judicial tribunals, for the " originally small party " positively refused to recognize and obey the courts, and the time had come when we might, as the Hartford convention said we had the right to do, become our own judges and execute our own decisions. The principles set forth by that convention were signed by a number of the leading men of that day, among them Nathan Dane, founder of the professorship of law in the Cambridge University, and who was author of the ordinance for the government of the Northwestern territory in 1787. He, like Rawle, understood what was meant by the framers of the Constitution. He lived in their day and with them, and we may regard his utterances as an authoritative construction of the instrument.

On November 9, 1860, Horace Greeley wrote: "The telegraph informs us that most of the cotton States are meditating a withdrawal from the Union because of Lincoln's election. Very well. They have a right to meditate, and meditation is a profitable employment of leisure. We have a chronic, invincible disbelief in disunion as a remedy for either Northern or Southern grievances. We cannot see any necessary connection between the alleged disease and this ultra heroic remedy. Still we say, if any one meditates disunion, let him do so unmolested. That was a base and hypocritical row that was raised at Southern dictation about the ears of John Quincy Adams because he presented a petition for the dissolution of the Union. The petitioner had a right to make the request; it was the member's duty to present it. And now, if the cotton States consider the value of the Union debatable, we maintain their perfect right to discuss it. Nay, we hold with Jefferson to the inalienable right of communities to alter or abolish forms of government that have become oppressive or injurious; and if the cotton States decide that they can do better out of the Union than in it, we insist on letting them go in peace. The right to secede may be a revolutionary one; but it exists, nevertheless, and we do not see how one party has a right to do what another party has a right to prevent. We must ever resist the asserted right of any State to remain in the Union and nullify or defy the laws thereof. To withdraw from the Union is quite another matter; and whenever a considerable section of our Union shall deliberately resolve to go out we shall resist all coercive measures designed to keep it in. We hope never to live in a Republic whereof once section is pinned to the residue by bayonets, . . . Let the people reflect, deliberate, then vote, and let the act of secession be the echo of an unmistakable popular fiat. A judgment thus rendered, a demand for separation so backed, would either be acquiesced in without the effusion of blood, or those who rushed upon the carnage to defy and defeat it would place themselves clearly in the wrong."

Judge Story, in his "Commentaries on the Constitution," says: "Though obvious deductions which may be and, indeed, have been drawn from considering the Constitution as a compact between the States are that it operates as a mere treaty or convention between them, and has an obligatory force upon each State no longer than it suits its pleasure or its consent continues; that each State has a right to judge for itself in relation to the nature, extent, and obligations of the instrument, without being at all bound by the interpretation of the Federal Government, or by that of any other State, and that each retains the power to withdraw from the confederacy and dissolve the connection, when such shall be its choice, and may suspend the operations of the Federal Government, and nullify its acts within its own territorial limits, whenever in its own opinion the exigency of the case may require—these conclusions may not always be avowed, but they flow naturally from the doctrine which we have under consideration."

Judge Tucker, professor of law in the University of William and Mary, in Virginia, and one of the earliest commentators on the Constitution, in 1803 wrote: " The Constitution of the United States then being that instrument by which the Federal Government had been created, its powers defined and limited, and the duties and functions of its several departments prescribed, the

government thus established may be pronounced to be a confederate republic, composed of several independent and sovereign democratic States united for their common defense and security against foreign nations and for the purpose of harmony and mutual intercourse between each other, each State retaining an entire liberty of exercising as it thinks proper of those parts of its sovereignty which are not mentioned in the Constitution or act of union as parts that ought to be exercised in common."
"In becoming a member of the federal alliance, established between the American States by the Articles of Confederation, she expressly retained her sovereignty and independence. The constraints put upon the exercise of that sovereignty by those Articles did not destroy its existence." "The Federal Government then appears to be the organ through which the united republics communicate with foreign nations and with each other. Their submission to its operation is voluntary. Its councils, its engagements, its authority are theirs, modified and united. Its authority is an emanation from theirs, not a flame in which they have been consumed, nor a vortex in which they are swallowed up. Each is still a perfect State, still sovereign, still independent, and still capable, should occasion require, to resume the exercise of its functions as such in the most unlimited extent."

In speaking of our separation from Great Britain, Chancellor Kent says: "The principle of self-preservation and the right of every community to freedom and happiness gave sanction to this separation. When the government established over any people becomes incompetent to fulfill its purposes or destructive to the essential ends for which it was instituted, it is the right of the people, founded on the law of nature and the reason of mankind and supported by the soundest authority and some illustrious precedents, to throw off such government and provide new guards for their future safety."

With a single exception, I have confined my citations of authority to the Northern antislavery States, the home of the "originally small party." No Southern man, no slave-holder ever more clearly announced and advocated the sovereignty of the States, or that the Constitution was a compact between the States, or that one party could not violate it in one or more particulars and require or expect the other to observe the residue. No stronger argument can be made that the Constitution is a whole, and to be binding on one side must be obeyed as a whole by the other. The Constitution was the chain that linked the States in union. The breaking of one link dissolved the tie.

The authorities all tend to the one inevitable conclusion that the Union exists alone by the Constitution and its observance in every particular. Being the terms of union, one party may not be permitted to violate it in any particular and insist on its observance by the other as to any of its terms, whatever they may be. The right to its enforcement as a whole, or its rejection as such, is inalienable and indestructible.

In the investigation of the question my trouble has not been in finding authority of the highest and clearest and most convincing character. It has been in avoiding its multiplicity. I have relied on the testimony of those not at all in sympathy with the institution of slavery, passing by the opinions and utterances of Southern statesmen and jurists.

Under the condition of things as slightly, and but slightly, portrayed in this address, the Southern States began the work of secession and organizing a new Government. They hoped, as they rightly might, that they would not be interfered with; that there would be no war. In this they were mistaken. The "originally small party," which had then come into power, ordered the relief squadron with eleven ships, carrying two hundred and eighty-five guns and twenty-four hundred men, from New York and Norfolk to re-enforce Fort Sumter—peaceably if permitted, forcibly if they must. This was of itself an act of war. After several attempts and failures on the part of General Beauregard to have some understanding with Major Anderson, and seeing that unless he took action his forces would be exposed in front and rear, and perhaps destroyed for usefulness, he fired the first gun of the war. This he did in self-defense. He was in command of the forces of a Government foreign to that of the United States. The harbor of Charleston belonged to the Confederate States, or rather to the independent Government of South Carolina. Being then the property of another Government, there was no authority resting with or in the Government at Washington to interfere with it. It was that Government's duty to withdraw its troops, at least when demand was made by General Beauregard. Failing to do so, it became his imperative duty to take the necessary steps to remove them, and to resort to such force, mild or violent, as would bring about that removal. It became necessary to strike the first blow. That blow was in self-defense. The overt act on the part of the United States justified it. Neither nation nor individual is required to wait until stricken after the assailant has assumed the attitude of offense with the present ability to strike.

The squadron was ordered to Fort Sumter to attack. The order will bear no other interpretation. There can be no authority to order the re-enforcement of a foreign port in times of peace and with hostile demonstrations. That was an act of war, was the first assault, the inauguration of the war by the United States. If ever there was a case of pure, unmitigated, unmixed, and positive justification and self-defense, the law and the testimony makes that case for the Confederate Government and the Confederate soldier.

We yielded to the logic of force. The right still lives. A new

Government has been built upon the downfall of the old ones. We have promised our allegiance to it. We will keep the faith plighted at all hazards and to the last extremity, so long as the Constitution is respected. The element of evils and discord has been removed. Old things have passed away, and there will be, we venture to hope, no other sectional jealousy. Our devotion to the Constitution at all times; our conduct as soldiers for four years, battling from field to field, from time to time, holding in check one million five hundred thousand soldiers with six hundred thousand, gives assurance that we will always be worthy citizens of a constitutional Union, and may be confidently relied on in times of need.

I know that in many things I have repeated an often told story; but, in the language of Mr. Webster, "to state things a thousand times is not enough in these days of misrepresentation, for there are persons whose consciences it would seem lead them to consider it their duty to deny, misrepresent, and cover up truths."

In this effort my purpose and desire have been to awake the Southern man and woman to the importance of having their children study our lost cause from constitutional, legal, and historical stand-points, that they be not misled. It is time we were seeking after their school-books ourselves, and not trusting too much to others.

Our cause was worth all we sacrificed to it. Though lost, it deserves vindication. Its defense by our arms at least checked centralization. Understanding the principles of self-government, for which our comrades battled and died, our children will stand at their graves with love, admiration, and approval of their course, and offer up the prayer: "God bless and perpetuate their memories!"
 HON. PETER TURNEY,
Chief-justice of the State of Tennessee.

RELIGION IN THE SOUTHERN ARMY.

The army is generally regarded as a great "school of vice." As a theory I have nothing to write anent it. I only state facts as I glean them from history and experience. I left my charge, Winchester, Tenn., July 9, 1861, and went directly to "Camp Sneed," Knoxville, East Tennessee, and continued in the Southern army until the surrender, and was paroled in Macon, Ga., in May, 1865, and reached my home July 13, 1865.

The centurions of whom we read in the Bible have much said to their credit, nothing in censure. The first of whom we read was noted for his great faith, humility, and charity. The next "glorified God" at the cross, and testified: "Truly this was the Son of God." Cornelius was "a devout man" who "feared God with all his house," "gave much alms," "and prayed to God always." Julius was kind and courteous in all his treatment toward Paul during the months that he was in the custody of the centurion.

"Tapsters and town people" Oliver Cromwell found would not defeat the Royalists, but when he rallied "men of religion" and went singing or shouting into the conflict, the "Lord of hosts" he thought gave them the victory, and he recognized God's hand in all results.

"Godly soldiers bore a conspicuous part" in the great work of the Wesleys; and Captain Thomas Webb, of the British army, a lay preacher, was converted under the preaching of John Wesley in Bristol, England, and there testified to others of God's saving power; and in America he was eminently useful, preaching in his military dress, and was a pioneer in planting Methodism on this continent.

"Colonel Gardiner found the army an inviting field for Christian work," and he was remarkably successful in winning officers and soldiers from the vices of camp life. His life was great in deeds of piety, his death was grand and triumphant.

Headley Vicars was eminent as a soldier of the cross.

General Joseph Warren, who fell at Bunker Hill, spent two hours in prayer the night before his gallant death.

General Andrew Jackson, when told by an officer that the articles of war forbid "an unusual noise in camp," and that some of the soldiers had been singing and praying in their quarters, replied: "God forbid that prayer should be an unusual noise in my camp!"

We all know how fully and frequently Jefferson Davis, Robert E. Lee, and Stonewall Jackson appealed to God for help, and to the people to look to him for aid during the time of the great conflict.

Much more of vice than virtue was manifest in the army of Tennessee during the first and second years of the war. Not a a few chaplains were so much discouraged with the army as a field of acceptability and usefulness that they resigned their commissions and left the camp. I am indebted to Dr. W. W. Bennett's "Great Revival in the Southern Armies" for the following extracts and much else that I furnish in this sketch:

> In the first months of the strife the call of the war-trumpet was heard above all other sounds. The young men rushed to the camps of instruction, and, freed from the restraints of home and the influence of pious relatives, thousands of them gave way to the seductive influences of sin.
>
> Legions of devils infest a camp. Vice grows in it like plants in a hot-bed, and yields abundant and bitter fruits. "In the Old Testament it is said, 'One sinner destroyeth much good.' If so, what destruction of good must be effected by a large body of ungodly soldiers in close and constant contact, where one may, without extravagance, consider them as inocu-

lating each other daily with the new infection of every debauch through which they pass!"

Before the "soldiers of Christ" addressed themselves in earnest to the work, gambling, profanity, drunkenness, and other kindred vices prevailed to an alarming extent.

The temptation to recklessness is strong among all soldiers. Religion is supposed to be well suited to the pursuits of peaceful life, but not to rough, uncertain army life. This reckless spirit, we must admit, greatly prevailed, and was much encouraged by many who had been long in the military profession, and brought with them into our armies the vicious habits of many years of sin. Among the soldiers the great, overshadowing evils were lewdness, profanity, and drunkenness; among the people at home, the "greed of gain" was the "accursed thing."

It was a melancholy fact that many men entered the army avowed enemies of all intoxicating drinks, who, alas! very soon fell victims to the demon of the bottle. With many there seemed to be a conviction that the fatigue and exposure of their new mode of life could not be endured without the artificial stimulant of ardent spirits. This was a great and fatal error. The soldier does not need, even in the worst climates, and in the hardest service, his rations of rum.

The cause of Christ was hindered, and that of Satan promoted, in the Southern armies by the influence and example of wicked and licentious officers and men.

One who had observed the course of intemperance in the army wrote: "The prevalence of vice—drunkenness and profanity—in our camps, is attributable to the officers themselves. By far the larger number of the officers of our Southern army are both profane and hard drinkers, where they are not drunkards."

Another says: "There is an appalling amount of drunkenness in our army. More among the officers than the men. This evil is now on the increase."

A surgeon, writing from the army, says: "I was greatly astonished to find soldiers in Virginia whom I had known in Georgia as somber, discreet citizens—members of the different Churches, some deacons and official members, even preachers—in the daily and constant habit of drinking whisky for their health."

An officer who had visited many portions of the army gave it as his opinion that with the exception of the reverse at Fort Donelson, we were defeated not by the Federals, but by whisky.

A distinguished general is said to have remarked that "if the South is overthrown, the epitaph should be: '*Died of Whisky.*'"

This was one of the giant evils. Hundreds all over the land, moved by an unholy desire for gain, engaged in the manufacture of ardent spirits. It was estimated that in one county in Virginia, and that not one of the largest, the distillers in one year consumed thirty-one thousand bushels of grain, enough to furnish six hundred families with food for the same period. While the commissioners appointed by the court of that county to procure grain to feed the families of soldiers could not purchase enough for that purpose, the smoke of fifty distilleries darkened the air; meantime, the cries of the poor mothers and helpless children went up in vain for bread.

The same was the case in other States. In one district in South Carolina one hundred and fifty distilleries were in operation. A gentleman in North Carolina said he could count from one hill-top the smoke of fourteen distilleries. One of the Richmond papers declared that a single distiller in that city made at one period of the war a profit of $4,000 a day.

In Augusta County, Va., it was estimated that fifty thousand bushels of grain were consumed monthly by the distilleries in operation there.

A writer on this subject estimated that in the second year of the war sixteen hundred barrels, or sixty-four thousand gallons, of ardent spirits of the worst sort were daily manufactured in the Confederate States.

The temptation to drink in the army was very strong: men were cast down in spirit, away from home, wife, children, mothers and sisters—all that makes life dear. Many that ventured to drink at all under such circumstances found it hard to avoid excesses.

But this evil was not confined to the soldiers. In the councils of the general Government and State Governments its baleful influence was felt.

The best and ablest officers of the army sought by example and by precept to suppress this vice, and the following noble language from General Bragg is a sample of the general orders issued from time to time against the evils which infested our armies:

"Commanders of all grades are earnestly called upon to suppress drunkenness by every means in their power. It is the cause of nearly every evil from which we suffer; the largest portion of our sickness and mortality results from it; our guard-houses are filled by it; officers are constantly called from their duties to form court-martials in consequence of it; inefficiency in our troops, and consequent danger to our cause, is the inevitable result. No one is benefited but the miserable wretch who is too cowardly to defend a country he is willing to sell by destroying those noble faculties he has never possessed. Gallant soldiers should scorn to yield to such temptations, and intelligent and honorable officers should set them an example. They should be encouraged to send to their families at home the pay they receive for their services, instead of wasting it in their own destruction, and at the risk of the holy cause in which they are engaged. Small as the amount is, it will cause many a dear one to rise up and call them blessed.

"'Give strong drink unto him that is ready to perish, and wine to those that be of heavy hearts;' but as for us, the glorious cause in which we are engaged should furnish all the excitement and enthusiasm necessary for our success."

When ardent spirits were offered to our great warrior Jackson, in his last illness as a medicine, he exclaimed: "Give me pure water and milk." And among the soldiers many followed the example of the great leader.

There was much of preaching and prayer-meeting in our army around Knoxville in the summer of 1861; less, of course, during the winter of 1861-2 at Cumberland Gap; but far more in the army about Tupelo, Miss., and Bean's Station and Tazewell, East Tennessee, in the spring and summer of 1862. Then, after our forced march across Eastern Kentucky to Richmond and Lexington, Ky., in the early autumn, while resting and recruiting in the beautiful blue-grass country, we had for some weeks our regular camp services in the midst of the handsome new tents captured from the Federal troops. During all these fifteen months I had seen no signs of a revival in our army.

Late in November and early in December, 1862, Chaplains Wexler, of the Twenty-ninth North Carolina; Allen Tribble, of the Fourth Tennessee; J. G. Bolton, of the Eleventh Tennessee; Rev. Captain Brady, of the Thirty-ninth Georgia; and myself, conducted a protracted meeting beginning at Normandy and ending at Manchester, Tenn. There were some happy public professions of faith and a number of penitents, the first I had witnessed during the war among the soldiers.

After the battle of Murfreesboro, or Stone's River, our army remained in camp for five months near Shelbyville, Tenn. Distinguished ministers of different Churches came to the help of the chaplains. Among those I remember were Dr. Teasdale, Missionary Baptist; Dr. Pease, Episcopal; and Dr. J. B. McFerrin, Methodist. Dr. Bunting, Presbyterian chaplain of Terry's Texas Rangers, was also with us. Chaplain Crouch, of Armstrong's Brigade, was killed in a skirmish at Thompson's Station, Tenn., March 5 or 6.

The Chaplains' Association was organized at the Presbyterian Church in Shelbyville February 18, 1862—Rev. Dr. Bryson, Chairman, and Rev. Mr. Bowde, Secretary. There were ten chaplains present. The destitution of regiments of chaplains, the word of God, tracts, etc., was discussed. Dr. (now Bishop) Quintard was recommended as agent for Polk's Corps to look after more preachers and religious reading for the soldiers. Chaplain Bennett and I were appointed on the 24th of March to wait upon Lieutenant-general Polk and request that the inspection of arms should be dispensed with on Sunday. Our bishop-general received us with marked courtesy, and assured us that there should be no interference with our hours for religious service.

On May 7 Dr. McFerrin preached the funeral of the Rev. S. S. Moody, and a revival was reported at the chaplains' meeting in Ector's Texas Brigade—seventeen conversions to date. Chaplains Morris and Finney organized a Soldiers' Christian Association of forty or fifty members in that brigade. April 5 I found Colonel Camp, of the Fourteenth Texas, reading his Bible. The flag of his regiment bore the inscription: "In God We Trust."

On May 10 we organized a Soldiers' Christian Association of ninety-nine members for the Thirty-seventh Georgia Regiment, and began a protracted meeting for the brigade. Captains Wilson and Carter, and Rev. S. S. Taylor, a worthy minister of the Primitive Baptist Church, and a true private soldier, rendered me valuable assistance during the three weeks the meeting continued.

At our chaplains' meeting on May 12 Chaplains C. S. Hearn, of the Fifth Tennessee, and W. T. Bennett, of the Twelfth Tennessee, reported eighty-five conversions in Vaughn's and forty-five in Strahl's Brigade. Rev. H. D. Hogan, a private soldier, held a fine revival in his regiment, the Twenty-fourth Tennessee. Since the war he has been a presiding elder in Kansas for several years.

At Shelbyville, on May 24, John P. McFerrin, son of the Rev. A. P. McFerrin, was recommended for license to preach. He gave us good help at Tyner's Station three months later, was terribly wounded at Chickamauga in September, and assisted us in another meeting near Augusta, Ga., in March, 1865. He is now pastor of the First Methodist Church in Chattanooga. Rev. Dr. J. B. McFerrin gave us invaluable help in Middle and East Tennessee in 1863, in Georgia in 1864, and was with us till the day of the surrender at Greensboro, N. C., and preached to the army that day. He did much for the spiritual welfare of our soldiers during the two active, efficient years of his army life.

At Fairfield, on June 2, a chaplains' meeting was organized—S. M. Cherry, Chairman; Dr. F. S. Petway, Secretary. Present: Chaplains Rush, of the Third Georgia; H. B. Moore, of the Seventeenth Tennessee; John A. Ellis, of the Twentieth Tennessee; —— McMurray, of the Forty-fifth Tennessee; and Rev. S. S. Taylor, of the Thirty-seventh Georgia. A good revival was conducted in Brown's Brigade near Fairfield and Beech Grove by Chaplains T. H. Davenport, of the Third Tennessee; —— Chapman, of the Thirty-second Tennessee; and —— Harris, of the

Twenty-sixth Tennessee, assisted by Dr. J. B. McFerrin. We had some revival at a meeting in Bate's Brigade. Rev. Lieutenant Curry, of the Ninth Alabama, assisted Chaplain Ellis and myself. We also had a splendid experience-meeting on June 7. Dr. McFerrin preached for us that day.

The conflict at Hoover's Gap closed our protracted meetings and the campaign in Middle Tennessee on the 24th of June, 1863.

In July and August the Army of Tennessee was in camp around Chattanooga, Tenn. Lieutenant-general D. H. Hill was in command of our corps. He preferred to attend service in camp rather than to "slink" off to town, as he expressed it, as was the custom of many. He was a true-blue Presbyterian, and a Christian indeed. He was also a great help to the chaplains in their camp service. Our army was now well furnished with chaplains, and amply supplied with missionaries of ability. Among the latter were the Revs. Messrs. Caldwell and Wills, Presbyterians; Revs. R. P. Ransom, William Burr, and Welborn Mooney, of the Tennessee Conference; and C. W. Miller, of the Kentucky Conference.

A protracted meeting of three weeks was conducted by Chaplain Ellis and myself for Bate's Brigade at Tyner's Station, near Chattanooga in August. We were assisted by the Rev. Colonel Wiley Reed, of the First Cumberland Presbyterian Church, Nashville, Tenn.; Dr. Bryson, Presbyterian; Revs. Caldwell, Wills, R. P. Ransom, W. Mooney, C. W. Miller, John B. Stevenson, and J. P. McFerrin. Dr. B. M. Palmer, of New Orleans, preached us two grand sermons at the close of these meetings, and was announced to preach on the night of August 23, but the long roll called us to the march, and there was no more regular camp service until after the terrible conflict at Chickamauga on the 19th and 20th of September. A general revival prevailed in our army around Chattanooga in the summer of 1863.

On the 3d and 4th of November, 1863, the chaplains and missionaries of the army held a council of two sessions daily at the Lookout Hotel, on Lookout Mountain. Dr. B. W. McDonald, of the Fiftieth Alabama, Chairman; Rev. A. D. McVoy, of the Fifty-eighth Alabama, Secretary.

The *Army and Navy Herald* was established in Macon, Ga., in October, 1863, and General Bragg was requested to designate some one to act as "Distributing Agent of Religious Reading for the Army of Tennessee." On the recommendation of Dr. McFerrin and chaplains and others in the army, I was appointed to that work, and took leave of the Fourth Tennessee and the Thirty-seventh Georgia Regiments, with which I had been so intimately associated for more than two years. My duties were still much in camp, but more general and extensive. I preached and labored much more in my wider field than while chaplain of the two regiments.

After the battle of Missionary Ridge our army went into winter-quarters at Dalton, Ga., where rough log houses were erected in many brigades, and we witnessed the most wonderful revivals that I ever saw anywhere in my life. But I prefer the testimony of others rather than what I could pen myself, so I clip from the "Great Revival," by Dr. Bennett, and copy from "Christ in the Camp," by Dr. Jones.

The venerable Dr. J. C. Stiles, about seventy years of age, preached a series of sermons at Dalton, Ga., in the winter of 1863–4 that impressed me as the finest series of revival sermons I ever heard. He thus wrote the *Christian Observer* of a revival in the Army of the Potomac near Winchester, Va., in 1862:

General Pryor, upon one hour's notice, marched up twelve to fifteen hundred men, who listened with so much interest to a long sermon that I was not surprised to hear of such a beginning of religious interest in various regiments of the brigade as issued in a half-way promise on my part to fall in with the proposal of the general to preach very early to his soldiers for a succession of nights. In General Lawton's Brigade there is a more decided state of religious excitement. The great body of the soldiers in some of the regiments meet for prayer and exhortation every night, exhibit the deepest solemnity, and present themselves numerously for the prayers of the chaplains and the Church. Quite a pleasant number express hope in Christ. In all other portions of General Early's Division (formerly General Ewell's) a similar religious sensibility prevails.

In General Trimble's and the immediate neighboring brigades there is in progress at this hour one of the most glorious revivals I ever witnessed. Some days ago a young chaplain of the Baptist Church, as a representative of three others of the same denomination, took a long ride to solicit my co-operation, stating that a promising seriousness had sprung up within their diocese. I have now been with him three days and nights, preaching and laboring constantly with the soldiers when not on drill. The audiences and the interest have grown to glorious dimensions. It would rejoice you over-deeply to glance for one instant on our night meetings in the wild woods under a full moon, aided by the light of our side stands. You would behold a mass of men seated on the earth all around you (I was going to say for the space of half an acre), fringed in all its circumference by a line of standing officers and soldiers—two or three deep—all exhibiting the most solemn and respectful earnestness that a Christian assembly ever displayed. An officer said to me last night on returning from worship that he had never witnessed such a scene, though a Presbyterian elder, especially such an abiding solemnity and delight in the services as prevented all whispering in the outskirts, leaving of the congregation, or restless change of position. I suppose at the close of the services we had some sixty or seventy men and officers come forward and publicly solicit an interest in our prayers, and there may have been as many more who, from the press, could not reach the stand. I have already conversed with quite a number who seem to give pleasant evidence of return to God, and all things seem to be rapidly developing for the best.

The officers, especially Generals Jackson and Early, have modified military rules for our accommodation. I have just learned that General A. P. Hill's Division enjoys as rich a dispensation of God's Spirit as General Early's.

P. S.—I have opened this letter the second time to inform you of the wide spread of holy influence. In General Pickett's Division also there are said to be revivals of religion.

Dr. Bennett thus continues the account of the revival in the Army of Northern Virginia:

There was scarcely a brigade in the army in which the work of revival did not go forward with deepening power. Some of the far Southern troops were signally blessed with great outpourings of the Spirit. The Sixtieth Georgia Regiment was favored with the services of a most excellent chaplain, Rev. S. S. Smith, under whose ministry many were brought to Christ. In a letter describing the revival among his men, he says: "About the first and middle of October we held a series of meetings in camps, during which time many souls were renewed and encouraged, several were made happy in the love of God, and the altar was crowded from day to day with seekers of religion. The like was hardly ever before witnessed in camps. I was blessed with the assistance of the Rev. Dr. Joseph Stiles, of the Presbyterian Church, to whom the army owes a debt of gratitude for his arduous labors and efforts to save sinners from the wrath to come."

The revival was not confined to the soldier in camp. In the towns in Virginia where military hospitals were located there were gracious displays of the power of God in the salvation of souls. The convalescent soldiers flocked to the churches and crowded the altars as humble penitents. In Farmville, under the ministry of Rev. Nelson Head, there was a most interesting revival, and the greater number of the converts were soldiers from Georgia and Alabama. In Lynchburg, Charlottesville, Petersburg, and Richmond the work was pervasive and powerful. A writer in one of the Richmond secular papers, speaking of the work of grace in the hospitals in that city and other places, says: "At Camp Winder, for some weeks, there has been in progress a revival of religion. Thirty-five soldiers have professed to be converted. Daily meetings are being held, and numbers are manifesting a deep interest in reference to spiritual things. A revival is also in progress at Chimborazo, and frequently from thirty to forty present themselves as 'inquirers.' Many have professed to experience the saving change. One hundred have professed conversion within a comparatively brief period in the hospitals in Petersburg. For more than a month a protracted meeting has been in progress at Lynchburg, at which some twenty soldiers have made the good profession. We learn from the post chaplain in Farmville that there is considerable religious interest among the hospitals there, and that eight have professed conversion. At other points the divine blessing is being richly bestowed upon the pious efforts of chaplains and colporteurs. There can be no more inviting field for Christian enterprise than that presented by the hospitals. In this city alone over ninety-nine thousand sick and wounded soldiers have been in the hospitals. At no time do men feel more grateful to the Giver of all good, and more like becoming pious, than when recovering from long spells of sickness."

The revival at this period of the war was undoubtedly greater and more glorious in the army in Virginia than in other portions of the Confederacy, but there were happy signs of spiritual life among the troops in the far South and West. On Sullivan's Island, near Charleston, S. C., there was a blessed work of grace, which powerfully checked the ordinary vices of the camp and brought many souls into the fold of the Good Shepherd. Speaking of his work, in a letter of October 9, Rev. E. J. Meynardie, chaplain of Colonel Keitt's Regiment of South Carolina Volunteers, says: "On Thursday evening, 25th ult., the religious interest, which for some time had been quite apparent, became so deep and manifest that I determined to hold a series of meetings, during which, up to last night, *ninety-three* applied for membership in the various branches of the Church, nearly all of whom profess conversion. Every night the church at which we worshiped was densely crowded, and obvious seriousness pervaded the congregation. To the invitation to approach the altar for prayer prompt and anxious responses were made, and it was indeed an unusual and impressive spectacle to behold the soldiers of the country, ready for battle, and even for death on the battle-field, bowed in prayer for that blessing which the warrior, of all others, so much needs. God was with us most graciously, and it was a period of profound interest and great joy. The influence of this meeting has pervaded the regiment, and is still operating most beneficially. To what extent it has improved the morals of the soldiers it is impossible to estimate. Suffice it to say, that it has struck at the very root of camp vices, and that the great crime which is more frequently committed in the army than any other, profanity, hides its deformed head."

It was now that the signs of that wonderful revival in the Army of the West began to appear. "I shall never forget," says Rev. W. H. Browning, "the look of astonishment in the Association of Chaplains in January, 1863, when Brother Winchester, a chaplain and a minister in the Cumberland Presbyterian Church, announced a conversion in his command, and stated that he believed that we were on the eve of one of the most glorious revivals ever witnessed on the American continent. His countenance glowed with an unearthly radiance, and while he spoke 'our hearts burned within us.' He urged us to look for it, pray for it, preach for it. A revival in the army! The thing was incredible. And yet, while we listened to this man of faith, we could almost hear the shouts of redeemed souls that were being born to God. We could not but catch the zeal of this good man, and went away resolved to work for a revival."

This pious man was not permitted to participate in the revival which he so feelingly predicted. He was soon called to the spirit world.

A General Association of Chaplains and Missionaries had been formed in this army in August of this year (1863), but the subsequent movements greatly interfered with its complete organization, and it was not until November following that it was properly organized and made really efficient. Rev. Dr. McDonald, President of Lebanon University, was the President, and Rev. Welborn Mooney, of the Tennessee Conference, was the Secretary. Mr. Browning supposes the proceedings of this association were lost in the subsequent reverses of the army, and hence we are cut off from most reliable information concerning the progress of the revival. The seeds of truth were sown by such faithful laborers as Rev. M. B. De Witt, chaplain of the Eighth Tennessee; Rev. Mr. Weaver, of the Twenty-eighth Tennessee; Rev. Tilmon Page, of the Fifty-second Tennessee; and Rev. W. H. Browning, chaplain of General Marcus Wright's Brigade. In other portions of the army, under the preaching of Rev. S. M. Cherry, Rev. Messrs. Petway, Taylor, Henderson, and scores of other devoted and self-sacrificing ministers, the revival influence became deep and powerful.

Rev. L. R. Redding, a Methodist of the Georgia Conference, began his work in Gist's Brigade, assisted by the Revs. F. Auld and J. P. De Pass. He thus writes of the revival near Dalton in 1864: "The gallant Colonel McCullough, of the Sixteenth South Carolina, himself a godly man, leads his men to the place of worship. The Twenty-fourth South Carolina falls into line, led by their chaplain, Mr. Auld, and their brave Colonel Capers, son of the deceased Bishop Capers, of the Southern Methodist Church. The benches and the pulpit have to be removed from the house, and a dense multitude of hearers crown the chapel hill. A clear, strong voice starts a familiar old hymn, and soon thousands of voices chime in and the evening air is burdened with a great song of praise. The preacher now enters the stand, and a thousand voices are hushed and a thousand hearts are stilled to hear the word of the Lord. Perhaps the speaker is Rev. William Burr, of Tennessee. As he rises with his theme, his silvery, trumpet-like voice, clear as a bugle note, rings far out over the mass of men, and hundreds sob with emotion as he reasons with them of righteousness, of temperance, and a judgment to come. At the close of the sermon hundreds bow in penitence and prayer, many are converted, tattoo beats—the men disperse to their cabins, not to sleep, but to pray and sing with their sorrowing comrades; and far into the night the camps are vocal with the songs of Zion and the rejoicing of newborn souls."

In this revival, described by an eye-witness, one hundred and forty were converted in two weeks, among them Colonel Dunlap, of the Forty-sixth Georgia, who united with the Presbyterian Church. Among the private soldiers that contributed to the success of this work we are glad to place on record the name of W. J. Brown, of Company I, Forty-sixth Georgia. His influence with his regiment was very great, and he threw it all in favor of religion. He entered the Protestant Episcopal Church, and, if we are not misinformed, is now in the ministry. Colonel Dunlap, converted in camp, became an earnest Christian, and labored with zeal and success to bring his men to Christ. He was five times wounded, but survived the war, and is now an honored citizen of Georgia.

General C. A. Evans was a Methodist and a class-leader before the war. He entered as a private in the Thirty-first Georgia, was elected major at its organization, and colonel at its reorganization six months afterward. He greatly distinguished himself at the battles around Richmond, at Manassas, and at Fredericksburg. He was promoted and put in command of General Gordon's celebrated brigade. The last year of the war he commanded Gordon's old division. He was an earnest, working Christian, and in the midst of war the call came to him to preach the gospel, but he wore his sword until the fatal day of Appomattox, when, with his noble comrades, he laid down the weapons of war, returned to his home, and was soon afterward licensed to preach and received into the Georgia Conference. It is a singular incident that his first circuit was called Manassas, and that his junior preacher was one of his old army couriers. He is still actively engaged in the ministerial work.

The revival was hardly less powerful in those regiments and brigades which were favored with the regular services of chaplains than in those that had none. The Second Arkansas, of Liddell's Brigade, Cleburne's Division, had no chaplain at the time of which we write; but they were led by pious officers, who strove to stem the tide of irreligion. Lieutenant-colonel Harvey, Captain H. D. Cregg, Lieutenant Wilfong, and others, being profoundly impressed with the great need of religious services, formed themselves into a band of Christian soldiers and began a moral warfare against the powers of darkness. They fought gallantly and well.

The main body of the Confederate army remained in winter-quarters, and here began one of the most powerful revivals witnessed during the war. Fredericksburg was the center of the work, and the minister who contributed more to its success in the town than any other was the Rev. William Benton Owen, connected with General Barksdale's Mississippi Brigade. Mr. Owen was earnest in calling to his help the ministers of all the different Churches, and, among others, he was favored at this time with the aid of Rev. Dr. J. C. Stiles, an eminent and eloquent minister of the Presbyterian Church. In the latter part of February he reached the town, and entered into the work with his well-known ardor. He says: "After my arrival we held three meetings a day—a morning and afternoon prayer-meeting, and a preaching service at night. We could scarcely ask of delightful religious interest more than we received. Our sanctuary has been crowded—lower floor and gallery. Loud, animated singing always hailed our approach to the house of God; and a closely packed audience of men, amongst whom you might have searched in vain for one white hair, were leaning upon the voice of the preacher as if God himself had called them together to hear of life and death eternal. At every call for the anxious the entire altar, the front seats of the five blocks of pews surrounding the pulpit, and all the spaces thereabouts ever so closely packed, could scarcely accommodate the supplicants, while daily conversions gave peculiar interest to the sanctuary services. Of this class we have numbered during the week say some forty or fifty souls. Officers are beginning to bow for prayer, and our house to be too strait for worshipers. The audience, the interest, the converted, the fidelity of the Church, and the expectations of the ministry, are all steadily and most hopefully increasing."

Rev. W. C. Dunlap, chaplain of the noble Eighth Georgia Regiment, wrote in reference to this work: "God has wonderfully blessed us of late. We have had going on in our midst a revival of religion, with more or less interest, since the battles in front of Richmond. Recently, however, it has grown greatly in interest, and before breaking up camps near Fredericksburg, the Lord was doing a mighty work in our midst. I have held prayer-meetings in my own regiment until ten o'clock many a night, and after closing the brethren would all retire to the woods, frequently accompanied by a half-dozen mourners, and there, with no other covering save the open canopy of heaven, pour out their souls in humble supplication at a throne of grace, often remaining until after midnight; and, what is remarkable, I never have known the meeting to close without the witnessing influences of the Holy Spirit."

The revival at Fredericksburg, already noticed, continued through the greater part of the spring with the greatest power. The labors of Dr. Stiles were blessed and honored in the salvation of many souls, but he was compelled to leave for other scenes of labor. Rev. James D. Coulling and other ministers went to the help of Mr. Owen, and, by their earnest and pointed preaching, greatly promoted the work. An eye-witness, writing at this time from the scene, says: "Last evening there were fully one hundred penitents at the altar. So great is the work, and so interested are the soldiers, that the M. E. Church, South, has been found inadequate for the accommodation of the congregations, and the Episcopal Church having been kindly tendered by its pastor, Rev. Mr. Randolph, who is now here, the services have been removed to that edifice, where devotions are held as often as three times a day. This work is widening and deepening, and, ere it closes, it may permeate the whole Army of Northern Virginia, and bring forth fruits in the building up and strengthening, in a pure faith and a true Christianity, of the best army the world ever saw."

In the churches, scarred and torn by the balls and shells from the Federal batteries, the meetings were held night after night for many weeks, and the scenes were such as thrill the angelic hosts in heaven. In the space of six weeks one hundred and sixty professed religion in Barksdale's Brigade, while scores of others were earnestly seeking salvation.

There was hardly a regiment of the army where the revival influence was not felt. Rev. W. A. Hemmingway rejoiced in a gracious revival in the Twenty-first South Carolina Regiment, which lasted for months. Rev. L. S. West, of the Thirteenth Mississippi, conducted a meeting for six weeks, in which many were happily converted. Rev. S. H. Smith, of the sixtieth Georgia (Lawton's Brigade) collected from the soldiers and officers $850 to purchase Bibles, Testaments, and hymn-books, and saw the men daily anxious "about the salvation of their souls." Rev. F. Milton Kennedy, chaplain of the Twenty-eighth North Carolina Regiment of Jackson's Corps, found "the men generally interested in their spiritual welfare." A Chaplains' Association was formed, and weekly meetings held to consult upon the best method of prosecuting our work and to pray for success. The chaplains of this corps issued an earnest appeal for more laborers. The fields were white to the harvest, but the laborers were few, while thousands of the noblest of the land, having left home and friends, were calling loudly and earnestly for the bread of life. To this and other calls the Churches responded by sending some of their ablest ministers into the army work, who, by their earnest labors, greatly extended the area of the revival.

The signs from other portions of the army in the West and South-west were equally cheering. Along the lines in East Tennessee the revival began to spread with great power. Rev. W. B. Norris, writing from Loudon, Tenn., says: "During the month (April) there has been a deep religious interest among the soldiers here. We have had a series of meetings for about two weeks, which, we hope, resulted in much good. The church in which we met was always crowded to the utmost, and there were always many seekers for the way of eternal life."

In the Fifty-ninth Tennessee Regiment there was a glorious work. Rev. S. Strick, the chaplain, says: "God is at work among our men. Many are earnestly seeking the pardon of their sins. Some have been converted. Our nightly prayer-meetings are well attended by anxious listeners, and my tent is crowded daily by deeply penitent souls. Never have I known such a state of religious feeling in our army as at this time. God's Spirit is moving the hearts of our soldiers."

The great concern of the people at home for the salvation of their fellow-countrymen in the armies soon bore fruit. In the Army of Tennessee there was a glorious work, which embraced hundreds and thousands in its influence. The Rev. F. S. Petway, chaplain of the Forty-fourth Tennessee Regiment, Johnson's Brigade, Cleburne's Division, in connection with other ministers, reported a wonderful revival in that celebrated command. "In the latter part of March," he says, " Chaplain Taylor, of the Twenty-third Tennessee Regiment, commenced a series of meetings at Tullahoma, assisted by Rev. A. W. Smith, of the Twenty-fifth, and myself, which continued for several weeks, until temporarily interrupted by military movements. These meetings have resulted in much spiritual benefit to professed Christians, while about one hundred and five souls have embraced Christ as their Saviour. In General Wood's Brigade a meeting of great interest has for several weeks been under the supervision of Rev. F. A. Kimball, chaplain of the Sixteenth Alabama, assisted mainly by Colonel Reed, Chief of Provost Marshal Department in Hardee's Corps, and Colonel Lowery, of the Forty-fifth and Thirty-second Mississippi, the result of which has been one hundred conversions. In the same brigade Chaplain Otkin, of Colonel Lowery's Regiment, has been conducting religious services, which, from the best information received, has been productive of great good in restoring many wanderers to their former enjoyments and inducting about forty-five souls into the kingdom of Christ. In General Polk's Brigade, Brothers Davis, of the First Arkansas, and Quarles, of the Forty-fifth Tennessee, have been laboring with commendable zeal and success in their respective commands, with occasional assistance from Chaplains Smith and Taylor, and as the fruit of their labors God has converted about seventy souls. In General Liddell's Arkansas Brigade, which is destitute of a chaplain, a meeting was commenced five weeks since by Brother G. W. Anderson, preacher in charge of Bedford Circuit, but who, in consequence of affliction, was forced to retire in the very incipiency of an encouraging revival. The charge of the meeting devolved on me, and, with the efficient aid of Brothers Taylor Smith and J. B. Stevenson, it has continued up to the present time without any abatement of interest. Each night crowds of penitents throng the altar for prayers—averaging from eighty-five to one hundred—and the number of conversions, according to the most correct estimate, will not fall below one hundred and forty."

The whole number converted at these meetings was four hundred and seventy-eight, while hundreds more, who had yielded to the vices and temptations of the camp, found the joy of salvation restored to their souls. Under the preaching of Rev. S. M. Cherry, in McCown's Division, the conversions in two regiments reached one hundred and forty. In the brigades of Generals A. P. Stewart and Wright the revival was powerful, and many were converted. "In these revivals," says Mr. Petway, "two encouraging facts are made manifest. We see officers, from colonels of regiments down to captains, lieutenants, and sergeants, giving their counsels and mingling their tears, songs, and prayers with those of the private soldier, and a good number of those who are thus engaged have recently been made partakers of God's converting grace."

To this work Rev. Dr. J. B. McFerrin, who had been recently appointed army missionary, contributed greatly by his able and fervent sermons. He was personally known to thousands of the Army of Tennessee, and his coming was like the visit of a father to his children.

The Presbyterian Church sent forth many of her ablest ministers. Rev. Dr. Waddell, Chancellor of the University of Mississippi, was appointed Superintendent of Army Missions in the West and South-west, and he was ably supported by such men as Dr. Palmer, of New Orleans,

Dr. Rutherford, Dr. E. T. Baird, Rev. J. H. Bryson, and many other earnest preachers. In the Army of Northern Virginia they had Dr. B. T. Lacy, Dr. R. E. Dabney, and others, who gave a great impetus to the revival by their unwearied and successful labors. Besides the regular missionaries, the pastors of the home Churches of all denominations visited and preached to the various camps on all occasions when they could spare time from their charges.

Rev. Messrs. McFerrin, Petway, and Ransom, of the M. E. Church, South, went to the help of General Bragg's army; Messrs. Thweat and Harrington, of the same Church, to the army in Mississippi; while Bishop Pierce, Dr. A. L. P. Green, and Rev. J. E. Evans went to General Lee's army in Virginia. Rev. Dr. Kavanaugh was sent to the army of General Price, and Rev. Mr. Marvin (now Bishop) was directed by Bishop Pierce to take position as missionary with any army corps west of the Mississippi. The work of these ministers, with that of other zealous men from sister Churches, gave a great impulse to the revival. In Colonel Colquitt's Forty-sixth Georgia Regiment, camped near Verona, Miss., the work was powerful, and great numbers were converted. "Last night," says Rev. T. C. Stanley, "there were about eighty presented themselves for prayer, kneeling upon the ground."

Rev. R. G. Porter, chaplain of the Tenth Mississippi Regiment, Bragg's army, says: "It makes my very soul happy to witness the manifestations of God's saving power as seen here in the army—from ten to forty at the altar of prayer. Have preaching every day when not hindered by the men being called off."

The Rev. Dr. Palmer, of New Orleans, preached with power and love, and under his word the revival deepened. Rev. C. W. Miller, army missionary, writes of the work in Georgia in General D. H. Hill's Corps: "Since I arrived here as missionary I have been engaged every night in religious services with the soldiers. A revival and extensive awakening have been in progress in General Bate's Brigade for four weeks. Every night the altar is crowded with weeping penitents. Several have been happily converted. To me it is the most interesting sight of my life."

Even under the fire of the Federal batteries the work went on. Rev. Mr. Browning, from Chattanooga, says: "Yesterday evening about five o'clock the enemy began to throw shells across the river again, firing slowly for about an hour. Notwithstanding this, at the usual hour (twilight) we had a very large crowd of anxious listeners at the rude arbor the men had erected for the worship of God. A short discourse was delivered, when the penitents were invited to the altar. Fifty or sixty came forward, earnestly inquiring the way of salvation. Ten of this number were converted and enabled to 'testify of a truth' that Christ was their Saviour. The work is still extending. Each night increases the attendance, the interest, and the number of penitents. During a ministry of a fourth of a century I have never witnessed a work so deep, so general, and so successful. It pervades all classes of the army (in this brigade), and elicits the co-operation of all denominations. We know no distinction here. Baptists, Cumberlands, Old Presbyterians, Episcopalians, and Methodists work together and rejoice together at the success of our cause."

Mr. Browning writes again from the same place: "The glorious work of God is still progressing in this brigade. About one hundred and thirty conversions up to this time. The interest is unabated—from sixty to seventy-five penitents at the altar each night. It is wonderful that for nearly five weeks we have been enabled to continue this work, with but one night's interference from rain and one on picket."

From General Bragg's army, that veteran soldier of the cross, Dr. J. B. McFerrin, wrote: "I have the pleasure of saying that, notwithstanding the recent numerous movements of the Army of Tennessee, the work of God still progresses. Many have been brought to Christ in various brigades, and whenever the troops remain long enough in one place religious services are observed with great effect. The chaplains and missionaries work with zeal, and have much good fruit. Let our friends at home thank God and take courage. Hundreds of soldiers are coming to Jesus. My health is good, though I feel weak with jaundice. We now have at work in this army, as missionaries from our Church, Revs. R. P. Ransom, C. W. Miller, Wellborn Mooney, W. Burr, Brother Allen, and your humble servant. We expect Brother Petway."

Soldiers were converted by thousands every week. From Virginia Rev. G. R. Talley wrote: "God is wonderfully reviving his work here and throughout the army. Congregations large, interest almost universal. In our chaplains' meeting it was thought, with imperfect statistics, that about five hundred are converted every week. We greatly need chaplains—men of experience and ministerial influence. Our Regimental Christian Association, as a kind of substitute for a Church, and our Bible classes are doing well."

Under the powerful *stimulus* of such a revival the Churches at home redoubled their efforts to supply preachers.

Rev. S. M. Cherry, one of the most faithful laborers among the soldiers of the Western army, gives an account of the blessed scenes that were witnessed among the wounded and dying men at Chickamauga. Of the work of the chaplains he says: "Dr. McFerrin was at Cleburne's Division hospital, where his son was, slightly wounded, and his nephew, Rev. John P. McFerrin, severely wounded, working with the sufferers. Dr. Cross, chaplain on General Buckner's staff, was on the field and at the hospital. Brothers Mooney and Miller were at Stewart's Division hospital, active and industrious in attending to the wounded and dying. Dr. Petway came in good time to render efficient aid in the double capacity of surgeon and minister. I saw Brothers Burr and Browning on the field; also Brothers Quarles, Harris, A. W. Smith, Fitzgerald, Daniel, and others, looking after their wounded and suffering soldiers. Chaplain Willoughby was with the dying, and superintended the burial of the dead of our division. Brother McVoy came in time to minister to the wants of his men at the hospital, and many others were at the post of duty, if not of danger."

"It was encouraging," he says, "to the Christian heart, to see the soldiers of the cross die so heroically. Said Mr. Pool, a member of the Methodist Church in Columbus, Ga., whose shoulder was shattered: 'Parson, write my wife a calm letter, and tell her how I died, for I will never be able to write to her again. Tell her I was ready and willing to die.' Mr. Turner, of Elbert County, Ga., was horribly mangled by a shell, and while on the gory litter said to me: 'I want to die; all is well.' Sam Robins, of Spring Place, Ga., amid the flying, falling, and exploding shells, handed me his hymn-book and his wife's ambrotype, having the night previous talked long with me about his religious enjoyments, pious mother, and praying father, sending messages of love to his youthful wife, and testifying that he had no fear of death."

We have already stated that the Presbyterian Church sent over fifty laborers into the army. At the session of the Synod of Virginia Dr. J. Leighton Wilson, Secretary of Missions, gave a sketch of the army revival, and urged that his Church prosecute its army mission-work with increased zeal. Dr. Wilson said: "There is a state of religion in the Army of Tennessee quite as interesting as that in the Army of Northern Virginia. The Rev. Dr. Palmer says he has never before seen so great a movement. Go where you will, and only let it be known that you are to preach—it hardly makes a difference who the preacher is—and crowds will attend to hear. Dr. Wilson thought it doubtful whether there had been any thing since the days of Pentecost equal to this wonderful work of the Holy Spirit of God in our army. If ever there was a mighty, an imperative call upon us, it is now. If we do not rise to the occasion, our Church will degrade herself before the world and before other denominations."

Of his work after the battle of Chickamauga Dr. J. B. McFerrin wrote: "The revival in the army progressed up to the time of the Chickamauga fight; and even since, notwithstanding the condition of troops moving to and fro, or engaged in erecting fortifications, the good work in some regiments still goes on. The good accomplished by the ministry of the word will never be appreciated by the Church till the light of eternity shall reveal it. Some of the fruits have already ripened: souls converted in the army have gone to the rest that remains for the people of God. The chaplains and missionaries will have many seals to their ministry."

We have already referred to the gallant band that General Price led from Missouri, and their deeds of valor at Corinth, Miss., and other places are well known to those who can recall the scenes in the South-west. One of the most faithful laborers in this corps of our army was Rev. Dr. B. T. Kavanaugh, who has kindly sent us the following account of the revival which prevailed in General Price's Corps on this side and beyond the Mississippi River: "Among those who came out of Missouri with General Price's army are John R. Bennett (your brother), W. M. Patterson, Nathaniel M. Talbott, and myself, besides Brothers Minchell, Harris, Dryden, and McCary. Subsequently we were joined by Brother E. M. Marvin (now Bishop) and others. But little visible effect followed our preaching for the first year or two, while the soldier's life was a novelty; but after two years' hard service the romance of the soldier's life wore off, and a more sober and serious mood seemed to prevail in our camps. The first decided revival that occurred under my observation and ministry was in the State of Mississippi, to which State I had followed General Price's army, while we were encamped near Tupelo. Here we kept up nightly meetings for several weeks in our camp, and there were some forty conversions or more. Brothers Bennett, Harris, and myself held a profitable meeting near Grenada, Miss., where we had some conversions; but for a length of time the army was kept in motion so constantly that we had but little opportunity for religious services. When the army retreated from Big Black into Vicksburg Brothers Bennett, Patterson, and myself rode together into that devoted city. The regiment to which I was then chaplain had been captured at Big Black, and as I had no duties to perform, I told those brethren that I should make my escape from the city before the enemy's lines were thrown around us, and requested them to join me. Brother Bennett refused, saying he should stick to his men, and Patterson refused to leave Bennett alone. I obtained leave of absence, and made my escape by riding all night alone, and found myself outside of Grant's lines the next morning, and went into Selma, Ala., where I spent the summer. I requested Bishop Paine to give me a commission as a missionary to General Price's army, which was then in Arkansas. I obtained it, and left the house of Robert A. Baker, my cousin, in Alabama, on September 15, 1863. I succeeded in making the trip, crossing the Mississippi River just below Bolivar, swimming my horse, and arrived in General Price's camp early in October. My first work was to organize all the chaplains and missionaries into an association for mutual aid and co-operation. When we went into camp at Camp Bragg, thirty miles west of Camden, we there commenced our work in earnest. Through the winter of 1863-4 we kept up our meetings in camp, had seats and pulpit prepared, and were successful in having more than one hundred conversions. After the battles of Mansfield and Pleasant Hill, in Louisiana, our armies returned to Arkansas, and made an encampment at a place called Three Creeks, on the southern line of the State of Arkansas. Here I commenced preaching on June 10, 1864, and continued our meetings until the 10th of September. An extensive revival commenced within a few days after our meeting commenced, and grew in interest and power to the close. We had preaching, beginning at early candle-light—or rather pine-knot fires on stands around the preaching-place. After about ten o'clock at night the preaching and other exercises at the stand closed; but this was but the beginning of the night's work. Like meetings were held in other camps by Dr. A. R. Winfield and Brother Jewell, of Camden. At Three Creeks I had the aid of Brothers Talbott, Dryden, and Minchell, of Missouri, and a Baptist chaplain from Arkansas, whose name I do not remember. To sum up the results of these gracious revivals in the army, we may safely say that at Three Creeks there were five hundred conversions, under Brothers Winfield and Jewell there were three hundred, at Camden and Camp Bragg there were two hundred—making in all in Arkansas one thousand souls. To show the genuineness of this work of grace upon the lives of these converts, we have to remark that after our camp was broken up, and the army was put upon the march to distant fields, wherever we went into camp but for a night our boys held prayer-meetings every night, greatly to the astonishment of the people in the country who were witnesses of their devotion. After the army was disbanded, in riding through the country in Arkansas and Texas, I met with some of our converts, who had returned to their families and parents, and they were still true to their profession and evinced a decidedly firm Christian character. The parents of some of these young men have since told me that in place of having the characters and habits of their sons ruined by being in the army they had returned to them as happy Christian men."

In a letter from the lines in front of Atlanta the Rev. S. M. Cherry gives an account of the scenes he witnessed on the first Sunday in August, 1864: "At 9 A.M. I reached the Missouri Brigade of General French's Division, and found the soldiers gathering for prayer-meeting. At eleven o'clock Chaplain E. M. Bounds, now editor of the *St. Louis Christian Advocate*, was to preach the funeral sermon of Rev. Mr. Manning, a pious young minister of the Cumberland Presbyterian Church, recently appointed chaplain of a Missouri regiment, but before he received his commission he was killed in battle while in the discharge of his duties as an officer of the line. As I approached Sears's Mississippi Brigade I saw a group of soldiers, with uncovered heads, bowing beside a row of new-made graves, two of which contained the forms of comrades now being consigned to the cold clay. Chaplain Lattimore was engaged in prayer. I joined in the solemn burial services of the soldiers slain in the strife of Saturday."

Next he came to the brigades of Ector, McNair, and Gholson: "I looked around for a suitable place for preaching. A central point to the three commands was selected, but not a single tree or shrub was to be found to screen us from the intense heat of an August sun. Soon the singing collected a large congregation of attentive soldiers. A caisson served for a pulpit, while the cannon, open-mouthed, stood in front of the foe. We were in full range and in open view of the enemy, but not a single shell or minie-ball was heard hissing or hurtling near during the hour's service. The soldiers sat on the ground, beneath the burning sun, listening seriously to the words of life. At the close of the sermon they crowded up to get Testaments and papers. I regretted much that I could only furnish five of the former to a regiment. On Friday an intellectual young officer came forward and joined the Church. The day following he was killed in a skirmish with the enemy. During the service in Sears's Brigade there was a sharp skirmish in the front of that command, and the pickets were so closely pressed that the officer in command of the brigade sent a re-enforcement at the close of the service, and there was a continuous cannonade to the left. Strange to see soldiers in the trenches with a sharp fire in front and a rapid roar of artillery on their flank, and a shower of rain falling, yet quietly sitting or patiently standing to hear the gospel."

Up to January, 1865, it was estimated that nearly *one hundred and fifty thousand* soldiers had been converted during the progress of the war, and it was believed that fully one-third of all the soldiers in the field were praying men and members of some branch of the Christian Church. A large proportion of the higher officers were men of faith and prayer, and many others, though not professedly religious, were moral and respectful to all the religious services, and confessed the value of the revival in promoting the efficiency of the army.

PRISON SERVICE.

Not only in the army at home did our soldiers manifest the deepest interest in religion, but even in the dreary prisons of the North they prayed for and received the divine blessing. An officer at Johnson's Island writes to the *Southern Presbyterian:*

"This is the last quarter of a long, long twelve-months' confinement. I try to pass my time as profitably as I can. We have preaching regularly every Sabbath, prayer-meeting two or three times a week, and worship in my room every night. We also have a Young Men's Christian Association, Masonic meetings, etc. I attend all of these, and fill out the rest of my time by reading the Bible. We have had some precious religious times. There have been about one hundred conversions—colonels, majors, captains, and lieutenants being among the number."

A lieutenant writes thus: "I am glad to state that I am a better man than when you saw me last. There are about two thousand officers here, and I never have seen so great a change in the morals of any set of men as has been here in the last four months."

We have referred to scenes in the prisons North and South where thousands languished and died. In Richmond was a prison noted over the whole country. We refer to the "Libby." Here were confined many hundreds of Northern soldiers; to them the gospel was preached by Southern ministers, and may we not hope that some at least found the peace of God in the midst of war? The writer himself had the privilege of offering spiritual consolation to Federal soldiers, sick, wounded, and dying, and he rejoices to believe that not a few rested their souls in the last trying hour upon the merits of Christ.

The following testimony comes from one who was personally engaged in the blessed work of leading soldiers on both sides to the fountain of life: "In Richmond the Rev. Dr. Woodbridge, of the Protestant Episcopal Church, and family (and this was true of other clergymen), were found ready to furnish books, papers, etc., to abate the rigors of prison life to

Federal soldiers in the Libby. One of the chaplains relinquished his other work, and devoted himself to visiting and preaching to the officers and soldiers, and to ministering to their wants. This was followed up by frequent visits and ministrations of various kinds; and it is said that all the supplies sent from the North to the prisoners of war were brought about by a chaplain in a North Carolina regiment."

Since the foregoing was in the hands of the compositor I have received the following from the Rev. J. G. Bolton, now presiding elder of the Savannah District, who was well known to me as a most gallant private soldier from 1861 till finally appointed chaplain in 1863, I believe, and was very faithful and zealous, and truly popular among the soldiers until the surrender in 1865. When the statement which he furnishes by my request was announced at our chaplains' meeting at Dalton, the question very naturally asked and discussed was: "What became of the ten penitents—or the eight, rather—who were instantly killed while upon their knees seeking salvation?" Without any hesitation I declared: "If they were truly penitent, forsaking and confessing their sins, praying for pardon, trusting with all their hearts in Christ for salvation, they were saved." Who questions it?

March 7, 1890.

After spending the winter near Dalton, Ga., some time in the spring—April, I think, of 1864—our (Maney's) brigade, Cheatham's Division, Army of Tennessee, was moved to a new encampment. After cleaning off the ground, burning the leaves and brush, and making ourselves as comfortable as possible, I, being chaplain of the Fiftieth Tennessee, got a number of my regiment and some members of the other regiments together. We cleaned off a place near the center of the brigade, and prepared seats for divine services, having had successful revival services in the command for several weeks previous. On Saturday evening we finished up our work, and at the time for evening service the bugle sounded the Church call and five or six hundred soldiers repaired to the place for worship. Rev. Allen Tribble, late a member of the Tennessee Conference, who was chaplain of the Fourth (Confederate) Tennessee Regiment of Maney's Brigade, was to assist in the meeting. After conferring with him, it was agreed that I should preach Saturday night and he Sunday morning; so after the preliminary services I preached from Luke xii. 31: "But rather seek ye the kingdom of God; and all these things shall be added unto you." Being young in the ministry, mine were not words of enticing wisdom; but the Holy Spirit was with us, and at the conclusion penitents were invited, and as well as I now remember, about fifty came to the altar for prayers, and the altar exercises had continued but a short while when the whole congregation was thrown into utter confusion. One penitent, a member of the Fourth Tennessee Regiment, whom I thought would be converted in a moment, and to whom I had just been talking, suddenly fell backward against my knees and remained perfectly motionless. I put my hand upon his head, and found his skull crushed to pieces. I then called for a surgeon; and soon after, the confusion subsiding to some extent, I learned that a tree had fallen in the midst of the congregation, killing eight instantly and mortally wounding two others who died during the night, making ten in all. We buried them next day (Sunday) with military honors, the Methodist burial service being read by Rev. Tilman Page, late of the Memphis Conference, but then chaplain of one of the Tennessee regiments. It seemed that while clearing up the encampment a small limbless tree had caught on fire, and, being overlooked, had burned sufficiently to cause its fall, resulting as above stated. We continued the services during our stay at that place, and they were finally closed by the brigade being ordered to the front to meet Sherman, who was threatening an attack on Joseph E. Johnston, near Tunnel Hill. We were assisted in the meeting by Rev. C. D. Elliott, D.D., chaplain in Maney's Brigade, and Rev. William Burr, late a member of the Tennessee Conference, and then a missionary to the Army of Tennessee.

Lawrenceburg, Tenn., March 4, 1890.

Chaplains W. C. Atmore, of the Fifteenth Kentucky Regiment, father of C. P. Atmore, of the L. and N. Railroad; J. E. Reed, of the Thirty-eighth Illinois Regiment; J. C. Thomas, of the Eighty-eighth Illinois Regiment of the Federal army, were captured by our army at Stone's River December 31, 1862, and I had a pleasant interview with them.

I am indebted to the Rev. Dr. J. William Jones's "Christ in the Camp" for the following list of chaplains in the Army of Northern Virginia:

First Maryland Regiment, Rev. Mr. Cameron.

Virginia Regiments.—First, Rev. Mr. Aldrich; Second, Rev. Mr. McVeigh and A. C. Hopkins; Third, Rev. Mr. Hammond and J. W. Ward; Fourth, Rev. F. C. Tebbs and William R. McNear; Seventh, J. H. Bocock, F. M. McCarthy, and —— Frazier; Eighth, T. A. Ware and G. W. Harris; Ninth, J. W. Walkup and G. W. Easter; Tenth, J. P. Hyde, S. S. Lambeth, and —— Balthis; Eleventh, Dr. J. C. Granbery and T. C. Jennings; Twelfth, S. V. Hoyle; Thirteenth, Dr. J. William Jones; Fourteenth, —— Crocker; Fifteenth, J. F. August; Seventeenth, J. L. Johnson and R. M. Baker; Eighteenth, J. D. Blackwell; Nineteenth, P. Slaughter; Twenty-first, J. H. Gilmer; Twenty-third, P. C. Morton; Twenty-fourth, W. T. Gardiner; Twenty-fifth, G. B. Taylor and J. W. Jones; Twenty-sixth, W. E. Wiatt; Twenty-seventh, L. C. Vass; Twenty-eighth, —— Tinsley; Twenty-ninth, —— Phillips; Thirtieth, W. R. D. Moncure; Thirty-first, A. D. Lepps; Thirty-third, J. M. Grandin; Fortieth, G. T. Bagley and J. M. Anderson; Forty-first, J. W. Pugh; Forty-second, Thomas Williams; Forty-fourth, R. I. McIlwane and James Nelson; forty-sixth, W. G. Miller; Forty-seventh, S. B. Meridith; Forty-eighth, George E. Booker; Forty-ninth, J. P. Garland; Fiftieth, J. W. Denny; Fifty-second, John Magill; Fifty-third, W. S. Penick, P. H. Fontaine, and —— Colton; Fifty-fifth, R. B. Beadles; Fifty-sixth, —— Robbins; Fifty-seventh, J. E. Joyner; Fifty-eighth, George Slaughter and L. B. Madison; Fifty-ninth, L. B. Wharton; Sixty-first, H. H. Hatcher.

North Carolina Regiments.—First, W. R. Gwaltney; Second Battalion, —— Tennent; Twelfth, J. H. Robbins; Fourteenth, W. C. Power; Fifteenth, S. W. Howerton; Sixteenth, —— Watson; Twentieth, L. A. Bickle and J. M. Sprunt; Twenty-second, F. H. Wood; Twenty-fourth, T. B. Neil; Twenty-sixth, A. N. Wells; Twenty-eighth, F. M. Kennedy; Thirtieth, A. D. Betts; Thirty-second, W. B. Richardson; Thirty-third, T. J. Eatman; Thirty-fourth, A. R. Benick; Thirty-seventh, A. L. Stough; Thirty-eight, —— McDiarmid; Forty-third, E. H. Thompson; Forty-fourth, R. S. Webb; Forty-fifth, E. H. Hardin; Forty-sixth, A. D. Cohen; Forty-seventh, W. S. Lacey; Forty-eight, C. Plyer; Fifty-first, —— Sanford and J. M. Cline; Fifty-third, J. H. Colton; Fifty-seventh, John Paris.

South Carolina Regiments.—First, George T. T. Williams; Second, W. E. Walters; Fifth, J. N. Craig; Sixth, W. E. Boggs; Seventh, J. M. Carlisle; Eighth, H. M. Brearly; Twelfth, —— Dixon and J. M. Anderson; Thirteenth, Wallace W. Duncan and J. N. Bouchelle; Fourteenth,

W. B. Carson; Fifteenth, H. B. McCallum; Sharp-shooters, James McDowel.

Georgia Regiments.—Third, J. M. Stokes; Fourth, R. F. Evans; Sixth, A. M. Thigpen; Seventh, —— Stokes; Eighth, W. C. Dunlap; Ninth, H. A. Tupper, A. B. Campbell, and J. C. Byrnham; Tenth, J. C. Camp; Eleventh, W. A. Simmons; Twelfth, A. M. Marshall and —— Pouldridge; Fifteenth, W. F. Robertson; Seventeenth, —— Hudson; Nineteenth, A. J. Jarrell and W. H. C. Cone; Twenty-second, W. H. McAfee; Twenty-third, W. A. Dodge; Twenty-seventh, G. S. Emory; Twenty-eighth, A. H. McVay; Thirty-first, J. L. Pettigrew; Thirty-fifth, J. H. Taylor; Thirty-eighth, J. M. Brittian; Forty-fourth, H. E. Brooks; Forty-fifth, E. B. Barrett; Forty-eighth, J. A. Lowery; Forty-ninth, J. J. Hymon; Fiftieth, W. L. Curry; Fifty-first, C. H. Toy; Sixtieth, S. H. Smith; Sixty-first, A. B. Woodfin; Second Battalion, J. O. A. Sparks; Wofford's Brigade, W. P. Dubose.

Florida Regiments.—Second, J. W. Timberlake; Seventh, J. H. Tomkies; Eleventh, —— Little.

Alabama Regiments.—Third, T. J. Rutledge; Fourth, Robert Frazier; Fifth, W. G. Curry; Sixth, G. R. Talley; Eighth, W. E. Massey; Ninth, M. L. Whitten; Tenth, J. J. D. Renfroe; Eleventh, —— Johnson; Twelfth, H. G. Moore; Thirteenth, T. H. Howell; Twenty-sixth, William E. Cameron; Forty-fourth, W. G. Perry; Forty-eighth, —— Price.

Mississippi Regiments.—Twelfth, C. H. Dobbs; Thirteenth, —— West; Sixteenth, A. A. Lomax; Seventeenth, W. B. Owen; Eighteenth, J. A. Hackett; Nineteenth, —— Duke; Twenty-first, —— McDonald; Twenty-sixth, M. B. Chapman; Forty-second, T. D. Witherspoon; Forty-eighth, A. E. Garrison.

Louisiana Regiments.—First, Father Sheran; Second, Robert Hardee; Fifth, William M. Strickler; Seventh, Father Hubert; Eighth, Father Schmilders; Ninth, F. McCarthy.

Tennessee Regiments.—First, W. T. Helm; Seventh, —— Harris; Fourteenth, J. E. King.

Third Arkansas Regiment, G. E. Butler.

First Texas Regiment, I. R. Vick.

Army Corps.—First, Dr. Theo. Pryor; Second, Dr. B. T. Lacey, Dr. L. Rosser, and Rev. E. J. Willis; Third, Dr. George D. Armstrong.

Cavalry Corps, Virginia Regiments.—Sixth, R. T. Davis; Ninth, C. H. Boggs; Tenth, James B. Taylor, Jr.

Artillery Battalions.—Haskell's, J. A. Chombliss; Washington's, William A. Hall; Cutsham's, —— Page; Nelson's, T. W. Gilmer; Braxton's, Dr. A. B. Brown and Jes. Nelson; Hardaway's, T. M. Niven and H. M. White; Pegram's, —— Rodman; Poague's, James Wheary.

Post Chaplains.—Petersburg, Thomas Hume, Sr., Thomas Hume, Jr., W. M. Young, and J. B. Hardwicke; Staunton, Dr. J. B. Taylor; Charlottesville, Dr. W. F. Broddus; Lynchburg, Rev. J. L. Johnson; Gordonsville, Dr. D. B. Ewing; Farmville, Rev. A. D. McVeigh; Danville, Rev. C. C. Choplin; Richmond, Dr. J. B. Taylor, Sr., Dr. Robert Ryland, Dr. W. W. Bennett, Revs. William H. Williams, J. E. Martin, and J. T. Carpenter— practically the pastors of Richmond, among whom were Drs. J. T. Burrows, J. B. Jeter, D. Shaver, J. B. Solomon, and L. W. Seely, Baptists; Drs. M. D. Hoge, T. V. Moore, and C. H. Read, Presbyterians; Drs. D. S. Doggett, J. A. Duncan, and J. E. Edwards, Methodists; Drs. C. Minnegerode, G. W. Woodbridge, Peterskins, and T. G. Dashiels, Episcopalian.

I record here some of the names of preachers I met ministering to the spiritual interests of the soldiers during the war:

Chaplains Rush, of the Third Georgia; —— McLean, of the Thirty-sixth Georgia; G. R. Kramer, of the Thirty-ninth Georgia; —— Thomson, of the Fortieth Georgia; Dr. Rosser, of the Forty-first Georgia; —— Oslin, of the Forty-third Georgia; —— Brown, of the Forty-sixth Georgia; W. A. Parks, of the Fifty-second Georgia; —— Daniel, of the Fifty-seventh Georgia; and J. H. Myers, —— Strickland, and —— Timmons; Drs. Harpe and A. G. Haygood. Missionaries to Georgia troops, L. R. Redding and L. B. Payne.

Chaplains J. G. Richards, of the Tenth South Carolina; J. P. De Pass, of the Sixteenth South Carolina; F. Auld, of the Twenty-fourth South Carolina; W. T. Hall, —— South Carolina.

Chaplains E. C. Wexler, of the Twenty-ninth North Carolina; —— Beauman, of the Forty-eighth North Carolina.

Chaplains R. L. Wiggins, of the Fourth Florida; J. H. Tomkies, of the Seventh Florida; —— Giles, —— Florida.

Chaplains L. C. Ransom, —— Alabama; J. H. Willoughby, Eighteenth Alabama; Elbert West, Twenty-fifth Alabama; W. W. Graham, Twenty-eighth Alabama; J. S. Holt, Thirty-fourth Alabama; C. M. Hutton, Thirty-sixth Alabama; W. F. Norton, Thirty-ninth Alabama; Dr. B. W. McDonald, Fiftieth Alabama; A. D. McVoy, Fifty-eighth Alabama; J. P. McMullen, missionary. Alabama Brigade, Revs. Lieutenants Curry and Jones.

Chaplain R. G. Porter ("Gilderoy"), Tenth Mississippi.

Chaplains Morris and Finney, Ector's Texas Brigade; Dr. Bunting, Terry's Texas Rangers.

Chaplains E. M. Bounds and —— Lattimore, Cockrill's Missouri Brigade.

Chaplains H. H. Kavanaugh, of the Sixth Kentucky; —— Riddle, —— Kentucky; and C. W. Miller, missionary to Kentucky troops.

Chaplains Dr. C. T. Quintard, First Tennessee; T. H. Davenport, Third Tennessee; Allen Tribble, Fourth Tennessee; C. S. Hearn, Fifth Tennessee; M. B. De Witt, Eighth Tennessee; Dr. F. E. Pitts and P. G. Jamison, Eleventh Tennessee; W. T. Bennett, Twelfth Tennessee; L. H. Miliken, Thirteenth Tennessee; H. B. Moore, Seventeenth Tennessee; J. A. Ellis, Twentieth Tennessee; J. F. McCutchon, Twenty-fourth Tennessee; A. W. Smith, Twenty-fifth Tennessee; —— Harris, Twenty-sixth Tennessee; J. C. Chapman, Thirty-second Tennessee; J. W. Johnson, Thirty-seventh Tennessee; —— McMurray, Forty-fifth Tennessee; J. H. McNeely, Forty-ninth Tennessee; J. G. Bolton, Fiftieth Tennessee; S. A. Kelly, Strahl's Tennessee Brigade. Drs. F. S. Petway and Joseph Cross, also Revs. J. W. Cullum, W. H. Browning, J. B. Allison, B. M. Stephens, and others were chaplains from Tennessee.

H. D. Hogan, J. H. Strayhorn, John Goal, John A. Thompson, J. R. Harris, John P. McFerrin, F. Tarrant, William H. Anthony, T. L. Duncan, B. W. Bond, W. D. Cherry, R. A. Wilson, M. G. Williams, J. G. Hinson, B. F. Smith, A. L. Hamilton, J. B. Hamilton, F. R. Hill, and others, were in the Southern army, some of whom I never saw during the war. Dr. J. B. McFerrin, William Burr, W. Mooney, and R. P. Ransom I met often in their active work as missionaries to the Army of Tennessee.

The following were appointed by the Missionary Board of the Methodist Episcopal Church, South: Revs. Leo. Rosser and J. C. Granbery, in the Army of Northern Virginia; J. B. McFerrin, C. W. Miller, W. Mooney, R. P. Ransom, and W. Burr, in the Army of Tennessee; J. S. Lane and E. B. Duncan, in the Department of Florida; J. J. Wheat and H. J. Harris, in Mississippi; W. C. Johnson, to General S. D. Lee's Corps, North Mississippi; J. J. Hutchinson, to the army about Mobile; and beyond the

Mississippi River, J. C. Keener to Louisiana troops, and B. T. Kavanaugh and E. M. Marvin to Missouri and Arkansas troops.

Dr. J. William Jones, in "Christ in the Camp," very truly said of the work of the chaplains and missionaries in the army: "One of the most potent factors in the grand success of our work was the union of hearts and hands of all Christian workers. Dr. Hoge wrote of the great revival in Barksdale's Brigade in 1863. We had a Presbyterian sermon introduced by Baptist services under the direction of a Methodist chaplain in an Episcopal church. That was but a type of what was usual all through the army. We found common ground upon which we could stand shoulder to shoulder and labor for the cause of our common Master. And I am glad to believe that the fraternal spirit which has so largely prevailed for some years among evangelical Christians at the South is in no small degree due to the habit of co-operation which so generally prevailed during the war."

I indorse all my good Baptist brother wrote anent the catholic spirit which prevailed among the preachers of different denominations in the army. We preached a full, free salvation to all, and when soldiers of the cross desired to enter the army of the Lord we gave them the privilege of selecting their own company and choosing the division in which they could best battle for God against Satan. Their names were taken and ministers of their choice were invited to baptize them, and there was no controversy on the mode of baptism, or proselyting, and all who repented and believed on the Lord Jesus Christ, and were obedient to his will as they understood his word, were recognized as Christians in the army.

If nothing else was gained by the war, the broad, strong bond of Christian charity, which binds the people of God closer together now than in other years, and manifests more of the spirit of our Lord than hitherto, is to me the best evidence that great good grew out of what seemed a great evil. During the thirty-five years of my ministry I regard the four years of my army life as the most useful. I have found no other field so fertile and fruitful for soul-saving, no other people more devout and spiritual than Christian soldiers, and no ministers more zealous and faithful than chaplains, whether Baptists, Presbyterians, Episcopalians, Methodists, Disciples, or Catholics.

S. M. CHERRY.

Near Vanderbilt University, March 10, 1890.

THE INSTITUTION OF DOMESTIC SLAVERY IN THE SOUTHERN STATES.

In a work like this the real facts with regard to the institution of slavery, and especially domestic slavery as it existed in the Southern States before the war, should have a place. These facts have been distorted and exaggerated long enough. It is due to the dead who have been misunderstood and misrepresented, and to their posterity who have a just pride in their ancestry, that the truth should be told, if but briefly, in these pages. What are the facts concerning slavery?

1. Slavery has existed in all ages and in almost all countries. It still exists in Africa (the original home of the Southern negroes) and elsewhere.

2. Slavery was recognized both in the Old and New Testament Scriptures. The patriarchs were slave-holders. Abraham, the friend of God and "Father of the Faithful," was a large slave-holder. Slavery existed when our Lord Jesus Christ was on the earth, and in the days of the apostles, but no word of condemnation of the institution was ever spoken by him or any of them. On the contrary, the Apostle Paul sent a runaway slave back to his master.

3. For thousands of years the institution of slavery was everywhere regarded as a matter of course. Every civilized nation of the earth has at some time or other been a slave-holding nation. While from time to time during past ages a solitary voice has been raised against the institution, the agitation against it is a thing of comparatively modern date.

4. The slave trade was carried on by the European nations for many years, especially by England and Holland. The English and the Dutch planted slavery in the United States, with some help from the Spaniards and Portuguese.

5. The New England States were extensively implicated in the slave trade, especially Massachusetts and Rhode Island. The Southern States have had but little to do with it at any period of their history.

6. Slavery once existed in all the original Northern States. When it ceased to be profitable with them their slaves were mostly sold and taken to the South, where because of the invention of the cotton-gin and the peculiarities of the climate, it was more remunerative. The title of the Southern people to their slaves emanated in a large degree from the people of the Northern States, who carried on the slave trade, and who sold to the South the slaves owned by themselves.

7. The institution of domestic slavery was recognized and protected by the Federal Constitution, which was the solemn compact of union between the States of the American Union. This provision of the Constitution was flagrantly violated by the Northern States—those very States that afterward went to war to coerce the Southern States to hold them to the observance of a compact so grossly violated by themselves.

8. Steps were taken by some of the older Southern States looking to the emancipation of the slaves sixty years ago, but the violence of the enemies of the institution and of the South became so great, and their methods so dangerous, that in self-defense the people of the Southern States were compelled to turn their attention to measures for the protection of civil society itself rather than for the gradual emancipation of their slaves, which they had tentatively begun to consider.

9. The slave population of the Southern States increased so

rapidly that at length the number was so great, and the institution was so interwoven into the social, industrial, and political life of the South, that emancipation by the peaceful methods once possible seemed to be an impossibility. Twelve hundred millions of dollars were invested in it, and the whole labor system of the South rested on it.

10. Under the influence of domestic slavery as it existed in the South every successive generation of the negroes made an advance in civilization over its predecessor. Savages and cannibals in Africa, here in the Southern States they were humanized and civilized under the influences brought to bear upon them. In all the world besides there could not be found an equal number of black people enjoying an equal degree of physical comfort or raised to an equal degree of moral development. Slavery redeemed them from savagery, and gave them the rudiments of civilization and Christianity. The great body of the slaves were kindly treated, and they were a healthy, contented, and prolific race, noted for their muscular development, musical genius, and jolly good humor. The relations existing between them and their owners were for the most part kindly. The material prosperity of the South, the rapid growth of the negro population, the absence of any considerable social convulsions or disorders, furnish the proofs of the truth of this statement.

11. The religious welfare of the slaves was not neglected. The leading religious denominations of the South made provision for their religious instruction, and hundreds of thousands of them were communicants of the several Churches engaged in this service. The best white ministers of the gospel preached to them in the city, town, and country, and in many Christian homes in the South the white and the black members of the household knelt together in family worship. There was manifest an increasing interest in the religious welfare of the slaves.

12. Those who are now working most successfully for the promotion of the religious welfare of the emancipated negroes are building upon the foundations laid during the days of slavery in the Southern States. The most of the reputable and reliable religious leaders among the negroes at the present time were once slaves and received their religious training under the direction of white masters previous to their emancipation. The significance of such a fact as this ought not to be overlooked by any who would reach a just conclusion with regard to this matter.

13. The question whether slavery should be confined within its then existing limits, with the threat of constant war upon it until it was destroyed, or whether it should be admitted into the new Territories of the Union as they were organized, had much to do in intensifying the sectional excitement which at last culminated in the long and bloody war. It may be said, therefore, that the crusade against slavery, if not the cause, was one of the occasions of the war, the Southern States contending for a constitutional right which the North had practically nullified and which was being assailed with constantly increasing violence.

14. The emancipation of the slaves finally came in the guise of a war measure, and was a sudden change of the civil relations of millions of people unparalleled in the history of the human race. That this tremendous revolution was effected without bloodshed or social disorder, the two races continuing to live side by side in peace, is a proof that as a rule under slavery the masters were kind.

15. Since the slaves were emancipated they seem content to remain where they are, preferring to take their chances with their former masters rather than to cross the line and seek their fortunes elsewhere. And here, under the political domination and social influence of the white people of the South, they are acquiring property and education, and getting ready for wha'

ever God may have in store for them in the future, which is known only to him.

The foregoing facts will stand the test of fair and thorough investigation, and they carry their own deductions with them. Whatever might be said with regard to the harsher features and incidents of slavery may safely and properly be left to the many writers who have shown a readiness not only to exaggerate evils such as are incident to all human institutions, but to invent what never had any existence save in the wild declamation of demagogues, the excited fancies of fanatics, the credulity of the weak-minded who take their facts at second-hand, and the malicious inventions of those who are always ready to take up a reproach against their neighbors.